ANTISOCIAL BEHAVIOR IN ORGANIZATIONS

To Karen, Drew, Elizabeth, and Joshua,
whose unconditional love comforts me whenever
I ponder the reasons for antisocial behavior.
—RG

To Carolyn, whose prosocial behavior
so pleasantly contrasts with the antisocial behavior
described on these pages.
—JG

ANTISOCIAL BEHAVIOR IN ORGANIZATIONS

ROBERT A. GIACALONE
JERALD GREENBERG

SAGE Publications
International Educational and Professional Publisher
Thousand Oaks   London   New Delhi

For information address:

 SAGE Publications, Inc.
2455 Teller Road
Thousand Oaks, California 91320
E-mail: order@sagepub.com

SAGE Publications Ltd.
6 Bonhill Street
London EC2A 4PU
United Kingdom

SAGE Publications India Pvt. Ltd.
M-32 Market
Greater Kailash I
New Delhi 110 048 India

Printed in the United States of America

Library of Congress Cataloging-in-Publication Data

Main entry under title:

Antisocial behavior in organizations / editors, Robert A. Giacalone,
   Jerald Greenberg.
    p.   cm.
    Includes bibliographical references (p.) and index.
    ISBN 0-8039-7235-0 (cloth: acid-free paper).—ISBN
0-8039-7236-9 (pbk.: acid-free paper)
    1. Employee crimes. 2. Violence in the workplace. 3. Problem
employees. I. Giacalone, Robert A. II. Greenberg, Jerald.
HF5549.5.E43A58   1996
158.7—dc20   96-25241

97 98 99 00 01 02 03 10 9 8 7 6 5 4 3 2 1

Acquiring Editor: Marquita Flemming
Editorial Assistant: Frances Borghi
Production Editor: Michèle Lingre
Production Assistant: Sherrise Purdum
Typesetter & Designer: Andrea D. Swanson
Indexer: Juniee Oneida
Cover Designer: Lesa Valdez
Print Buyer: Anna Chin

Contents

Preface

If this book does nothing else, it surely will prompt the reader to ask, "What do you mean by 'antisocial behavior in organizations'?" Insofar as the question involves the title of this book, an immediate response is called for. To the point, we conceive of antisocial behavior in organizations as *any behavior that brings harm, or is intended to bring harm, to an organization, its employees, or stakeholders.* It is the opposite of prosocial behavior, which is designed to help, to bring good. Antisocial behavior falls into the same category as *deviant* or *dysfunctional behavior,* terms that also have been used in the literature, although we believe the term *antisocial behavior* is more encompassing. Specifically, we consider the following to be examples of antisocial behaviors that occur in organizations:

- Arson
- Blackmail
- Bribery

- Discrimination
- Espionage
- Extortion
- Fraud
- Interpersonal violence
- Kickbacks
- Lawsuits
- Lying
- Sabotage
- Sexual harassment
- Theft
- Violations of confidentiality
- Whistle-blowing

Both the popular press and scholarly literature have pointed to an increase in antisocial behavior in organizations in recent years. Interpersonal violence on the job, most notably at offices of the U.S. Postal Service, coupled with repeated instances of attacks on company facilities (especially computers), have brought the problem of aggressive workers to the front pages of the news. Financial dishonesty—evidenced in the scandals at large organizations, both for-profit (e.g., Phar-Mor) and nonprofit (e.g., the United Way), including specific allegations against highly regarded religious leaders (e.g., Rev. Jim Bakker) and political leaders (e.g., U.S. Senator Dan Rostankowski)—have elevated the visibility of white-collar crime, leading to the undeniable conclusion that antisocial behavior pervades even the highest levels of our most esteemed institutions. If all of these difficulties were not enough concern to organizations, there are additional challenges. In an era in which lawsuits are on the rise, predicting, identifying, and apprehending antisocial employees before they can raise havoc in organizations must be tempered by management's exposure to the potential lawsuits that may arise from wrongful accusations and dismissals.

Traditionally, the study of antisocial behavior has been of less interest to management scholars than to other social scientists. Industrial/ organizational psychologists, for example, have studied the prediction of various forms of dishonest behavior, whereas their clinical counterparts have focused on the development and treatment of antisocial personality disorders. Sociologists and anthropologists have examined the impact of various factors, such as group structure and class differences, on antisocial behavior. Extending these approaches, criminologists have actively examined the impact of different factors as deterrents of antisocial behavior in the workplace.

Despite the widespread occurrence of incidents of antisocial behavior in organizations, and guidance from related social science disciplines, it is curious that the topic of antisocial behavior has received little attention from management scholars. Such neglect stems largely from the fact that matters of antisocial behavior traditionally have been relegated to security officials. To the extent that managers believed that their security departments could handle such concerns, there was no need for them to get involved in the problem themselves. However, it is now becoming clear that matters of antisocial behavior not only may be controlled by management but may be triggered by various management practices. As such, we contend that problems of antisocial behavior in organizations are management problems and need to be addressed as such.

It is with this in mind that we have prepared the present book. There has been—until now, at least—no single volume that could provide an easy reference for professionals interested in various forms of antisocial organizational behavior. Instead, interested students, professors, and practitioners were forced to look at interdisciplinary journals or specialized field books to learn about the problem areas—a most intimidating task. However, we expect that academics and practitioners in such fields such as management, industrial/organizational psychology, sociology, social psychology, legal studies, and criminal justice will benefit by reading the present collection of original essays.

In preparing *Antisocial Behavior in Organizations*, we intended to provide a book that would examine some of the most popular forms of antisocial organizational behavior from both theoretical and practical perspectives. It was not our intent to provide complete coverage of all the forms of antisocial organizational behavior that exist. Such a task would be far too ambitious for a single volume. Instead, our goal was to provide an overview of some of the most important, promising, and underrepresented aspects of antisocial behavior for the field of management. Specifically, the chapters of this book are arranged in order roughly from individual-level processes to organizational-level processes. We begin by looking at the general phenomenon of frustration, which underlies many forms of antisocial behavior. We then consider specific forms of antisocial behavior, such as revenge, aggression, lying, employee theft, and sabotage. Following this, we turn our attention to two forms of behavior that may be considered antisocial, although their stated goals may be prosocial: whistle-blowing and litigation. Finally, we conclude on a broader note—a chapter making connections between antisocial behavior and organizational climate. The present collection of original chapters by subject-matter experts is designed to provide academicians, students, and practitioners with an understanding of the various forms of antisocial behavior in organizations and how they can be identified and managed, if not prevented altogether.

It is our hope that this book will stimulate others to take a more comprehensive look at antisocial behavior in organizations. Undoubtedly, there is much work left to be done. There are still other types of antisocial behavior to be considered, emerging legal and ethical problems with antisocial workers, developing techniques for detection and prevention that must be generated and tested, and a continued need to bridge theory and practice so that more effective approaches can be developed and implemented. We recognize that dealing with these issues will be a multidisciplinary challenge for the future and that new approaches in theory, research, and practice will develop in and out of the organizational sciences. If nothing else, the present book should provide a useful beginning.

Robert A. Giacalone
Jerald Greenberg

The Role of Frustration in Antisocial Behavior at Work

Paul E. Spector

Antisocial behavior at work is a common occurrence in many organizations. Although such acts are carried out for a variety of reasons, often they can be explained as reactions to frustration. Events and conditions of work can induce anger and frustration that are accompanied by antisocial acts such as aggression, sabotage, theft, and the intentional withholding of output. Earlier, I presented a model of how frustration leads to these antisocial behaviors (Spector, 1978). It is the purpose of this chapter to update this model by incorporating an expanded role for cognitive processes and individual differences. These additional factors provide a more complete picture than the original model of how frustration can lead to antisocial behavior at work. In addition, this chapter will discuss strategies for reducing antisocial behavior at work, based on the expanded frustration model.

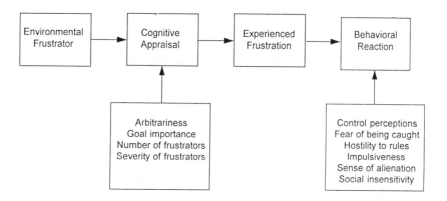

Figure 1.1. A Model of Organizational Frustration

My earlier frustration model (Spector, 1978) was based on the social psychological work on aggression in general and the frustration-aggression hypothesis in particular (Dollard, Doob, Miller, Mowrer, & Sears, 1939). The frustration-aggression hypothesis outlined several environmental conditions that lead to frustration and aggression. One of the biggest limitations to Dollard et al.'s work was its deemphasis of cognitive processes and individual differences in response to frustration. Subsequent research has provided a basis for adding these elements to the frustration model, as I will discuss in this chapter.

A Model of Frustration

A model of the job frustration process is illustrated in Figure 1.1. The model is intended to show how certain environmental conditions can lead to antisocial behavior at work. The leftmost box in the model represents the environmental frustrator. As discussed below in detail, this can be any event or situation at work that interferes with employees' goals. The next step in the process is the appraisal or interpretation of the situation. To experience frustration, an individual must perceive that the frustrator interferes in some way with a goal. Experienced frustration (Step 3) is associated with an emotional reaction that can range from minor annoyance to rage. The last step in the process is the behavioral reaction of the employee. The model describes factors that can lead an employee to engage in an antisocial act.

Frustrators

The experience of frustration at work begins with an event or situation that I call a *frustrator*. A frustrator is an environmental event or situation that interferes with or prevents an individual from achieving or maintaining a personal goal at work. Goals can be long term, such as being promoted to division manager, or short term, such as exceeding a weekly sales quota. Following Locke and Latham's (1990) goal-setting theory, I assume that human behavior is intentional. Behavior is directed toward achieving goals and purposes as opposed to being random or reflexive. Goals can be the accomplishment of some large task or the completion of a quite small and seemingly inconsequential objective. Both becoming company president and leaving for lunch by noon would be considered the achievement of a goal.

Many frustrators (events or situations) at work can interfere with the accomplishment of a goal. Some frustrators prevent the reaching of a goal, such as being given an urgent assignment that prevents leaving for lunch on time. Other frustrators can threaten the continuation of a goal. For example, anything that threatens self-esteem can be threatening to the goal of maintaining a positive self-image.

Frustrators can arise from many sources in an organization. Anything that interferes with an individual's task performance can be considered a frustrator. Peters and O'Connor (1980) outlined eight organizational constraint areas that can involve frustrators: (a) job-related information, (b) tools and equipment, (c) materials and supplies, (d) budgetary support, (e) required services and help from others, (f) task preparation, (g) time availability, and (h) work environment. Keenan and Newton (1984) noted that job stressors also can be considered frustrators. Role ambiguity can be considered as insufficient job-related information, which is one of the above constraint areas. Role conflict can be a frustrator in that it prevents achievement of competing goals. Workload can be a frustrator in that having too much work can prevent pursuing other goals. Finally, interpersonal conflicts can be frustrators because they interfere with goals of maintaining good relations with others. Keenan and Newton (1984) showed that measures of these job stressors related to experienced frustration.

Appraisal

An environmental situation only can become a frustrator for an individual if that individual appraises it as such. Lazarus (1995) discussed the important role of appraisal in the work stress process. He noted that a person's emotional reaction to work is dependent on his or her appraisal of the work situation in the context of personal goals. Although Lazarus was concerned with the broader question of job stress and a variety of emotional responses, the experience of frustration is certainly one of the emotions relevant to job stress (see Chen & Spector, 1992).

Both environmental and personal factors combine to determine the individual's appraisal of the situation as being a frustrator. Situations appraised in this way lead to the experience of frustration. Figure 1.1 identifies several factors that influence the appraisal of the frustrator and the subsequent experience of frustration. These include the importance of the goal, the extent to which it is blocked, the number of frustrators that occur per unit of time, and the intent of the agent of the frustrator (arbitrariness).

The goal's importance to the individual is a critical element in the process. The blocking of important goals is likely to be interpreted as frustrating. The extent of interference is another important factor. A frustrator can represent a minor interference that requires little effort to overcome or a major obstacle that requires a great deal of time and effort to overcome. The greater the extent of interference, the greater will be the experienced frustration. Major interferences with very important goals are likely to result in high levels of experienced frustration that lead to antisocial behavior. Buss (1963) provided evidence for this in a laboratory aggression study.

The number of frustrators experienced per unit of time affects reactions to events. The effects of frustrators can be cumulative over time. This means that the effects of several relatively minor frustrators can be the same as a single major frustrator. Evidence for this comes from laboratory aggression research (e.g., Spector, Penner, & Hawkins, 1975).

An important factor is the perceived intent of the agent of a frustrator. An arbitrary frustrator (Pastore, 1952) is one that was caused by someone for no apparent good reason. A person might be perceived as having produced the frustrator on purpose or to be mean. A nonarbitrary frustrator occurs by accident or for a good reason. For example, a supervisor might ask a subordinate to work late to finish a project because an equipment breakdown prevented completion by the end of the shift. Given the same objective event, the nonarbitrary frustrator will result in less experienced frustration.

Experienced Frustration

A situation that is appraised as a frustrator will lead to *experienced frustration*. Experienced frustration is the affective reaction to the situation. The affect is a form of anger that can range from minor irritation to rage. This is not meant to imply that experienced frustration is an emotional state distinct from anger. Anger is distinguished from experienced frustration in that the former term is a general emotional response, whereas the latter is a response to a specific situation.

Antisocial Behavior

Individuals who experience frustration may respond by engaging in antisocial behavior. Antisocial behavior can be directed at the agent of the frustrator and can serve to remove the obstacle. Aggression, for example, sometimes is effective at getting another person to remove a frustrator that is interfering with goal attainment. In some organizations, work group production norms are enforced with physical violence (Coch & French, 1948). Often the agent of the frustrator cannot be directly attacked. This may be because the person is not available or because of the fear of punishment. Aggressing against one's supervisor will usually result in losing one's job, so most antisocial behavior is displaced or indirect. Instead of aggressing directly against the supervisor, an individual may engage in hidden sabotage.

Not all instances of experienced frustration result in antisocial behavior. Most frustrators are probably seen by most people as challenges to be overcome and result in increased effort to achieve the goal. Often people will make repeated attempts to reach their objective, or they will devise strategies to get around obstacles. Ultimately, someone may change his or her goal if it is blocked by major impediments. The process of goal abandonment was discussed by Klinger (1975). For important goals, it can involve a process of anger and depression. Learned helplessness is another phenomenon that concerns how people abandon goals after experiencing severe frustration in uncontrollable situations (Seligman, 1975).

Figure 1.1 shows several factors that lead a person to respond to a frustrator with antisocial behavior. Given a moderate to high level of experienced frustration, an individual may choose any of a number of behaviors, some of which are antisocial. Factors that influence choice of behavior include fear of punishment for antisocial behavior and perceptions of little situational control (Allen & Greenberger, 1980). Hogan and Hogan (1989) outlined four personality factors that lead to antisocial behavior: hostility to rules, impulsiveness, sense of alienation, and social insensitivity. These four characteristics define the Hogans' organizational delinquency concept.

Fear of punishment has been shown to be an inhibitor of aggressive behavior (e.g., Graham, Charwat, Honig, & Weltz, 1951). Often the inhibited behavior is displaced to a safer form or target (e.g., Gambaro & Rabin, 1969). This is undoubtedly one reason that direct aggression against coworkers or supervisors is relatively rare at work (Geddes, 1994). However, less direct forms of antisocial behavior are likely to occur when fear of punishment is high. Sabotage and theft are possible indirect responses when direct aggression is blocked. Such displaced behavior is performed even though it does not overcome the obstacle to the goal.

Research on Organizational Frustration

Only a handful of studies have investigated frustration in organizations. A few of these have been concerned with the role of frustration in antisocial behavior at work. This is why many of the studies discussed so far have been conducted in the laboratory. A major impediment to studying these behaviors in organizations is that people are reluctant to admit to them. Researchers who study antisocial behavior often must rely on anonymous questionnaires (Giacalone & Rosenfeld,

1987), the use of which limits the sorts of conclusions that can be reached. The results of organizational studies relevant to the frustration model will be summarized here.

Linkage From Frustrators to Experienced Frustration

A literature search uncovered 12 studies that reported correlations of experienced frustration with other work variables. The search was conducted by using the PsycLIT bibliographical database (1980 to 1994) and by checking the reference lists of all studies found. Limiting the review to field studies resulted in the deletion of one additional study. Ten of these studies used the Peters, O'Connor, and Rudolf (1980) scale of experienced frustration at work. Keenan and Newton (1984) used a scale they developed to assess perceptions of both environmental frustration and experienced frustration. Spector (1975) used a scale he devised to assess frustration at work. Twelve work variables were included in at least three of the studies.

A meta-analysis was conducted to summarize the results of the 12 studies, using the approach advocated by Rosenthal (1991; see Table 1.1). This approach involves computing the mean effect size (correlation) for a group of studies. The first column of the table lists the variables correlated with experienced frustration. The second column shows the number of studies that included each variable. The third column contains the total sample size across all studies including the variable. The fourth column contains the unweighted mean correlation. Because of the small number of studies, more extensive statistics were not calculated.

The first six variables in the table are job stressor variables that can be considered frustrators. Experienced frustration was found to correlate with autonomy (negatively) as well as with interpersonal conflict, organizational constraints, role ambiguity, role conflict, and workload. Organizational constraints in all but one study were those described by Peters and O'Connor (1980) and are conditions that interfere with performance. Thus they can be considered to fit the current definition of frustrators.

The frustrators assessed in these studies were self-report measures, which are likely to be influenced by subjects' experienced frustration. The correlations here reflect relations between the cognitive interpretation

Table 1.1 Results of a Meta-Analysis of Studies That Related Experienced Frustration to Other Work Variables

Variable	Number of Studies	Total Sample Size	Mean Correlation
Autonomy	4	613	–.22
Constraints	7	2,876	.49
Interpersonal conflict	4	762	.37
Role ambiguity	5	916	.33
Role conflict	3	614	.43
Workload	4	762	.49
Aggression	3	617	.25
Health symptoms	5	991	.25
Hostility	3	617	.49
Intent to quit	5	1,066	.45
Job satisfaction	8	2,996	–.30
Sabotage	3	617	.20
Work anxiety	6	1,168	.49

and perceptions of the environment and the affective response of frustration. It is not clear from these studies that experienced frustration is linked to the environmental or objective frustrators. Stronger evidence for the link between environmental frustrators and experienced frustration is provided by Spector, Dwyer, and Jex (1988) in a study that gathered data on experienced frustrators from multiple sources, including both job incumbents and their supervisors. Frustration experienced by incumbents was significantly correlated with constraints, interpersonal conflict, role ambiguity, and workload as reported by supervisors (rs ranged from .19 to .23). These results suggest that experienced frustration might be a reaction to environmental frustrators. The cross-sectional nature of the design makes it difficult to draw firm causal conclusions about the possible effects of environmental frustrators.

Linkage From Experienced Frustration to Behavior and Other Reactions

Table 1.1 summarizes the results of studies relating experienced frustration to antisocial behavior and other reactions. As shown in the table, experienced frustration correlates with affective reactions other than anger. Both job satisfaction and work anxiety were associated with experienced frustration. Individuals who reported experiencing high levels of work frustration tended to report high levels of work anxiety and low levels of job satisfaction. These findings are consistent with Keenan and Newton's (1984) model of work frustration. In addition, experienced frustration was associated with physical health symptoms. Individuals who reported high levels of experienced frustration tended to report high levels of physical health symptoms.

Experienced frustration showed some significant associations with employee withdrawal behavior. It correlated with intention of quitting the job (see Table 1.1). In O'Connor et al. (1984), experienced frustration showed a small (.08) but significant correlation with turnover itself. People who quit reported higher levels of experienced frustration than people who did not. Spector et al. (1988) did not find a significant correlation between absence and experienced frustration.

The table summarizes results relating experienced frustration with antisocial behaviors of aggression, hostility, and sabotage. Chen and Spector (1992) used both an anger measure (Spielberger, 1979) and an experienced-frustration measure (Peters et al., 1980) in their study of antisocial behavior. Although the anger measure correlated significantly with theft, the experienced-frustration measure did not. The anger measure also correlated more strongly than the experienced-frustration measure with aggression, hostility, and sabotage. It seems likely that the anger measure is more sensitive to affective reactions than the Peters et al. measure of frustration, resulting in higher correlations with criteria.

Two studies provide indirect evidence for a linkage between frustrators and antisocial behavior. Geddes (1994) conducted a survey of managers to find out about their experiences with giving negative performance appraisal feedback to subordinates. This sort of feedback can be considered a frustrator in that it can interfere with goals in several ways. For example, in many organizations rewards are tied to performance. Poor evaluations can result in an employee's being denied a merit raise or promotion. Furthermore, negative feedback can be an attack on an individual's self-esteem. In both cases, the individual is likely to experience frustration from the situation.

Geddes found that antisocial responses to negative feedback were very common. Her subjects reported that subordinates engaged in aggression, sabotage, withdrawal, and withholding of output. Direct forms of physical aggression were one of the least common responses. It is not clear from these data how much the various antisocial behaviors were associated with experienced frustration. However, the respondents reported that anger was a common response.

Greenberg (1990; Chapter 5 of this volume) conducted a field experiment to determine the effects of pay reduction on theft. A company had to reduce salaries temporarily in two of three plants. In one plant, employees were told that their pay would be reduced, but little justification was given. In the second plant, employees were given a complete explanation for the necessity of reducing salaries because of a lost contract. The third plant had no reduction and served as a control. The amount of material stolen was recorded for each plant before, during, and after the temporary salary reduction.

Both pay reduction plants had an increase in thefts during the time of the pay reduction and a decrease back to baseline when salary levels were restored to their normal levels. However, the theft rate was significantly higher in the plant with little justification for the pay cuts. The third plant, which served as a control, experienced about the same level of theft during the entire study. Greenberg interpreted these results using an equity framework (Adams, 1963), but they also could be viewed from a frustration perspective. Subjects in the no-justification condition might well have interpreted the pay reduction as an arbitrary frustrator, and some responded by stealing. The justification condition would have been interpreted by employees as a nonarbitrary frustrator, thereby inducing less experienced frustration and resulting in less antisocial behavior.

Perceived Control as a Determiner of Antisocial Behavior

A factor that has been linked to antisocial behavior is lack of control. Allen and Greenberger (1980) discussed how lack of perceived control is a contributing factor in destructive behavior. Perlow and Latham (1993) found that scores on the personality variable locus of control predicted later client abuse by workers in a mental retardation facility. Individuals who believed that they did not have personal control (externals) were more likely to engage in abuse than people who believed they had control (internals).

Storms and Spector (1987) conducted a more direct test of how perceived control might affect a person's antisocial responses to experienced frustration. They conducted a questionnaire study in which they assessed behavior, constraints, experienced frustration, and locus of control. They found that both constraints and experienced frustration were correlated with antisocial behaviors of aggression, hostility and complaining, sabotage, and withdrawal. Locus of control moderated the relation between experienced frustration and all these behaviors except hostility and complaining. The correlations were all significant for externals, ranging from .48 to .62. None of the correlations were significant for the internals, ranging from –.06 to .24. Insofar as these data were collected from a cross-sectional survey, causal conclusions are difficult to draw. However, the findings are consistent with the hypothesized role of perceived control in antisocial behavior.

Using a similar survey methodology, DeMore, Fisher, and Baron (1988) found results for college student vandalism that were consistent with Storms and Spector (1987). Students who reported low levels of perceived control and high levels of perceived inequity (which can be considered experienced frustration) reported high levels of vandalism.

Delinquent Personality and Antisocial Behavior

Hogan and Hogan (1989) identified four personality traits that they hypothesized would lead to delinquent behaviors. These behaviors included those considered antisocial in this chapter. They developed an employee reliability scale from the Hogan Personality Inventory (Hogan, 1986; a scale assessing the traits hypothesized to lead to delinquency and initially developed by comparing college students to convicted felons). Hogan and Hogan (1989) reported that scores on employee reliability correlated with several delinquent behaviors, including discharges from work, number of equipment failures, aberrant behavior, injuries, absence, and job performance.

There can be many reasons that an individual who has the delinquency characteristics would engage in antisocial behavior at work. Frustration is one factor that might contribute to these behaviors. The impulsiveness of the delinquent individual makes it likely that he or she will respond to experienced frustration with antisocial behavior. The hostility to rules, sense of alienation, and social insensitivity should reduce the person's inhibitions against engaging in these behaviors. Thus the delinquent individual is more likely than the nondelinquent to resort to antisocial behavior as a response to experienced frustration. It should be noted that these ideas are speculative, as there are apparently no empirical tests of them.

Possible Interventions

The frustration model discussed in this chapter leads to several suggestions for interventions designed to reduce antisocial behavior. Unfortunately, little research has been conducted to determine what types of interventions might be effective. Companies concerned about behaviors such as theft usually have taken one of two approaches: integrity testing to identify applicants with the tendency to engage in unwanted behavior, or surveillance (e.g., hidden cameras or lie detector tests) to inhibit behavior. More positive approaches that focus on reducing experienced frustration are more difficult to find. Interventions can focus on any one of the elements of the frustration model. They can focus on reducing frustrators or on enhancing people's ability to cope with frustrators. The increasing of perceived control might be an effective approach to reducing antisocial behavior.

Interventions to Reduce Frustrators

If we accept the frustration model, it makes sense that we could reduce antisocial behavior by reducing frustrators at work. Greenberg's (1990) study showed how theft could be reduced by giving people a clear explanation of the need for a salary reduction. The turning of an arbitrary to a nonarbitrary frustrator would be expected to reduce the negative impact of the salary reduction. Although they did not measure antisocial behavior, Schaubroeck, May, and Brown (1994) found that a justification for a pay freeze positively affected employee attitudes and turnover intentions.

Geddes (1994) found that negative performance appraisal feedback can lead to antisocial behavior on the part of employees. Meyer, Kay, and French (1965) reported that limiting the amount of criticism in performance appraisal interviews reduced the negative impact on employees. The reduction in negative reactions by limiting the amount of negative feedback is consistent with the idea that the effects of frustrators are compounded when they occur together. This suggests that a way to reduce antisocial behaviors arising from negative performance feedback is to administer that feedback in small doses continually during the year rather than all at once during an annual appraisal session (Meyer et al., 1965).

Interventions to Reduce Experienced Frustration

Frustrators can often be reduced at work, but they cannot be totally eliminated. Interventions to reduce frustration-related antisocial behavior should focus on reducing experienced frustration. Individuals who are in inherently frustrating jobs (e.g., police) could be given stress management training to enhance their coping skills. Individuals who are having a difficult time coping with work frustration could be referred to an employee assistance program by their supervisors. Employee counseling has been shown to improve performance relevant behavior such as absence and alcohol use (Cooper & Sadri, 1995) and might be effective for enhancing employee skills at handling frustrators in a constructive rather than a destructive manner.

Interventions to Enhance Feelings of Control

Enhancing employee feelings of control should help reduce antisocial behavior. Coch and French (1948) noted that employee resistance to production changes involved antisocial behaviors in response to frustration. In this study, an effective solution was to allow employees to participate in the planning of these changes. Thus one might assume that participation enhanced employee feelings of control and perhaps made changes seem less arbitrary because fellow workers were involved.

Employee Screening

An approach that could be effective in reducing antisocial behavior is to use integrity or personality tests to avoid hiring individuals who are prone to these behaviors. Several important personality variables have been discussed in this chapter. As noted earlier, Hogan and Hogan (1989) showed that their employee reliability test was a valid predictor of antisocial behavior. Perlow and Latham (1993) showed that locus of control predicted subsequent client abuse by employees. Storms and Spector (1987) also showed a link between locus of control and antisocial behavior. Ones, Viswesvaran, Schmidt, and Reiss (1994) conducted a meta-analysis that showed how integrity tests can significantly predict violence and other antisocial behaviors.

There are two limitations to using the selection approach for the problem of antisocial behavior. First, to use this method, one must have a sufficiently large applicant pool from which to choose. If there are few applicants, one may have to hire everyone with the required job skills, regardless of his or her likelihood of engaging in antisocial behavior at work. Second, from a societal point of view, what happens to the potentially delinquent individuals if they are not hired by organizations? Organizations that use personality tests will merely push these individuals onto other employers who use other hiring criteria. Furthermore, these delinquent individuals may cause more social problems if they are unemployed than if they are working. In the long run, it may be better to find ways to control antisocial behavior in the potentially delinquent than trying to avoid hiring them.

Conclusion

Frustration in the workplace and its relation to antisocial behavior have been almost ignored in the organizational literature. Although there has been increased interest in the past few years in antisocial behavior, most research has focused on selection of individuals who are less likely to commit these acts. Research with integrity and personality tests has shown that such tests can successfully predict antisocial behavior (Ones et al., 1994). However, our understanding of the psychological processes underlying acts such as aggression, sabotage, theft, and withholding output is quite limited.

One difficulty in studying these behaviors is that they can occur for a variety of reasons. Some antisocial behavior is in response to frustrators at work. The model of frustration shows how conditions and events at work might lead to antisocial behavior. This model is preliminary and includes only those limited factors that have been shown to relate to antisocial behavior. There are probably many more important variables that have not yet been studied.

The limited research evidence supports the model presented in Figure 1.1. Most of this research used cross-sectional designs with self-report data. Although these data show that experienced frustration is associated with reports of behavior, it is not clear to what extent experienced frustration is the result of environmental frustrators. This connection is important because of its implications for interventions. If experienced frustration is an idiosyncratic reaction by an individual, the focus of interventions should be the individual. If certain environmental conditions reliably lead to experienced frustration and to antisocial behavior, interventions should focus on the environment.

The difficulty of studying behaviors that occur occasionally and are illegal is certainly a major reason for the limited amount of research on this topic. Giacalone and Rosenfeld (1987) noted that we are often limited to anonymous surveys to study antisocial behavior. They suggested several additional methods that could be used as well. Antisocial behavior at work is a serious problem that deserves far more research attention than it has been given.

References

(Those with an asterisk are studies included in the meta-analysis)

Adams, J. S. (1963). Toward an understanding of inequity. *Journal of Abnormal and Social Psychology, 67*, 422-436.

Allen, V. L., & Greenberger, D. B. (1980). Destruction and perceived control. In A. Baum & J. E. Singer (Eds.), *Applications of personal control* (Vol. 2, pp. 85-109). Hillsdale, NJ: Lawrence Erlbaum.

Buss, A. H. (1963). Physical aggression in relation to different frustrations. *Journal of Abnormal and Social Psychology, 67*, 1-7.

*Chen, P. Y., & Spector, P. E. (1991). Negative affectivity as the underlying cause of correlations between stressors and strains. *Journal of Applied Psychology, 76*, 398-407.

*Chen, P. Y., & Spector, P. E. (1992). Relationships of work stressors with aggression, withdrawal, theft and substance use: An exploratory study. *Journal of Occupational and Organizational Psychology, 65*, 177-184.

Coch, L., & French, J. R. P., Jr. (1948). Overcoming resistance to change. *Human Relations, 1*, 512-532.

Cooper, C. L., & Sadri, G. (1995). The impact of stress counseling at work. In R. Crandall & P. L. Perrewé (Eds.), *Occupational stress* (pp. 271-282). Washington, DC: Taylor & Francis.

DeMore, S. W., Fisher, J. D., & Baron, R. M. (1988). The equity-control model as a predictor of vandalism among college students. *Journal of Applied Social Psychology, 18*, 80-91.

Dollard, J., Doob, L. W., Miller, N. E., Mowrer, O. H., & Sears, R. R. (1939). *Frustration and aggression*. New Haven, CT: Yale University Press.

Gambaro, S., & Rabin, A. (1969). Diastolic blood pressure response following direct and displaced aggression after anger arousal in high- and low-guilt subjects. *Journal of Personality and Social Psychology, 12*, 87-94.

Geddes, D. (1994, August). *The relationship between negative feedback and increased organizational aggression*. Paper presented at the meeting of the Academy of Management, Dallas, TX.

Giacalone, R. A., & Rosenfeld, P. (1987). Reasons for employee sabotage in the workplace. *Journal of Business and Psychology, 1*, 367-378.

Graham, F. K., Charwat, W. A., Honig, A. S., & Weltz, P. C. (1951). Aggression as a function of the attack and the attacker. *Journal of Abnormal and Social Psychology, 46*, 512-520.

Greenberg, J. (1990). Employee theft as a reaction to underpayment inequity: The hidden cost of pay cuts. *Journal of Applied Psychology, 75*, 561-568.

Hogan, J., & Hogan, R. (1989). How to measure employee reliability. *Journal of Applied Psychology, 74*, 273-279.

Hogan, R. (1986). *Hogan Personality Inventory manual*. Minneapolis: National Computer Systems.

*Jex, S. M., & Gudanowski, D. M. (1992). Efficacy beliefs and work stress: An exploratory study. *Journal of Organizational Behavior, 13*, 509-517.

*Keenan, A., & Newton, T. J. (1984). Frustration in organizations: Relationships to role stress, climate, and psychological strain. *Journal of Occupational Psychology, 57*, 57-65.

Klinger, E. (1975). Consequences of commitment to and disengagement from incentives. *Psychological Review, 82*, 1-25.

Lazarus, R. S. (1995). Psychological stress in the workplace. In R. Crandall & P. L. Perrewé (Eds.), *Occupational stress* (pp. 3-14). Washington, DC: Taylor & Francis.

Locke, E. A., & Latham, G. P. (1990). *A theory of goal setting and task performance*. Englewood Cliffs, NJ: Prentice Hall.

Meyer, H. H., Kay, E., & French, J. R. P., Jr. (1965). Split roles in performance appraisal. *Harvard Business Review, 43*, 123-129.

*O'Connor, E. J., Peters, L. H., Pooyan, A., Weekley, J., Frank, B., & Erenkrantz, B. (1984). Situational constraint effects on performance, affective reactions, and turnover: A field replication and extension. *Journal of Applied Psychology, 69*, 663-672.

*O'Connor, E. J., Peters, L. H., Rudolf, C. J., & Pooyan, A. (1982). Situational constraints and employee affective reactions: A partial field replication. *Group and Organization Studies, 7*, 418-428.

Ones, D. S., Viswesvaran, C., Schmidt, F. L., & Reiss, A. D. (1994, August). *The validity of honesty and violence scales of integrity tests in predicting violence at work*. Paper presented at the meeting of the Academy of Management, Dallas, TX.

Pastore, N. (1952). The role of arbitrariness in the frustration-aggression hypothesis. *Journal of Abnormal and Social Psychology, 47*, 728-741.

Perlow, R., & Latham, L. L. (1993). Relationship of client abuse with locus of control and gender: A longitudinal study. *Journal of Applied Psychology, 78*, 831-834.

Peters, L. H., & O'Connor, E. J. (1980). Situational constraints and work outcomes: The influences of a frequently overlooked construct. *Academy of Management Review, 5*, 391-397.

Peters, L. H., O'Connor, E. J., & Rudolf, C. J. (1980). The behavioral and affective consequences of performance-relevant situational variables. *Organizational Behavior and Human Performance, 25*, 79-96.

Rosenthal, R. (1991). *Meta-analytic procedures for social research*. Newbury Park, CA: Sage.

Schaubroeck, J., May, D. R., & Brown, F. W. (1994). Procedural justice explanations and employee reactions to economic hardship: A field experiment. *Journal of Applied Psychology, 79*, 455-460.

Seligman, M. E. P. (1975). *Helplessness: On depression, development, and death*. San Francisco: W. H. Freeman.

*Spector, P. E. (1975). Relationships of organizational frustration with reported behavioral reactions of employees. *Journal of Applied Psychology, 60*, 635-637.

Spector, P. E. (1978). Organizational frustration: A model and review of the literature. *Personnel Psychology, 31*, 815-829.

*Spector, P. E. (1987). Interactive effects of perceived control and job stressors on affective reactions and health outcomes for clerical workers. *Work and Stress, 1*, 155-162.

*Spector, P. E., Dwyer, D. J., & Jex, S. M. (1988). The relationship of job stressors to affective, health, and performance outcomes: A comparison of multiple data sources. *Journal of Applied Psychology, 73*, 11-19.

*Spector, P. E., & Jex, S. M. (1991). Relations of job characteristics from multiple data sources with employee affect, absence, turnover intentions and health. *Journal of Applied Psychology, 76*, 46-53.

*Spector, P. E., & O'Connell, B. J. (1994). The contribution of individual dispositions to the subsequent perceptions of job stressors and job strains. *Journal of Occupational and Organizational Psychology, 67*, 1-11.

Spector, P. E., Penner, L. A., & Hawkins, H. L. (1975). The effect of the thwarting of aggression on subsequent aggression. *Social Behavior and Personality, 3*, 233-241.

Spielberger, C. D. (1979). *Preliminary manual for the State-Trait Personality Inventory (STPI)*. Unpublished manuscript, University of South Florida, Tampa.

*Storms, P. L., & Spector, P. E. (1987). Relationships of organizational frustration with reported behavioral reactions: The moderating effect of perceived control. *Journal of Occupational Psychology, 60*, 227-234.

2

At the Breaking Point

Cognitive and Social Dynamics
of Revenge in Organizations

Robert J. Bies
Thomas M. Tripp
Roderick M. Kramer

I was so angry. He betrayed me, he used me. With each second I could feel the pressure building inside of me. I could feel the rage in my veins, pulsing, pushing me to get even.

—A mid-level manager at a Fortune 500 company

And if you wrong us, shall we not revenge?

—Shakespeare, The Merchant of Venice

Revenge . . . vengeance . . . "getting even." For most people, hearing those words conjures up frightful images of anger and violence, as in the case of U.S. postal service employees murdered by angry former coworkers (Swisher, 1994), or vivid historical examples of hatred and violence across the centuries, as in the case of Bosnia (Pomfert, 1995). Given such mental images and vivid examples, it is not surprising that revenge is viewed as an emotional and volatile act, and one that always carries destructive consequences—an irrational and socially deviant response in any "civilized" organization or society (Barreca, 1995; Jacoby, 1983).

However, this view of revenge represents an incomplete and skewed picture of it as a motive and as behavior (Bies, 1987; Cahn, 1949; Solomon, 1990). Though it is true that revenge can be *destructive* and *antisocial,* as in the cases of employee theft (Greenberg, 1990), workplace violence (Swisher, 1994), and other forms of social deviance in organizations (Robinson & Bennett, 1995), it is also true that revenge can be *constructive* and *prosocial.* For example, the threat of revenge can act as a powerful deterrent against power abuse by authority figures and organizational decision makers (Bies & Tripp, 1995b). Similarly, a retaliatory "tit-for-tat" response to the aggressive act of another can actually promote cooperation between conflicting parties in organizations (Axelrod, 1984). Indeed, revenge occurs every day (Black, 1990; Wall & Callister, 1995), and organizations still function without disintegrating. In fact, in some organizations, revenge is a *socially* acceptable form of conflict management (Morrill, 1992).

In this chapter, we outline a broader theoretical framework for understanding and explaining revenge cognitions and behavior in organizations. We argue that revenge cognitions and behavior are in response to a perceived personal harm or violation of the social order (Bies & Tripp, 1995a). When events occur that threaten their understanding of the social order, avengers (i.e., anyone who seeks revenge—the victim or observers) are motivated to make sense of those events (Weick, 1993). Similarly, when events occur that seem unjust or disrupt perceived equity in their relationships, avengers attempt to restore balance and equity through their actions (Adams, 1965).

Our framework is grounded in research from organizational behavior, social psychology, and sociology. This research suggests that revenge cognitions and behaviors follow a pattern of "heating up" and "cooling down." In what might be described as a "thermodynamic" model (Lave & March, 1975), a revenge episode begins with a precipitating event (e.g., interpersonal abuse, demotion), and this event *sparks* revenge cognitions and emotions. These revenge cognitions and emotions can create a *heating-up* process within the victim or observer, the intensity and duration of which depends on a variety of cognitive, motivational, and social processes that influence how the sparking event is construed.

If the heat continues to build and intensify, the revenge cognitions and motivation will ultimately find some release—that is, *cool down*. Cooling down may follow one of four different paths, each reflecting different revenge behaviors. First, the heat may escape through *venting* outlets. Second, the heat may *dissipate* relatively quickly, with no manifestation of revenge behavior. Third, if the heat does not dissipate, then revenge cognitions and emotions may *fatigue* the individual slowly over time. Finally, the heat may intensify and reach a breaking point, releasing an *explosion* involving a targeted revenge behavior.

The "Thermodynamics" of Revenge: Heating Up, Cooling Down

A revenge episode begins with a sparking event. Revenge behavior reflects an interplay of heating up and cooling down processes.

Sparking Events

A series of empirical studies have identified a variety of events and actions that can motivate individuals to "get even" in organizations. One category of events involves violations of explicit rules, norms, or promises; the other category centers on status and power derogation (Bies & Tripp, 1995a).

Violations of Rules, Norms, and Promises

Employees are motivated to seek revenge when the formal rules of the organization are violated. One such example involves organizational decision makers who change the rules or criteria of decision making after the fact to justify a self-serving judgment (Bies & Tripp, 1995a). Another example of rule violation involves a formal breach of a contract between an employee and employer, which can lead to litigation (Bies & Tyler, 1993).

Violations are not limited to formal rules but also include breaches of social norms and etiquette. For example, when bosses or coworkers make promises but then break them or even lie outright, the victims may be motivated to avenge such wrongs (Bies & Tripp, 1995a). More broadly, any perceived inequities on the job (Wall & Nolan, 1987) or violations of fairness norms (Aram & Salipante, 1981) can motivate revenge. Examples of such inequities and violations include bosses or coworkers who shirk their job responsibilities, take undue credit for a team's performance, or outright "steal" ideas (Bies & Tripp, 1995a). The revenge motive may also be salient when private confidences or secrets are disclosed to others inside or outside the organization—that is, when people feel "betrayed" by someone they trusted (Bies, 1993).

Status and Power Derogation

Several studies suggest that attempts to derogate a person's status or power can motivate revenge. For example, bosses who are hyper-critical, overdemanding, and overly harsh—even cruel—in their dealings with subordinates over time can spark revenge cognitions and emotions (Bies & Tripp, 1995a). Other revenge-provoking incidents include destructive criticism (Baron, 1988b), public ridicule intended to embarrass a subordinate or coworker (Morrill, 1992), or situations in which the employee is accused wrongly by boss or peer (Bies & Tripp, 1995a). Power struggles (Blalock, 1989) and, in particular, attempts to reduce another person's power (Ferguson & Cooper, 1987) can also elicit the revenge motive.

Heating Up

The initial revenge cognitions and emotions are often quite *hot*. For example, respondents in the Bies and Tripp (1995a) study reported that after they were harmed, they were "mad, angry, and bitter," and felt engulfed in "white-hot" emotions. One person in the Bies and Tripp study described herself as "inflamed and enraged," and "consumed by the thought of revenge," and another person "needed to satisfy the burning desire of revenge" (p. 254). At the time of these initial cognitions and emotions, a heating-up process may begin. This process will be shaped by cognitive, motivational, and social processes.

Cognitive Processes

Several prototypic patterns of social perception may explain revenge behavior in the workplace. The first is a tendency to make *overly
personalistic attributions* about the behavior of other organizational members, particularly those who occupy higher status roles or positions of
power (Kramer, 1994). A number of studies have demonstrated, for
example, that when individuals feel self-conscious or under evaluative
scrutiny, they tend to make overly personalistic attributions about
others' intentions and motives (Kramer, 1995). These overly personalistic attributions can motivate revenge (Anderson, Deuser, & DeNeve,
1995; Baron, 1988a; Thomas & Pondy, 1977).

Bies and Tripp (1995a) identified two kinds of motives in personalistic attributions: selfishness and malevolence. A selfish harm-doer
causes harm for personal profit, picking the victim/avenger purely on
the basis of opportunity. A malevolent harm-doer causes harm for the
sake of hurting a particular victim. When individuals overattribute
sinister and malevolent motives to others' actions, they may perceive
harmful intent or believe they are being belittled even in their otherwise seemingly benign social encounters. Goodwin (1988) provided an
excellent example of this "sinister attribution error" (Kramer, 1994) in
his description of the events that led Herb Stempel to take revenge
against NBC executives who decided to replace him with Charles Van
Doren as the star of the popular quiz show *Twenty One*. Goodwin
describes the "acute precipitating event" that pushed Stempel toward
revenge:

> A few weeks earlier I had asked Stempel: "Herbie, why do you hate
> Van Doren?" "I don't hate him," he objected. "Come on, Herbie," I
> replied, "You've been after him from the beginning." "I did get mad
> about one thing," he explained. "We were on some kind of a benefit
> show together. You know, a quiz show rematch for charity. After the
> show, he was talking to some people behind stage, and I went over to
> shake his hand, and he completely ignored me. It was like I wasn't
> even there." . . . The story was an illuminating metaphor. Whatever
> Van Doren's flaws, he was not a snob. He was much too well bred to
> spurn a handshake. *He just hadn't seen Stempel, and Stempel had inter-
> preted that momentary inattention as confirmation of his most painful
> misconceptions* [italics added]. (p. 55)

From that moment, Stempel found himself driven to exact his measure of revenge on both Van Doren and the network executives whom he felt had betrayed him.

A second important cognitive process contributing to individuals' perceptions that they are being intentionally harmed or singled out unfairly is the *biased punctuation of conflict*. Biased punctuation of conflict refers to a tendency for individuals to construe the history of conflict with others in a self-serving and provocative fashion. For example, in an interpersonal conflict with a manager *M*, a disgruntled employee *E* may reinterpret the history of interpersonal conflict between them as a sequence of exchanges *M-E, M-E, M-E, M-E*, in which the initial hostile or aggressive move was made by *M* (e.g., "She passed me over for promotion just because I was a white male, even though I was clearly the most qualified candidate"). From *E*'s perspective, each of his reactions is a legitimate and proportionate response to a malicious, provocative act by the other.

However, the manager *M* may punctuate the same history of interaction between them as *E-M, E-M, E-M, E-M*, in which the roles of "offender" and "responder" are reversed. Thus, for her, their conflict began because he was always late in completing his assignments and seemed passive aggressive toward her, resulting in her decision to select someone else for the management trainee position.

In terms of its role in the etiology of revenge behavior, the importance of biased punctuation of conflict is twofold. First, it contributes to self-justificatory motives. As Frank (1987) perceptively noted in this regard, construing the history of conflict in this way can be used to justify the claim that one needs "to defend against a powerful and evil enemy, *thereby shifting responsibility for one's own aggressive actions to the opponent* [italics added]" (p. 340). Bies and Tripp (1995a) found a similar justification for revenge behavior by avengers, who viewed their actions as "morally right" and "in service of justice." Second, biased punctuation of conflict tends to generate self-fulfilling patterns of action-reaction between the parties as each tries to restore balance to the relationship by "evening" the score (Kahn & Kramer, 1990). In other words, both sides view their own actions as purely defensive behaviors made in response to the other's unwarranted actions.

The phenomenon of biased punctuation reminds us that even though revenge behavior often appears to be a response to a specific precipitating event (e.g., a dismissal that is perceived as unjust), such acts are almost always embedded in a protracted history of perceived injustices or conflict (Tjosvold & Chia, 1989; Wall & Callister, 1995). In this regard, acts of revenge within organizations are seldom "bolts from the blue." Instead, managers and coworkers usually report, especially with the advantage of hindsight, that there had been a protracted history of behaviors and exchanges suggesting that something was seriously wrong with the individual (e.g., mutterings, withdrawal, veiled threats). From the perspective of outsiders, these events often seem minor and unrelated. In the avenger's mind, however, they form a coherent and cumulative pattern of egregious insult and injury, necessitating a *proportionate* retaliatory response against the organization or one or more of its members. What seems to outsiders like a minor insult becomes perceived as the "straw that broke the camel's back" to the aggrieved avenger (Morrill, 1992).

A third perceptual pattern that contributes to the perceived need to engage in revenge behavior is the *exaggerated perception of conspiracy* associated with paranoid cognitions (Colby, 1981). This term refers to the paranoid perceiver's tendency to view the actions of others in the organization as more tightly connected or coupled than they actually are. President Lyndon Johnson, who manifested many signs of organizational paranoia as he fought his critics over management of the Vietnam war, provides a nice illustration of this phenomenon. According to his aide and eventual biographer, Doris Kearns-Goodwin (1976), Johnson viewed the attacks against him as part of a vast concerted conspiracy to undo his Presidency. As he once confided to her:

> Two or three intellectuals started it all, you know. They produced all the doubt, they and the columnists in the *Washington Post,* the *New York Times, Newsweek,* and *Life.* And it spread and spread. . . . Bobby began taking it up as his cause and, with Martin Luther King on his payroll, he went around stirring up the Negroes. . . . Then the communists stepped in. They control the three networks, you know, and the forty major outlets of communication. It's all in the FBI reports. They prove everything. Not just about the reporters, but about the professors too. (p. 316)

The three patterns of social perception (more accurately, perhaps, misperception) described thus far—overly personalistic attribution, biased punctuation of conflict, and exaggerated perception of conspiracy—can be thought of as tendencies to overprocess social information in ways that promote the misattribution and overattribution of benign organizational exchanges and encounters. If we think of these as outgrowths of otherwise normal modes of social information processing in organizations (see Salancik & Pfeffer, 1978), the question arises: What might contribute to these three forms of overattribution and misattribution? Research suggests that two cognitive processes, hypervigilance and dysphoric rumination, play a prominent role in the development of these forms of misperception. Accordingly, our model posits that these cognitive processes play a particularly prominent role in the intensification or heating up of revenge cognitions.

Hypervigilance. The first process is *hypervigilance.* Numerous organizational theorists (Janis, 1983; Pfeffer, 1992; Weick, 1993) have noted the adaptive role that social vigilance plays within organizations. Given the often competitive and political nature of organizational life, vigilance increases the likelihood that individuals will detect threats and opportunities and respond effectively to them (Morrill, 1992). *Hyper*vigilance, however, represents an extreme and less adaptive mode of perception in which individuals overprocess information, prompting the drawing of erroneous inferences from it (Janis, 1983). For the hypervigilant organizational actor who perceives him- or herself as harmed or threatened, every social interaction becomes scrutinized for hidden meaning and sinister purpose. Thus the hypervigilant avenger dissects every act, no matter how seemingly benign, for hints of insult, humiliation, and derogation. From this vantage point, even the meaningless averted glance or failure to return a greeting takes on sinister significance and malevolent import, thus increasing the likelihood of revenge.

Dysphoric rumination. The second cognitive process contributing to the development of revenge cognition is a pattern of obsessive and dysphoric *rumination.* Dysphoric thinking involves the negative framing and editing of social information. Empirical studies have shown that dysphoric rumination following negative events tends to increase negative thinking about those events and also prompts a pessimistic attributional style when one tries to explain why they happened (Kramer, 1995; Lyubomirsky & Nolen-Hoeksema, 1993; Pyszczynski & Greenberg,

1987). Somewhat ironically, rumination also appears to increase individuals' confidence in their interpretations, further exacerbating the problem of reality testing (Wilson & Kraft, 1993). Thus the more one ruminates about the insults one has experienced, the more convinced one becomes of their intentionality and hidden significance.

Such confidence and feelings of aggravation are further amplified when rumination occurs publicly, in the company of coworkers and/or friends, in so-called "bitch sessions" (Morrill, 1992). When victims receive social support and reinforcement of their suspicion and outrage, it can strengthen their initial beliefs, deepen their resolve to seek revenge, and become the basis for "conspiracy theories" in organizations (Bies & Tripp, 1995a).

Motivational Processes

To explain revenge behavior, it is important to go beyond considering the purely cognitive social information-processing factors that influence how events are construed by organizational members. In particular, it is essential to take account of the motivational factors that underlie cognition and behavior in such situations. Psychological researchers have long recognized the need for individuals to maintain a view of their social and organizational worlds as just (Lerner, 1980) and knowable (Weick, 1993) places. When events occur that threaten those worldviews, individuals become highly motivated to make sense of those events and bring psychological closure to them (Janoff-Bulman, 1992).

Researchers also have recognized the need for individuals to maintain positive personal and social identities (Brewer, 1991) and a sense of self-efficacy and control over their worlds (Bandura, 1986; Seligman, 1975). When events occur that threaten their self-esteem or control, they take actions to affirm a positive self and to restore perceptions of control (Janoff-Bulman, 1992; Steele, Spencer, & Lynch, 1993)

In some cases, the exaggerated sense of harm and threat associated with paranoid cognitions may prompt consideration of extreme remedies to restore a sense of self and to "get even" again in one's relationship with the offending party. A good example of this process is the notion of *Pyrrhic revenge* described by Berglas and Baumeister (1993). Social scientists have long recognized the notion of Pyrrhic victory, in which decision makers escalate commitment to a course of action in the hope of winning, even if the price of victory is severe. With Pyrrhic revenge, however, there is no expectation of conquest, merely of retaliation. The goal, according to Berglas and Baumeister (1993), is "payback rather than current conquest" (p. 151).

Contextual Factors

An analysis of revenge cognitions and behaviors must include consideration of the organizational and institutional settings in which interpersonal relationships are embedded and in which revenge acts unfold. Such relationships are almost invariably hierarchical and are characterized by significant asymmetries in the information available to the parties, their relative power and status in the relationship, and the extent to which they can influence the processes and outcomes that affect them within the workplace.

These objective differences in power, status, and influence can translate into potent differences in the parties' perceived control over each other and perceptions of dependence, vulnerability, and threat (Kramer, 1995). We suggest that these differences, in turn, at least partially account for the differences we have hypothesized in vigilance and rumination. Those "on the top" of a hierarchical relationship, for example, often have little (or less) inclination to pay attention to the social relational dimensions of their interactions with those below them (Pfeffer, 1992). For those "on the bottom," in contrast, relational issues are relatively more salient and psychologically significant because they have perceived implications for one's status or standing in the organization and how well one is doing (Lind & Tyler, 1988). As Ashford and Cummings (1983) noted, individuals in organizations are proactive information seekers interested in assessing where they stand and how they are doing. This portrait might be applied with special force to those who perceive their role in the organization as uncertain and under the control of a more powerful actor. The interaction of these two divergent perceptual and motivational orientations can intensify the heating process, leading ultimately to an eruption in the form of revenge behavior.

Another important underlying contextual factor is the tendency for emerging conflicts within many contemporary American corporations and institutions to remain suppressed or "hidden" from view (see Kolb

& Bartunek, 1992). That is, conflicts tend to be denied or minimized (Nord & Doherty, 1994). For example, they may be discounted as merely "interpersonal friction" between a particular manager and employee or between two manager peers (Morrill, 1992), rather than acknowledged as symptomatic of a more pervasive and fundamental problem in the culture (e.g., a problem of trust between those with the power and those without it).

Because of the discomfort and ambivalence about attending to conflict or even acknowledging its existence, conflicts within such organizations tend to be treated as "exceptional" events that require formal or stylized interactions and interventions such as bargaining and mediation. As Barley (1991) noted, these formal conflict resolution activities become treated as special, "bracketed" activities that interrupt the normal ebb and flow of interaction and occur during experiential "time-outs." At the extreme, parties may be viewed through a "legalistic lens" as if they were litigants in a courtroom (see Sitkin & Bies, 1994).

In contrast with this formalistic approach to dealing with revenge feelings that pervades many contemporary Western organizations, organizations in other cultures often provide alternative mechanisms for more informal and effective handling of feelings of revenge (Augsburger, 1992). For example, Van Maanen (1992) described how a British police agency used drinking occasions and rituals as "organizational time-outs" to surface and manage revenge. The life of a police officer, he noted, is full of recurrent strains, not only because of the intrinsic stresses of the job but also because of the friction between the officers who find themselves daily "on the front lines" and the managing officers, who seem bureaucratic and out of touch with current conditions in the field. "Given this hothouse microenvironment," Van Maanen argued,

> the office party allows for some often blunt discourse across the CID ranks. With alcohol obvious and everyone drunk, an officer is not responsible for what he says and does. *Higher officials can criticize lower ones and, more important, lower ones can "come on about their complaints" with the higher ranks.* [italics added] (p. 49)

Van Maanen's analysis thus chronicled the functional adaptiveness of "off-duty" social processes that help police officers resolve their grievances and provide a mechanism for venting problems before their causes and consequences accumulate.

Some Japanese corporations utilize similar social conventions to manage psychological and social dynamics more effectively (March, 1989). For example, within the workplace, rules of hierarchy may be strictly observed, with displays of proper deference for authority and suppression of overt conflict clearly in evidence. However, off site and after hours, regular rituals of drinking and socializing provide opportunities for complaints to be raised and suggestions made. Verbal retaliation and apologies can flow back and forth, with greatly reduced sense of accountability and concern about losing face. In particular, the other's face can be restored without the loss of one's own.

Cooling Down

A review of the research identified four different patterns of cooling down: *venting, dissipation, fatigue,* and *explosion.*

Venting

One way people satisfy their revenge motive is to *vent* (Thomas, 1992). Venting involves victims talking heatedly and animatedly to their friends or coworkers about what a "jerk" the harm-doer is and the wrongful harm they endured (i.e., "blowing off steam"), with little or no intention of acting out their feelings. Interestingly, though we have discussed the role of "social" rumination in increasing revenge cognitions and emotions, social rumination also can have an opposite effect and act to cool down an avenger. As a result, venting can be relatively satisfying and constructive (Bies & Tripp, 1995a).

Venting can also have an intrapsychic dimension. For example, people may satisfy their revenge impulses by *fantasizing* about the "painful and sordid" revenge they will inflict on the harm-doer (Bies & Tripp, 1995a). Such fantasies may be shared publicly in the venting sessions described in the previous paragraph.

Some organizations provide *procedural mechanisms* to facilitate the venting process (Sitkin & Bies, 1994). For example, some organizations set up *grievance procedures* in which victims often do no more than file a complaint (Aram & Salipante, 1981), yet that can satisfy their revenge motive. These procedures may be more informal, as in the case of managers who have *open-door policies* in which they listen to the victims and often cool them down as a result (Bies, 1995).

Dissipation

Dissipation involves the release of emotional energy without targeted revenge behavior. It can occur in a variety of ways. For example, people may give the harm-doer the "benefit of the doubt" (Bies & Tripp, 1995a) and search for a plausible external explanation or attribution (i.e., nonpersonalistic) for the harm (e.g., the perpetrator was under a lot of pressure or was "forced" to cause the harm by top management). Whether the victim discovered such an explanation through an investigation or was provided *social accounts* (e.g., explanations, excuses) by the perpetrator, a *nonpersonalistic* attribution mitigates avenging responses (Bies, 1987; Greenberg, 1990; Sitkin & Bies, 1993).

Dissipation also can occur because avengers do not believe that they could successfully avenge. In some cases, dissipation takes the form of victims' *doing nothing* out of fear of retaliation by the harm-doer, especially when the harm-doer was their boss; in other cases, victims may do nothing because they cannot successfully invent a method of revenge (Bies & Tripp, 1995a). In either case, victims who do nothing often report a loss of status and self-respect (Bies & Tripp, 1995a).

Victims who do nothing may view that course as the best means to advance their own calculated self-interest. For example, as one person put it, "I needed his recommendation for my promotion. I was not going to do anything to jeopardize that. I was angry, not stupid" (Bies & Tripp, 1995a, p. 256). Matthews (1988, p. 111) reported a similar perspective on revenge and self-advancement espoused by some politicians, with such sayings as "Don't get mad; don't get even; get ahead"; "Don't spend your life looking through a rearview mirror"; and "Don't let [the harm-doers] live inside [your head] rent free."

Dissipation can occur also when victims *forgive* the harm-doers (Shriver, 1995). Victims may be more likely to forgive when they receive an apology (Bies, 1987). In forgiving, victims report that when they "let go," it releases the anger and desire for revenge, thus ending the conflict; as such, forgiveness is viewed as personally and socially constructive (Bies & Tripp, 1995a).

Fatigue

Sometimes, however, people can maintain the energy for very long periods of time. These people do not forgive, forget, or otherwise "let go." Indeed, some people *obsessively ruminate* about incidents that occurred years earlier, expressing regret about not getting even with the harm-doer and becoming cynical about life in organizations (Bies & Tripp, 1995a). For these people, such reflections and ruminations may distract them from their professional responsibilities.

Explosion

An explosive act of revenge is one that expends the built-up energy through an overt behavioral action, which on completion may leave the avenger with little desire for further revenge—but not in all cases, as will be noted below. Some explosions are not extreme or destructive, but limited, focused, and constructive. For example, some people, in response to humiliating public criticism of their work performance, *work harder* to "prove" the critic wrong and restore their status (Bies & Tripp, 1995a; Kidder, 1981). Other examples include a constructive *private confrontation* with the perpetrator to *solve the problem and negotiate a resolution to the situation* (Bies & Tripp, 1995a; Morrill, 1992). *Avoiding the harm-doer* for a short period of time (Bergman & Volkema, 1989; Bies & Tripp, 1995a) and *transferring out of the job or department* may also be viewed as constructive revenge responses, particularly if one's career is not adversely affected by such actions.

However, explosive acts of revenge can be destructive as well. For example, the revenge can be targeted at the organization directly in the form of *employee theft* (Greenberg & Scott, 1996) and *sabotage* (Robinson & Bennett, 1995). *Litigation* (Bies & Tyler, 1993) and *whistle-blowing* (Miceli & Near, 1992) can also be revenge targeted at the organization. These revenge acts can prove costly not only to the organization but also to the individual, as in the case of whistle-blowing.

Explosive revenge can also escalate, as in the case of *feuding* (Bies & Tripp, 1995a). In a feud, conflict escalates because one party's explosion is another party's spark. That is, conflict escalates as the revenge act invites counter-retaliation, which invites yet further retaliation. Feuding can take a variety of forms, such as *public complaints designed to humiliate another person* (Morrill, 1992), *public demands for apologies that are intended to embarrass the harm-doer* (Bies & Tripp, 1995a; Morrill, 1992), *"bad-mouthing" the harm-doer* (Bies & Tripp, 1995a; Morrill, 1992), *verbal threats of retaliation* (Morrill, 1992), *blocking the harm-doer's goals* (Wall & Callister, 1995), and *mobilizing opposition to harm-doer* (Morrill, 1992). In some cases, the feud may result in *physical violence* (Morrill, 1992; Sternberg & Dobson, 1987; Sternberg & Soriano, 1984).

Discussion

Taken together, the research suggests that revenge is a multifaceted social and organizational phenomenon. Indeed, revenge has many "faces"—the good, the bad, and the ugly. For example, contrary to conventional wisdom, which views revenge only in behavioral terms, we found that the revenge response can be primarily or solely cognitive, as in the case of revenge fantasies and obsessive rumination. In other words, the revenge response must be viewed in *intra*personal as well as interpersonal terms.

The empirical evidence we reviewed supports a broader view of revenge and its functionality. More specifically, revenge is not always destructive and antisocial; the evidence we uncovered suggests that revenge can also be constructive and prosocial, as in the cases of private confrontation followed by forgiveness. If revenge by a victim or observer can stop the harm-doer, then it serves a very valuable organizational function. Ironically, then, if the revenge act deters the harm-doer in the future, it is, in a sense, "deviance stopping deviance." As such, revenge should be viewed as an important and informal social control mechanism (Bies & Tripp, 1995b), one that is a necessary supplement to more formal, legalistic social control procedures (Sitkin & Bies, 1994).

To continue this line of reasoning, revenge is not always "irrational." Indeed, revenge has its own rationality. Though people may pursue revenge to achieve calculated political ends (Morrill, 1992), it is also clear that revenge is often rooted in justice terms (Hogan & Emler, 1981). Indeed, while engaging in revenge, avengers invoke moral justification and strongly believe that they are "doing the right thing" (Bies & Tripp, 1995a).

Our analysis of the "virtue" of revenge must be tempered with caution. For example, the assessment of functionality is usually based on the self-reports of the avenger. Clearly, data from other respondents and observers are needed to validate the assessment that the revenge response was constructive or destructive. Related to that point is a broader theoretical question: From whose perspective does one assess functionality? In a multiple stakeholder view of the world, the same revenge response may be viewed as constructive or destructive, depending on one's vantage point or self-interest.

Our framework also suggests new directions for future research on revenge. Though it is clear that attributional processes play a "trigger" role in eliciting revenge, more work is needed to explore the links between revenge cognitions and behavior, particularly in the case of extreme or violent forms of revenge. For example, what cognitive processes and information-processing activities "push" a person past the breaking point, resulting in workplace violence? Our framework suggests that extreme forms of revenge, as in violence, often begin with "everyday" sense-making activities that somehow go awry.

Forgiveness as a revenge response represents an intriguing variable and an important direction for future research. Not often viewed as a means of "getting even," it may be constructive because it restores control to the victim (Bies & Tripp, 1995a). Research is needed to untangle the psychological and social factors that lead a person to forgive and be "merciful," as well as to determine whether people can actually "forgive and forget." Answers to these and related questions would contribute to an important and broader discussion of the "ethics" of forgiveness (Shriver, 1995).

Finally, how organizations respond to revenge, or even try to manage it, represents another research direction (Bies & Tripp, 1995b). Organizational responses to manage revenge can be quite formalistic and legalistic (Sitkin & Bies, 1994), as in the case of grievance procedures (Aram & Salipante, 1981). But attempts to manage revenge can be more informal, as in the case of social accounts (Bies, 1987). Whether it concerns formal or informal responses or some combination of the two, research is needed on how these organizational efforts not only mitigate but also may paradoxically amplify revenge behavior. For we must remember that revenge is an integral part of the social fabric of organizations and that its consequences are both negative and positive. Moreover, revenge has been with us since the beginning of time, and it will continue to be with us into the new millennium of organizational life.

References

Adams, J. S. (1965). Inequity in social exchange. In L. Berkowitz (Ed.), *Advances in experimental social psychology* (Vol. 2, pp. 267-299). New York: Academic Press.

Anderson, C. A., Deuser, W. E., & DeNeve, K. M. (1995). Hot temperatures, hostile affect, hostile cognition, and arousal: Tests of a general model of affective aggression. *Personality and Social Psychology Bulletin, 21,* 434-448.

Aram, J. D., & Salipante, P. F. (1981). An evaluation of organizational due process in the resolution of employee/employer conflict. *Academy of Management Review, 6,* 197-204.

Ashford, S. J., & Cummings, L. L. (1983). Feedback as an individual resource: Personal strategies of creating information. *Organizational Behavior and Human Performance, 32,* 370-398.

Augsburger, D. W. (1992). *Conflict mediation across cultures: Pathways and patterns.* Louisville, KY: Westminster/John Knox.

Axelrod, R. (1984). *The evolution of cooperation.* New York: Basic Books.

Bandura, A. (1986). *Social foundations of thought and action.* Englewood Cliffs, NJ: Prentice Hall.

Barley, S. R. (1991). Contextualizing conflict: Notes on the anthropology of disputes and negotiation. In M. H. Bazerman, R. J. Lewicki, & B. H. Sheppard (Eds.), *Research on negotiation in organizations* (Vol. 3, pp. 165-202). Greenwich, CT: JAI Press.

Baron, R. A. (1988a). Attributions and organizational conflict: The mediating role of apparent sincerity. *Organizational Behavior and Human Decision Processes, 69,* 272-279.

Baron, R. A. (1988b). Negative effects of destructive criticism: Impact on conflict, self-efficacy, and task performance. *Journal of Applied Psychology, 73,* 199-207.

Barreca, R. (1995). *Sweet revenge: The wicked delights of getting even.* New York: Harmony.

Berglas, S., & Baumeister, R. F. (1993). *Your own worst enemy: Understanding the paradox of self-defeating behavior.* New York: Basic Books.

Bergman, T. J., & Volkema, R. J. (1989). Understanding and managing interpersonal conflict at work: Its issues, interactive processes, and consequences. In M. Rahim (Ed.), *Managing conflict: An interdisciplinary approach* (pp. 7-19). New York: Praeger.

Bies, R. J. (1987). The predicament of injustice: The management of moral outrage. In L. L. Cummings & B. M. Staw (Eds.), *Research in organizational behavior* (Vol. 9, pp. 289-319). Greenwich, CT: JAI Press.

Bies, R. J. (1993). Privacy and procedural justice in organizations. *Social Justice Research, 6,* 69-86.

Bies, R. J. (1995). *The injustice of procedural justice: A critical perspective.* Unpublished working paper, Georgetown University.

Bies, R. J., & Tripp, T. M. (1995a). Beyond distrust: "Getting even" and the need for revenge. In R. M. Kramer & T. Tyler (Eds.), *Trust in organizations* (pp. 246-260). Newbury Park, CA: Sage.

Bies, R. J., & Tripp, T. M. (1995b). The use and abuse of power: Justice as social control. In R. Cropanzano & M. Kacmar (Eds.), *Organizational politics, justice, and support: Managing social climate at work* (pp. 131-145). New York: Quorum.

Bies, R. J., & Tyler, T. (1993). The "litigation mentality" in organizations: A test of alternative psychological explanations. *Organization Science, 4,* 352-366.

Black, D. (1990). The elementary forms of conflict management. In School of Justice Studies (Ed.), *New directions in the study of justice, law, and social control* (pp. 43-69). New York: Plenum.

Blalock, H. M., Jr. (1989). *Power and conflict: Toward a general theory.* Newbury Park, CA: Sage.

Brewer, M. B. (1991). The social self: On being the same and different at the same time. *Personality and Social Psychology Bulletin, 17,* 475-482.

Cahn, E. (1949). *The sense of injustice.* New York: New York University Press.

Colby, K. M. (1981). Modeling a paranoid mind. *Behavioral and Brain Sciences, 4,* 515-560.

Ferguson, E. A., & Cooper, J. (1987). When push comes to power: A test of power restoration theory's explanation for aggressive conflict escalation. *Basic and Applied Social Psychology, 8,* 273-293.

Frank, J. D. (1987). The drive for power and the nuclear arms race. *American Psychologist, 42,* 337-344.

Goodwin, R. N. (1988). *Remembering America: A voice from the sixties.* New York: Harper & Row.

Greenberg, J. (1990). Employee theft as a reaction to underpayment inequity: The hidden costs of pay cuts. *Journal of Applied Psychology, 75,* 561-568.

Greenberg, J., & Scott, K. S. (1996). Why do workers bite the hands that feed them? Employee theft as a social exchange process. In L. L. Cummings & B. M. Staw (Eds.), *Research in organizational behavior* (Vol. 18, pp. 111-156). Greenwich, CT: JAI Press.

Hogan, R., & Emler, N. P. (1981). Retributive justice. In M. J. Lerner & S. C. Lerner (Eds.), *The justice motive in social behavior* (pp. 125-143). New York: Plenum.

Jacoby, S. (1983). *Wild justice: The evolution of revenge.* New York: Harper & Row.

Janis, I. L. (1983). *Groupthink* (2nd ed.). Boston: Houghton Mifflin.

Janoff-Bulman, R. (1992). *Shattered assumptions: Towards a new psychology of trauma.* New York: Free Press.

Kahn, R. L., & Kramer, R. M. (1990). Untying the knot: De-escalatory processes in international conflict. In R. L. Kahn & M. N. Zald (Eds.), *Organizations and nation-states: New perspectives on conflict and cooperation* (pp. 139-180). San Francisco: Jossey-Bass.

Kearns-Goodwin, D. (1976). *Lyndon Johnson and the American dream.* New York: New American Library.

Kidder, T. (1981). *The soul of a new machine.* New York: Avon.

Kolb, D. M., & Bartunek, J. M. (Eds.). (1992). *Hidden conflict in organizations: Uncovering behind-the-scenes disputes.* Newbury Park, CA: Sage.

Kramer, R. M. (1994). The sinister attribution error. *Motivation and Emotion, 18,* 199-231.

Kramer, R. M. (1995). The distorted view from the top: Power, paranoia, and distrust in organizations. In R. Bies, R. Lewicki, & B. Sheppard (Eds.), *Research on negotiation in organizations* (Vol. 5, pp. 119-154). Greenwich, CT: JAI Press.

Lave, C. A., & March, J. G. (1975). *An introduction to models in the social sciences.* New York: Harper & Row.

Lerner, M. J. (1980). *The belief in a just world.* New York: Plenum.

Lind, E. A., & Tyler, T. R. (1988). *The social psychology of procedural justice.* New York: Plenum.

Lyubomirsky, S., & Nolen-Hoeksema, S. (1993). Self-perpetuating properties of dysphoric rumination. *Journal of Personality and Social Psychology, 65,* 339-349.

March, R. M. (1989). *The Japanese negotiator.* New York: Kodansha International.

Matthews, C. (1988). *Hardball: How politics is played—told by one who knows the game.* New York: Summit.

Miceli, M., & Near, J. P. (1992). *Blowing the whistle.* New York: Lexington.

Morrill, C. (1992). Vengeance among executives. *Virginia Review of Sociology, 1,* 51-76.

Nord, W. R., & Doherty, E. M. (1994). Toward an improved framework for conceptualizing the conflict process. In R. J. Bies, R. J. Lewicki, & B. H. Sheppard (Eds.), *Research on negotiation in organizations* (Vol. 4, pp. 173-240). Greenwich, CT: JAI Press.

Pfeffer, J. (1992). *Managing with power*. Cambridge, MA: Harvard Business School.

Pomfert, J. (1995, December 18). Atrocities leave thirst for vengeance in Balkans. *Washington Post*, p. A1.

Pyszczynski, T., & Greenberg, J. (1987). Self-regulatory perseveration and the depressive self-focusing style: A self-awareness theory of reactive depression. *Psychological Bulletin, 102*, 122-138.

Robinson, S. L., & Bennett, R. J. (1995). A typology of deviant workplace behaviors: A multidimensional scaling study. *Academy of Management Journal, 38*, 555-572.

Salancik, G. R., & Pfeffer, J. (1978). A social information processing approach to job attitudes and task design. *Administrative Science Quarterly, 23*, 224-253.

Seligman, M. E. (1975). *Helplessness*. San Francisco: W. H. Freeman.

Shriver, D. W., Jr. (1995). *An ethic for enemies: Forgiveness in politics*. New York: Oxford University Press.

Sitkin, S. B., & Bies, R. J. (1993). Social accounts in conflict situations: Using explanations to manage conflict. *Human Relations, 46*, 349-370.

Sitkin, S. B., & Bies, R. J. (Eds.). (1994). *The legalistic organization*. Newbury Park, CA: Sage.

Solomon, R. C. (1990). *A passion for justice: Emotions and the origins of the social contract*. Reading, MA: Addison-Wesley.

Steele, C. M., Spencer, S. J., & Lynch, M. (1993). Self-image resilience and dissonance: The role of affirmational resources. *Journal of Personality and Social Psychology, 64*, 885-896.

Sternberg, R. J., & Dobson, D. M. (1987). Resolving interpersonal conflicts: An analysis of stylistic consistency. *Journal of Personality and Social Psychology, 52*, 794-812.

Sternberg, R. J., & Soriano, L. J. (1984). Styles of conflict resolution. *Journal of Personality and Social Psychology, 47*, 115-126.

Swisher, K. (1994, May 8). Working under the gun. *Washington Post*, p. H1.

Thomas, K. W. (1992). Conflict and negotiation processes in organizations. In M. D. Dunnette & L. M. Hough (Eds.), *Handbook of industrial and organizational psychology* (pp. 651-717). Palo Alto, CA: Consulting Psychologists Press.

Thomas, K. W., & Pondy, L. R. (1977). Toward an "intent" model of conflict management among principal parties. *Human Relations, 30*, 1089-1102.

Tjosvold, D., & Chia, L. C. (1989). Conflict between managers and workers: The role of cooperation and competition. *Journal of Social Psychology, 129*, 235-247.

Van Maanen, J. (1992). Drinking our troubles away: Managing conflict in a British police agency. In D. M. Kolb & J. M. Bartunek (Eds.), *Hidden conflict in organizations: Uncovering behind-the-scenes disputes* (pp. 32-62). Newbury Park, CA: Sage.

Wall, J. A., Jr., & Callister, R. R. (1995). Conflict and its management. *Journal of Management, 21*, 515-558.

Wall, J. A., Jr., & Nolan, L. L. (1987). Small group conflict: A look at equity, satisfaction, and styles of conflict. *Small Group Behavior, 18*, 188-211.

Weick, K. E. (1993). Sensemaking in organizations. In J. K. Murnighan (Ed.), *Social psychology in organizations: Advances in theory and practice* (pp. 10-37). Englewood Cliffs, NJ: Prentice Hall.

Wilson, T. D., & Kraft, D. (1993). Why do I love thee? Effects of repeated introspections about a dating relationship on attitudes towards the relationship. *Personality and Social Psychology Bulletin, 19*, 409-418.

3

Aggression in the Workplace

Joel H. Neuman
Robert A. Baron

Even the most casual observer would have to agree that contemporary society is replete with examples of human aggression—individuals intentionally harming or injuring others (Baron & Richardson, 1994). In the extreme, aggression may involve physical attack resulting in serious injury or death. In less severe forms, it may range from verbal insults and biting sarcasm through much more subtle but nonetheless harmful acts, such as spreading false rumors about others, consuming resources they require, or withholding crucial information from them. In all its many guises, "aggression, whether harmful to life and limb or merely painful to the ego, seems to be a real and important part of the human condition" (Geen, 1991, p. 1). In recognition of this fact, a significant amount of research has been devoted to factors that cause, facilitate, or

Authors' Note: We gratefully acknowledge the helpful comments of Robert Giacalone and Jerald Greenberg on earlier drafts of this chapter.

exacerbate aggression or that tend to prevent or reduce it (R. A. Baron, 1993). Unfortunately, there is little evidence to suggest that this large body of knowledge has been systematically applied to the study of aggression in the social context in which most adults spend the majority of their time—the workplace (Baron & Neuman, 1996; Hogan & Hogan, 1989; Robinson & Bennett, 1995).

In the discussion that follows, we examine the nature and prevalence of aggression in the workplace, some of its major causes, and its varied effects on both individuals and organizations. We then discuss the potential impact of recent changes in many work environments on aggressive behavior and conclude with some recommendations on the control of this particular form of antisocial behavior.

What Is Workplace Aggression?

In common usage, the word *aggression* is employed to describe many different behaviors, not all of which are antisocial in either their intentions or their effects. For example, most retail organizations would be pleased to employ an "aggressive" salesperson but less enthusiastic about employing an "aggressive" customer service representative. In this chapter, we employ the term *aggression* to refer to hostile, as opposed to assertive, forms of behavior. In our conceptualization, workplace aggression involves efforts by individuals to harm others with whom they work, or have worked, or the organizations in which they are currently, or were previously, employed. This harm-doing is intentional and includes psychological as well as physical injury.

With respect to intent, we refer to behaviors that inflict harm by design, as opposed to those acts in which harm-doing is inadvertent. For example, if a manager purposely withholds information needed by a coworker to harm this person, this constitutes aggression. If, instead, the manager simply forgets to provide this information and has no intention of harming this person, this action does not constitute aggression.

In addition, an attempt at harm-doing need not be successful for aggression to have taken place. For example, attempting to make others look bad in the hopes of getting them fired is, in itself, an act of aggression, even if the attempt does not result in the target's dismissal. Finally, our definition includes both *affective* (otherwise referred to as *hostile, reactive,* or *annoyance-motivated*) aggression and *instrumental* (also known as *operant* or *incentive-motivated*) aggression (Buss, 1961; Dodge & Coie, 1987; Feshbach, 1964, 1970; Hartup, 1974; Zillmann, 1979). In the case of affective aggression, the ultimate objective is to harm the target. However, in the case of instrumental aggression, the aggressor harms the target as a means of obtaining some other valued outcome. If I spread untrue, damaging rumors about you in an attempt to get you fired so that I can obtain your job, that constitutes an act of instrumental aggression. Alternatively, if the goal is simply to inflict harm by getting you fired, that is an example of affective (hostile) aggression. In either case, the harm done was intentional, and only the final goal state differed.

Forms of Aggression

As noted previously, aggression takes many different forms. One useful framework for classifying these diverse actions—a framework that has been found to have considerable heuristic value—was suggested by Buss (1961) in his now-classic treatise on human aggression. According to Buss, aggression can be categorized along three dimensions: physical/verbal, active/passive, and direct/indirect. These three dimensions describe the form of the aggressive behavior and the way in which harm is delivered to the target. Physical forms of aggression include such actions as attack with a weapon, physical restraint, unwanted touching, pushing, hitting, or punching, whereas verbal aggression is inflicted through words as opposed to deeds. This may involve threats, insults, sarcasm, or language that is offensive to the target.

Active forms of aggression inflict harm through the performance of some behavior, whereas passive aggression is accomplished through the withholding of some action. Accordingly, insults are a form of active verbal aggression, whereas failing to provide the target with needed information (withholding communication) is a form of passive verbal aggression.

With respect to direct forms, the source of the aggression delivers harm directly to the intended target, whereas in the case of indirect aggression, the harm is delivered through an intermediary or by attacking something that the target values. Insulting the target to his or her face is an example of direct, verbal aggression, whereas spreading false

Table 3.1 Examples of Eight Types of Workplace Aggression Categorized
According to the Buss (1961) Typology

Physical-Verbal Dimension	Active-Passive Dimension	Direct-Indirect Dimension	
		Direct	*Indirect*
Physical	Active	*(Cell 1)*	*(Cell 2)*
		Homicide	Theft
		Assault	Sabotage
		Sexual assault	Defacing property
		Dirty looks	Consuming needed resources
		Interrupting others	Hiding needed resources
		Obscene gestures	Removing needed resources
	Passive	*(Cell 3)*	*(Cell 4)*
		Intentional work slowdowns	Showing up late for meetings
		Refusing to provide needed resources	Delaying work to make target look bad
		Leaving area when target enters	Failing to protect the target's welfare
		Preventing target from expressing self	Causing others to delay action
Verbal	Active	*(Cell 5)*	*(Cell 6)*
		Threats	Spreading rumors
		Yelling	Whistle-blowing
		Sexual harassment	Talking behind target's back
		Insults and sarcasm	Belittling opinions
		Flaunting status	Attacking protégé
		Unfair performance evaluation	Transmitting damaging info
	Passive	*(Cell 7)*	*(Cell 8)*
		Failing to return phone calls	Failing to transmit information
		Giving target the silent treatment	Failing to deny false rumors
		Damning with faint praise	Failing to defend target
		Refusing target's request	Failing to warn of impending danger

rumors behind his or her back is a form of indirect, verbal aggression.
Table 3.1 presents examples of the eight forms of aggression identified
by the Buss (1961) framework.

At this point, we should briefly note the relationship between this
framework and a broader typology of deviant workplace behavior
proposed by Robinson and Bennett (1995). The Buss (1961) framework
focuses only on interpersonal forms of aggression—actions that are

designed to inflict some kind of harm on the target person or persons or, presumably, an organization. In contrast, the typology of deviant workplace behavior suggested by Robinson and Bennett is broader in scope and considers a wide range of deviant behaviors that may or may not involve intentions to harm others or the organization. Although many deviant actions do indeed inflict harm, they may stem from many motives other than, or in addition to, that of inflicting harm. For instance, wasting resources—one of several forms of *production deviance* identified by Robinson and Bennett—may stem from simple carelessness or a lack of concern with the organization's welfare rather than from a desire to harm it. Similarly, blaming coworkers, a form of *political deviance,* may involve efforts to protect one's own reputation and image rather than an intention to harm rivals. In short, although there is considerable overlap between actions identified in the Buss (1961) and Robinson and Bennett (1995) frameworks, the latter should be viewed as broader in scope and as concerned with many forms of behavior that would not be considered aggressive, as the term is defined in this chapter.

Workplace Aggression: The Need for Systematic Research

Table 3.1 suggests two points germane to the present discussion. First, although aggressive behavior takes many different forms, all such actions involve the desire to inflict harm on some target person or entity. Second, many of the behaviors represented in Table 3.1 have received little or no attention in systematic research (e.g., belittling others' opinions, delaying work to make others look bad, removing or needlessly consuming required resources, flaunting status, and intentionally showing up late for meetings). Instead, past research on workplace aggression (e.g., S. A. Baron, 1993; Mantell, 1994) has focused almost exclusively on physical forms of assault that are active and direct (refer to Cell 1 in Table 3.1). We contend that although these are certainly both dramatic and important, they are not the entire story where workplace aggression is concerned. Thus, we believe that research related to workplace aggression must include a focus on behaviors that are primarily verbal, passive, and indirect.

Inspection of Table 3.1 raises two additional questions: (a) Why has the aggression literature overlooked these potentially important—and damaging—forms of aggressive behavior? and (b) Why has the extant research in organizational settings failed to view these behaviors as aggressive?

With respect to the first question, our definition of aggression as intentional harm-doing behavior is consistent with the views held by many aggression researchers (see Berkowitz, 1974, 1981; Feshbach, 1970), but it is not universally accepted (e.g., Buss, 1961). Some definitions restrict aggression to infliction of physical injury (Zillmann, 1979), whereas other formulations require that the harm be successfully administered (Buss, 1961). The definition that is employed serves to delimit the forms of behavior of interest.

Another reason for the lack of research by aggression investigators may involve the extent to which the behavior is an exemplar of aggression: What comes to mind when they think about this form of behavior? We suspect that the answer to this question involves primarily acts of physical violence or direct verbal assaults (threats, taunts, insults). Accordingly, most aggression research has tended to focus on related issues. Finally, most research has tended to focus on affective (hostile) as opposed to instrumental aggression (Geen, 1991). Clearly, much aggression in organizational settings is instrumental.

With respect to the question of why organizational researchers have not typically viewed many of the behaviors listed in Table 3.1 as aggressive, we suspect the following. First, because much behavior in organizations is goal directed (e.g., directed toward the attainment of status, power, and/or material or financial gain), research in this setting tends to focus on instrumental as opposed to hostile motives. Accordingly, many behaviors, such as those listed in Cells 3, 4, 7, and 8 of Table 3.1, have been studied within the context of organizational politics (see Drory & Romm, 1990; Feldman, 1988; Ferris & Kacmar, 1992; Ferris & King, 1991; Velasques, Moberg, & Cavanaugh, 1983) rather than as instances of workplace aggression. Second, many of the actions included in Table 3.1 simply may not be recognized as aggressive. Insofar as the intentions behind such actions may be easily concealed, these behaviors may go completely unnoticed or be perceived as inadvertent or coincidental. Finally, these behaviors are not always motivated by aggressive intent: People do show up late for meetings or fail to return phone calls for reasons completely unrelated to aggression. This fact, too, makes it less likely that organizational researchers will identify such actions as instances of workplace aggression.

The Prevalence of Workplace Aggression

Data on the prevalence of workplace aggression are extremely limited and are associated primarily with acts of physical assault. For example, with respect to workplace homicide, no single agency or institution is responsible for collecting data. In fact, it was not until 1991 that the U.S. Department of Labor's Bureau of Labor Statistics (BLS) released its initial data on fatal occupational injuries (Strunk, 1993). In addition to the BLS initiative, data are now being collected by the Occupational Safety and Health Administration (OSHA) and the National Institute for Occupational Safety and Health (NIOSH). State agencies are also being mobilized in this effort. In New York, for example, data are being collected by the New York State Department of Labor, the New York State Workers' Compensation Board, and the New York City and New York State Departments of Health (New York Committee for Occupational Safety and Health [NYCOSH], 1995).

As limited as the data are with respect to workplace homicide, they are extensive when compared with data for nonfatal physical assault. None of the agencies that compile statistics on death in the workplace require organizations to report threats or attacks in which no one dies. Therefore, most of the data that exist are derived from police reports, workers' compensation claims, and surveys by employee unions and professional organizations.

Finally, with respect to more indirect and passive forms of aggression, which we believe represent the largest portion of workplace aggression (see Baron & Neuman, 1996), our knowledge derives from a limited number of professional surveys and empirical investigations. With these caveats in place, we now present an overview of current knowledge concerning the prevalence of several important forms of workplace aggression.

Fatal Occupational Injury

Homicide is the most serious and visible form of workplace aggression; accordingly, it has received the most attention by the mass media (e.g., "A Postal Employee," 1995), as well as the social science community (S. A. Baron, 1993; Mantell, 1994). From 1980 to 1988, homicide was the third leading cause of occupational injury death in the United States, accounting for 12% (7,603) of all such deaths (Centers for Disease Control, 1993; Jenkins, Layne, & Kisner, 1992). Studies conducted on a state-by-state basis have resulted in similar findings. Sniezek and Horiagon (1989) found an occupational homicide rate of 12% in North Carolina, and research by the Centers for Disease Control established an occupational homicide rate of 14% in Texas (Centers for Disease Control, 1985). In 1992 and 1993, workplace homicide was the third leading cause of traumatic occupational death in New York State (outside of New York City) and the leading cause of occupational death in New York City (NYCOSH, 1995).

As dramatic as these data are, they are somewhat misleading. The impression created is that workplaces are filled with disgruntled employees who are a hair-trigger away from committing mayhem. Although workplaces may contain many disaffected workers, these persons do not typically resort to murder. According to the BLS (1992), the vast majority of workplace homicides are the result of robberies and related crimes (81.9%) as opposed to personal disputes among coworkers (3.9%). To put this in perspective, in one recent year (1993), 1,063 people were killed while at work or on duty, out of a total workforce of approximately 120.8 million people. Of those 1,063 deaths, 59 were attributed to "disgruntled" coworkers (Larson, 1994).

Nonfatal Occupational Injury

Although the data on nonfatal physical assaults are difficult to obtain, what we are able to establish is sufficiently alarming. In 1992, the New York State Department of Labor reported over 11,000 work-related assaults that were serious enough to cause injuries resulting in at least one lost workday (NYCOSH, 1995). Nationally, 11% of all violent crimes were committed against people at work.

In a recent study, the Society for Human Resource Management (1993) surveyed 479 human resource professionals about violence in their respective organizations. These professionals reported incidents involving fistfights (74.8% of those responding), shootings (17%), stabbings (7.5%), and rape/sexual assault (6.5%). In a similar study by the American Management Association (1994), 500 private sector managers reported hand-to-hand violence (4.8% of those responding), assault with a weapon (5.2%), and rape/sexual assault (1.0%). In both these studies, the overwhelming majority of incidents reported did not result in death (95% and 92.3%, respectively) and therefore would not have been included in workplace violence statistics, although they are clearly examples of violence/aggression and certainly merit attention.

Sabotage, Vandalism, and Theft

Destruction of machinery or goods, interference with production, work slowdowns, passing on defective work, flattening tires, scratching cars, writing on company furniture, and intentionally misplacing important paperwork have all been identified as acts of sabotage in the workplace (DiBattista, 1991; Giacalone, Riordan, & Rosenfeld, Chapter 6 of this volume). Some acts, such as snipping cables on personal computers, may be easily discovered, whereas other forms of sabotage, such as destroying mail or company records, may go undetected.

Although sabotage is by definition an act of aggression, such is not the case with theft: That is, theft is probably not perceived by a majority of individuals as an aggressive act. Rather, it is commonly viewed as an action performed for economic gain. However, within the context of our definition, theft may sometimes qualify as aggression. This would be the case in situations in which employees steal items that they do not intend to use or sell because they realize that taking them will inflict economic loss on the organization or, in other instances, will inconvenience or harm specific individuals who need these items. In such cases, theft may well constitute an aggressive action.

Some acts of theft may be annoyance motivated as opposed to incentive motivated and therefore are examples of affective aggression. For example, research by Greenberg and others (e.g., Greenberg, 1990, 1993b, 1994a, Chapter 5 of this volume; Greenberg & Scott, 1996) suggests that many individuals steal from their companies because they believe this is justified. In their eyes, their companies are not providing them with fair outcomes—outcomes proportionate to their contributions. So, to even the score, they simply appropriate company property. Support for this contention is provided by the fact that such theft often occurs in the total absence of feelings of guilt: Employees view such thefts as simply "getting even." In sum, one important cause underlying epidemic levels of employee theft—one form of workplace aggression—seems to be the belief, on the part of many employees, that they are not being treated fairly by their employers. We will have more to say about this link between perceived fairness and workplace aggression below.

With respect to the frequency and impact of theft in organizations, employee theft exacts a high toll from many businesses (Greenberg & Scott, 1996). The U.S. Chamber of Commerce, for example, suggests that it is 10 times more costly to American companies than street crime (Govoni, 1992). With respect to its frequency of occurrence, it has been estimated that three quarters of all employees steal from their employers at least once (McGurn, 1988) and that many of these repeat such actions on a regular basis (Delaney, 1993).

Sexual Harassment

Another important form of workplace aggression involves sexual harassment, which is defined by the federal government as unwelcome sexual advances, requests for sexual favors, and other verbal or physical conduct of a sexual nature when (a) submission to such conduct is made either explicitly or implicitly a term or condition of an individual's employment, (b) submission to or rejection of such conduct by an individual is used as the basis for employment decisions affecting such individual, or (c) such conduct has the purpose or effect of unreasonably interfering with an individual's work performance or creating an intimidating, hostile, or offensive work environment.

Questions can be raised as to the threshold that must be broached before behavior is considered offensive, but to the extent that this behavior is intentional and inflicts harm, it constitutes an aggressive act. A survey of federal employees in 1980 revealed that 42% of females and 15% of males said that they had been sexually harassed on the job, and a follow-up survey in 1987 yielded similar results. Since 1980, more than 38,500 charges of sexual harassment have been filed with the federal government (Service Employees International Union, AFL-CIO, CLC, 1995), and the complaints are mounting: More than 12,500 complaints were filed with the Equal Employment Opportunity Commission in 1993 alone (Cascio, 1995). Ninety percent of Fortune 500 companies have dealt with sexual harassment complaints, and more than one third have been sued at least once (Fisher, 1993).

Work Harassment

Although sexual harassment has received a good deal of attention in the United States, especially following the 1991 confirmation hearings for Supreme Court Justice Clarence Thomas, considerably less attention has been given to other forms of harassment. For example, little research has examined the prevalence, or consequences, of being shouted at loudly or being exposed to insulting comments, undue criticism, unfairly damaging performance evaluations, insinuating glances, negative gestures, or threats of physical violence. The few studies that do exist suggest that research of this nature is badly needed.

For example, in a survey of 338 university employees in Finland, 32% of the respondents indicated that they had observed others being exposed to this type of harassment at their workplace (Björkqvist, Österman, & Hjelt-Bäck, 1994). Similarly, a study involving 178 full-time workers in the United States demonstrated the prevalence of these types of aggression (Baron & Neuman, 1996). Indeed, they were rated by participants in this study as being far more frequent in occurrence than direct, physical assaults.

In the American Management Association study cited previously, 33.2% of the 500 private-sector managers surveyed indicated that their organizations had received threats of violence from current employees (American Management Association, 1994). When asked to describe the nature of the most recent incident of workplace violence they experienced, 8.4% indicated harassment and 24.6% indicated threat of violence. In another survey of 600 full-time American workers, 19% reported being subject to harassment, and 7% reported threat of physical harm (Northwest National Life, 1993).

The various forms of workplace aggression described above could undoubtedly be studied as individual phenomena defined in terms of their own antecedent conditions, intervening processes, and outcomes, but by recognizing them as instances of aggression, we are able to draw on an extensive literature related to the causes, control, and prevention of human aggression. It is to this body of knowledge that we now turn our attention.

An Integrated Model of Aggression

Aggression, like other forms of complex behavior, is multidetermined: It stems from the interplay of a wide range of biological, individual, cognitive, social, situational, and environmental factors (Baron & Richardson, 1994; Geen, 1991). This basic fact is illustrated by Figure 3.1, which presents a conceptual model based on a substantial amount of empirical research related to human aggression and responses to stress (see Anderson, Deuser, & DeNeve, 1995; Berkowitz, 1990; Geen, 1991; Lazarus & Folkman, 1984). We introduce this model to illustrate the current state of theorizing with respect to the causes of human aggression and to set the stage for a discussion in which we argue that recent changes in many organizations may increase the likelihood of workplace aggression. The model further serves to suggest approaches that can be useful in the control and prevention of aggression.

As can be seen in Figure 3.1, aversive antecedent events, such as frustration, verbal threats, or violation of important social norms, have a direct effect on an individual's thoughts, feelings, and physiological responses (see Berkowitz, 1989, 1994). That is, aversive events may trigger hostile thoughts, feelings of anger, and sensations of physiological arousal. Consequent to these reactions, people attempt to make sense of the emotional and physiological sensations they are experiencing and to evaluate the causes of the antecedent event. In the final stage of the process, individuals consider what can be done, and what should be done, to respond to the antecedent event. Specifically, they assess the consequences associated with various responses, consider the various coping alternatives at their disposal, and weigh alternative explanations that may mitigate against an aggressive response.

Perhaps the following example will prove useful in illustrating this process. Imagine an employee whose pet project is rejected by her or his boss and who chooses another, competing project instead. How does this individual react? Initially, this rejection may trigger thoughts, memories, and images of similar, unpleasant events, feelings of anger, and increased tension and arousal. On reflection, however, the employee may conclude that the rejection was justified, that his or her project was actually inferior to the one chosen. Under these circumstances, the individual in question may conclude that the best strategy is to get to work immediately on a better plan, and an aggressive response is unlikely. In contrast, if this person concludes that the rejection was unfair and illegitimate—that the boss was "out to get him or her"—he or she may decide, instead, to seek revenge. Given that he or she also wishes to avoid retaliation for such actions, the employee

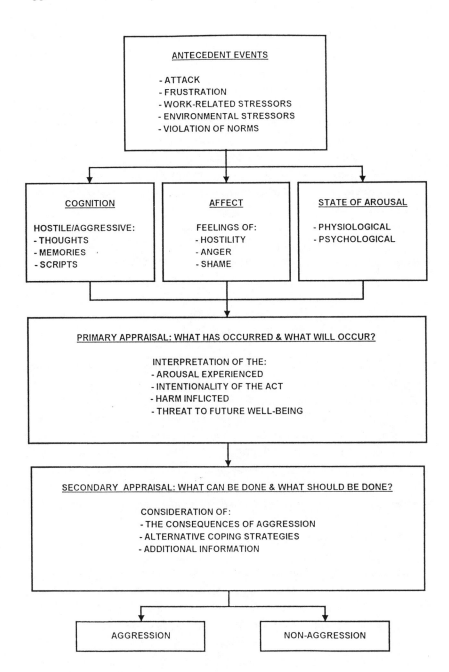

Figure 3.1. Integrated Model of Aggression

may then choose to aggress in a relatively covert manner—for example, by failing to deny false rumors about the boss, by withholding information needed by this person, or by taking some action that indirectly causes the boss to lose face or look bad.

We trust that the main point of this example is clear: In this and countless other instances, whether aggression occurs, the precise form it takes, and the magnitude of such reactions are determined by complex interactions among a very large set of variables. The central outcome—a decision to engage in aggression or other forms of behavior—may occur very quickly. The process leading to this decision, however, is anything but simple.

Using this model of aggression as a guide, we now turn our attention to several contemporary business practices that we believe may lead to an escalation of aggression in many workplaces.

The American Workplace:
Leaner, Meaner . . . and More Aggressive?

American business is currently being challenged by intense global competition, rapid technological change, volatile markets, and shrinking profit margins. In responding to these challenges, organizations may engage in behavior that is harmful to employees and then "rationalize their destructive behaviors in terms of policy shifts, quality shifts, and appropriate business conduct" (Williams, 1994, p. 4). We believe that some of these business practices may "set the stage" for increased aggression—especially, as we have argued previously, for relatively subtle forms of aggression (verbal, passive, and indirect acts of aggression).

Today's Workplace: Leaner and Meaner

In responding to the pressures outlined above, organizations have reengineered (Hammer & Champy, 1993), restructured (Tomasko, 1993), rightsized (Hendricks, 1992), and downsized (Tomasko, 1990). Ostensibly, these structural and process-oriented changes are being employed to increase organizational efficiency and effectiveness. In application, this most often results in reductions in force (Cameron, 1994; Cascio, 1993), increased use of part-time and temporary workers (Fierman, 1994b), increasing pressure for greater worker productivity (Fierman, 1994a), and abandonment of long-standing covenants between employers and employees (Williams, 1994).

Reductions in Force

More than 85% of the *Fortune* 1,000 firms downsized their white-collar workforces between 1987 and 1991, affecting more than 5 million jobs (Cameron, Freeman, & Mishra, 1991). Companies large and small are slashing jobs at a pace never before seen in American economic history (Cascio, 1993), and despite strong evidence that the economy is robust, evidence suggests that downsizing is far from over (McKinley, Sanchez, & Schick, 1995).

A national study of the changing workforce found that 42% of respondents were victims of organizational downsizing, 28% had seen management cutbacks, and 20% feared being fired (Shellenbarger, 1993). Between 1980 and 1982, 79% of managers surveyed and 75% of non-managers rated their job security as good or very good. However, for the period 1992 to 1994, those figures decreased dramatically—to 55% and 51%, respectively (O'Reilly, 1994).

Increased Pressure for Greater Worker Productivity

Employees today work more than they did 25 years ago—the equivalent of a 13th month every year—and 8% of 200 CEOs recently surveyed by *Fortune* magazine said they will have to push their people harder than ever before to compete in the 1990s (Fierman, 1994a). People-related issues are taking a back seat to bottom-line business concerns. In a recent survey by Towers Perrin, 300 senior-line and human resource executives who responded placed people-related issues at the bottom of a list of organizational priorities (American Management Association, 1995). The top three priorities were customer satisfaction, financial performance, and competition.

Violations of Preexisting Employment Norms

The social contract that once existed between employee and employer has been abandoned. In prior times, management and labor were party to an implicit psychological or social contract in which employees contributed loyalty in return for job security. Those long-term employee-employer relationships have been replaced by temporary and part-time affiliations. The number of people working for temporary employment agencies has jumped 240% in the past 10 years, and temporary or part-time positions accounted for approximately 20% of the 18 million jobs created since 1983 (Fierman, 1994b).

The Consequences to Employees

Growing evidence suggests that the survivors, as well as victims, of layoffs experience considerable frustration and stress (Brockner et al., 1994), as well as depression, resentment, and hostility (Catalano, Dooley, Novaco, Wilson, & Hough, 1993). Studies show that following reductions in force, survivors experience declining morale and an increasing distrust of management (Brockner, 1988; Cascio, 1993) and frequently have to cope with increased workloads (Tomasko, 1990). Adding insult to injury, survivors are frequently referred to in very disparaging terms. For example, one observer "heard personnel departments referring to remaining employees as 'backfill,' a term more commonly used in building roads and sewers" (Tomasko, 1990, p. 43). Tomasko (1990) further observed that because most management attention is focused on the mechanics of downsizing, many psychological issues are ignored or delegated to low-level staff. For example, while management's attention is focused on process reengineering or departmental reorganization, little attention may be paid to the social loss and insecurity experienced by employees as a result of these changes.

Beyond the effects associated with reductions in force, employees report higher levels of stress and frustration as a function of their participation in contingent employment relationships (e.g., part-timers, freelancers, subcontractors, and independent professionals). Some of this frustration may stem from the fact that roughly 6.4 million workers in 1993, out of 21 million contingent workers, said that they would prefer full-time positions (Fierman, 1994b).

Today's Workplace: More Aggressive?

Considering that the business practices described above appear to be associated with increasing levels of worker frustration, stress, and emotional disturbances (Kilborn, 1993; O'Reilly, 1994; Shellenbarger, 1993; Williams, 1994), what implications does this have for workplace aggression?

Frustration

Frustration has long been viewed as an antecedent to aggression (Berkowitz, 1989; Dollard, Doob, Miller, Mowrer, & Sears, 1939; Feshbach, 1984; Spector, Chapter 1 of this volume). In organizational settings, frustration has been found to be positively correlated with aggression against others, interpersonal hostility, sabotage, strikes, work slowdowns, stealing, and employee withdrawal (Spector, 1975, 1978, Chapter 1 of this volume; Storms & Spector, 1987).

Stress

The experience of stress also has been linked to human aggression. Chen and Spector (1992) found a relationship between work stressors and interpersonal aggression, hostility, sabotage, complaints, and intentions to quit. They also reported a modest relationship among work stressors, theft, and absence. Anecdotally, workplace stressors have been cited as the cause for the unusually large number of coworker-involved homicides among employees of the U.S. Postal Service (Kilborn, 1993); in the past 9 years, 10 postal workers have been responsible for the deaths of 38 coworkers.

Emotional Disturbances

As previously mentioned, stress and frustration experienced by layoff survivors also has been linked to emotional disturbances such as guilt, depression, resentment, and hostility (Catalano et al., 1993). Unpleasant feelings such as these may activate tendencies toward aggression, increased physiological arousal, and unpleasant thoughts related to these experiences (Berkowitz, 1989, 1994). Negative affect also has been found to be associated with increased aggression and reduced helping behavior (Cialdini & Kenrick, 1976; Weyant, 1978).

In short, it seems possible that changes currently occurring in many organizations are, in a sense, "setting the stage" for increased workplace aggression by providing antecedent events producing aggression-enhancing shifts in the cognitive and affective states of large numbers of employees (see Anderson et al., 1995). Findings from our own research (Baron & Neuman, 1996) offer at least preliminary support for these contentions. In a study conducted with more than 200 employees of several different organizations, we found that the greater the extent to which several changes had occurred in these organizations—changes such as downsizing, layoffs, increased workplace diversity, and increased use of part-time employees—the greater the incidence of reported workplace aggression. And, as noted earlier, most of this aggression was described as being relatively covert: that is, indirect, passive, and verbal rather than direct, active, and physical. Although these findings are far from conclusive, they provide at least suggestive evidence for the view that certain changes in modern organizations may indeed be contributing to elevated levels of workplace aggression.

Assuming that these findings and the reasoning offered above are accurate, an important question arises: Can anything be done to deal with this problem? It is to this issue that we turn next.

Prevention and Control of Workplace Aggression

The model of aggression presented in Figure 3.1 suggests several tactics that may prove useful in the prevention and control of workplace aggression, but we will confine our discussion to (a) the use of personnel selection procedures designed to screen for potentially aggressive employees, (b) the use of punishment to discourage aggressive acts, (c) the use of strategies that reduce feelings or perceptions of injustice, and (d) the implementation of training programs that provide individuals with improved social skills, coping strategies, and alternatives to aggression. In the following discussion, we elaborate briefly on each of these strategies.

Screening for Aggressive Individuals

Whether as a function of nature or nurture, some individuals are more predisposed to aggression than others. These individuals may be inclined (a) to attribute others' actions to hostile intentions (Dodge, Pettit, McClaskey, & Brown, 1986; Sancilio, Plumert, & Hartup, 1989),

(b) to experience negative affect (Watson, & Clark, 1984), or (c) to respond in an aggressive manner when exposed to mild frustration or minor provocation (Glass, 1977; Strube, 1989). Our point is not to suggest that these predispositions lead inexorably to aggression but rather that antecedents to aggression are associated with individuals as well as situations and environmental conditions (e.g., Folger & Skarlicki, 1995). This being the case, a good time to identify individuals with a strong propensity toward aggression is before they are hired.

Background Investigations and Reference Reports

The use of background data as a predictor of on-the-job performance has had a long history in employment settings (McDaniel, 1989; Owens, 1976), and recent attention has focused on using these data in screening for violence-prone employees (S. A. Baron, 1993; Mantell, 1994; Slora, Joy, Jones, & Terris, 1991). Mantell (1994) suggested that background investigations in such a screening process include a check of the applicant's work, military, criminal, and credit histories, as well as inspection of his or her driving record. The purpose of this type of investigation is not to uncover a single, minor indiscretion in the applicant's past; rather, it is an attempt to uncover a pattern of aggressive behavior or serious episodes of violence (e.g., convictions for crimes of violence, spousal abuse, child abuse, or workplace assaults).

A fundamental part of any background investigation involves contacting personal references supplied by the applicant. This has long been a popular method for obtaining information relating to personality traits possessed by the candidate, such as cooperativeness, honesty, and social adjustment (Peres & Garcia, 1962; Sleight & Bell, 1954). Unfortunately, reference reports of this type are nearly always supportive of the candidate, so it comes as little surprise that they are characterized by low inter-rater reliability and low criterion-related validity (Muchinsky, 1979). Although reference reports may not be particularly useful as selection devices, they may prove useful in identifying people who should *not* be considered for employment. Muchinsky (1979) suggested using the reference report to "screen out unsatisfactory candidates rather than to predict gradations of success among the satisfactorily performing employees" (p. 295). Accordingly, any negative reference reports or reports suggesting "faint praise" should raise concern.

Although background investigations and reference reports are very useful, there are practical problems associated with their use. Extensive investigative procedures such as the one outlined above may simply be too costly, time consuming, or impractical. Also, legal considerations may limit the scope of your investigation. For example, some of the information may violate the applicant's right to privacy or violate federal and/or state equal employment opportunity laws (Felsenthal, 1995). Further, individuals may be hesitant to provide unflattering information about the applicant for fear of being sued. It should be noted that organizations also are being sued when they fail to screen applicants properly: If an employee proves dangerous and the employer "should have known," litigation for negligent hiring practices can result (Ryan & Lasek, 1991).

Even when successful, background investigations and reference checks are able to identify only those persons who have engaged in overtly aggressive acts or those who have been apprehended and prosecuted for violence. For these reasons, organizations have turned to other screening techniques to identify potentially troublesome employees.

Pre-Employment Testing

Polygraph machines (lie detectors) and paper-and-pencil integrity tests have long been used in personnel selection to screen out "dishonest" and "counterproductive" job applicants (see Ash, 1991; Dalton, Metzger, & Wimbush, 1994; Murphy, 1993). Before the passage of the Employee Polygraph Protection Act of 1988, which severely limits the use of polygraph examinations in the personnel selection process, pre-employment screening accounted for more than 75% of all polygraph tests administered—approximately 4 million pre-employment tests per year (Ash, 1991). In response to this law, emphasis has shifted to the use of paper-and-pencil integrity tests (Sackett, Burris, & Callahan, 1989).

At first glance, a discussion about integrity testing may seem unrelated to workplace violence, but closer examination suggests otherwise. As suggested by Murphy (1993):

> Workers may vary considerably in the extent to which they engage in
> a variety of undesirable or forbidden behaviors, theft being only one
> of these; programs designed to detect, prevent, or deter theft may

capture only a small part of a broad cluster of behaviors indicative of dishonesty at work. (p. 15)

Consistent with this observation, some researchers have described honesty in terms of employee reliability and deviance (Hogan & Hogan, 1989; Hollinger & Clark, 1983). More directly relevant to the present discussion, scales that measure a person's predisposition to engage in violent on-the-job activities are included in some paper-and-pencil personnel selection tests (Slora et al., 1991). For example, a version of the London House Personnel Selection Inventory (PSI; London House, 1980) contains scales that measure propensity toward physical assault, intentional damage and waste, and hostile customer relations. The Personnel Decisions Inc. (PDI) Employment Inventory (Personnel Decisions Incorporated, 1985) contains scales that measure trouble with authority, hostility, and thrill seeking, and the Reliability Scale of the Hogan Personnel Selection Series (Hogan & Hogan, 1986, 1989) measures hostility to authority, thrill seeking, and social insensitivity. Although the use of these types of tests is not without controversy (e.g., Camara & Schneider, 1994; Lilienfeld, Alliger, & Mitchell, 1995; Ones, Viswesvaran, & Schmidt, 1995), there is evidence to suggest that standardized psychological instruments such as those cited above may prove useful in screening for potentially aggressive employees (Slora et al., 1991).

Situational and Stress Interviews

Potentially aggressive employees can also be identified through carefully structured job interviews. In addition to questions designed to assess an applicant's job-related knowledge, skills, and abilities, Mantell (1994) strongly recommends asking every applicant the following seven questions: (a) When have you felt that you have been treated unfairly in your life? (b) What did you do about it? (c) What would you have liked to do about it? (d) Why did you feel you had been treated unjustly? (e) What complaints have you had about your supervision in the past? (f) What could a supervisor do to make you angry? (g) What has a supervisor done in the past to make you really angry? Responses to these questions reflecting unjust or unfair treatment in past employment should raise concern. As Mantell (1994) observed, "In nearly every case involving disgruntled employees who resorted to some type of violence on the job, their perception of unjust or unfair treatment has been one key to their motivations" (p. 58). In fact, perceptions of inequity are related to many forms of aggression, not just instances of physical violence. We will have more to say about this relationship below.

Another useful interview technique involves describing a potentially difficult on-the-job situation and asking applicants how they would respond. For example, applicants might be asked how they would deal with a hostile customer or an antagonistic exchange with their boss or a coworker. Applicants also can be exposed to mild provocation from the interviewer to determine how they react. Similar procedures are used to assess the presence of the hostility component of the Type A personality dimension (e.g., Glass, 1977), so there is some precedent for their use. Needless to say, however, such procedures must be used only after careful preparation and with extreme caution.

Even the best procedures will not be totally effective in screening all potentially aggressive individuals, and given the right situational factors, even the most nonaggressive individuals may, on occasion, engage in intentional harm-doing (e.g., Folger & Skarlicki, 1995). We now turn, therefore, to techniques that have proven to be effective in controlling aggression.

Punishment and Workplace Aggression

Under certain circumstances, punishment or the threat of punishment can be effective in controlling overt forms of aggression (e.g., Berkowitz, 1962; Dollard et al., 1939). For this reason, all organizations should have a well-defined, consistently enforced policy related to workplace violence and sexual harassment. However, the threat of punishment is generally not effective when provocation and resulting anger arousal are high (e.g., Baron, 1973; Rogers, 1980). Moreover, although threatened retaliation may suppress direct forms of aggression, it can actually increase the occurrence of indirect (covert) forms of aggression (Donnerstein & Donnerstein, 1976). Because, as we contend, the vast majority of workplace aggression is covert, it appears that threats of punishment for engaging in various forms of workplace aggression may be of limited use in restraining such behavior.

Perceptions of Injustice and Workplace Aggression

In contrast to the use of threats and punishment, strategies that reduce feelings or perceptions of unfairness among employees may be much more effective in reducing the frequency and intensity of workplace aggression. Two forms of organizational justice, in particular, may be of central importance: interpersonal justice and informational justice (Greenberg, 1993a). *Interpersonal justice* refers to the demonstration of sensitivity to, and concern for, individuals within the organization—especially as relates to the distribution of outcomes they receive. *Informational justice* refers to providing individuals with adequate explanations of, and reasons for, the procedures used to determine those outcomes.

The model presented in Figure 3.1 suggests that these classes of social justice may be important determinants of aggression. Within this model, the interpretation of events (during the primary appraisal stage) strongly determines the likely response to such events. Aggression is most frequently associated with perceptions of intentional provocation by others (Mantell, 1994; Torestad, 1990) and also with feelings of exploitation (Hollinger & Clark, 1983). Therefore, strategies that minimize or eliminate perceptions of having been treated unfairly should prove useful in reducing aggression.

Support for this reasoning is provided by the results of an ingenious field study by Greenberg (1990). In this investigation, theft rates were measured in manufacturing plants during a period when pay had been reduced by 15%. Employees who received thorough and sensitive explanations as to the reasons for these cuts were significantly less likely to engage in theft than their colleagues who were not similarly informed. A follow-up laboratory study by Greenberg (1994b), designed to examine these results more precisely, demonstrated an independent effect for both informational and interpersonal justice. Specifically, the incidence of theft behavior was reduced as a function of the validity of the information provided about underpayment and the interpersonal sensitivity demonstrated toward the underpayment victim. Enhanced interpersonal justice and informational justice also have been found to reduce negative reactions to employee layoffs (Brockner et al., 1994).

We feel compelled to make one final point about social justice. An understandable reaction to our plea for a more humane and considerate workplace is probably to suggest that in the present business environment, management cannot afford to shift its attention from more pressing "bottom-line" concerns. Although we agree that the business community is justified in its concern for higher levels of worker productivity, we believe that managers have lost sight of an important fact: A high concern for productivity is not incompatible with a high concern for people. In fact, successful and effective leadership is more likely to result when management demonstrates high concern for both people *and* productivity (Blake & Mouton, 1964). Thus, some evidence suggests that high levels of interpersonal and informational justice may contribute to the attainment of key organizational goals.

Training

Formal training can provide individuals with skills that are useful in defusing, managing, and responding to aggression. For example, one major reason that individuals become involved in repeated aggressive encounters is that they are severely lacking in basic social skills such as sensitivity to the emotional states of others, ability to express their wishes properly, and ways of responding to provocation that are not inflammatory (Baron & Richardson, 1994). People lacking in such skills account for a significant proportion of violence in many societies (Toch, 1992). Fortunately, research demonstrates that training is effective in teaching social skills, and the acquisition of these competencies is associated with significant reductions in aggressive behavior (Goldstein, 1981; Schneider, 1991; Schneider & Byrne, 1987).

In addition to social skills training, instruction in conflict management (Rahim, 1992), interpersonal communication (Johnson, 1978), and stress management (Huesmann, 1994) all have demonstrated their effectiveness in reducing interpersonal aggression, and more specific forms of training targeted at particular work-related variables also may prove useful. For example, instruction related to designing and conducting performance evaluations may reduce the perceptions of unfairness and the feelings of frustration and hostility often associated with this process (Carroll & Schneier, 1982). Training in the appropriate administration of discipline (Grote & Harvey, 1983), as well as guidance in dealing with "difficult" subordinates, peers, and superiors (Solomon, 1990), may decrease the potential for confrontation and reduce the level of stress and anxiety associated with these unpleasant situations. All of these factors, as we have argued previously, may serve as antecedents to aggression.

Finally, although instances of serious physical violence are rare, they do occur. Training should be provided in responding to threats posed by present and previous employees, as well as customers (Anfuso, 1994). Efforts to develop systematic programs for equipping managers with the skills needed to recognize potentially dangerous situations and, perhaps, to defuse them are currently underway (e.g., S. A. Baron, 1993; Mantell, 1994).

Conclusion

Admittedly, we have focused on a limited number of issues related to workplace aggression and its control. However, we have touched on several issues that have been largely ignored in the growing literature on workplace aggression: (a) the tremendous range and variety of acts of workplace aggression; (b) the fact that such actions can be linked to a wide variety of social, cognitive, and environmental variables; and (c) the potential contribution of recent, continuing changes in many businesses to increasing levels of workplace aggression.

Most previous research on workplace aggression has focused primarily on workplace *violence*—an understandable tendency given the dramatic nature of such actions. However, we firmly believe, with some empirical support from our own ongoing research (Baron & Neuman, 1996), that the overwhelming majority of acts of workplace aggression are far more subtle, tending, in general, to be indirect and passive rather than direct and active. Such forms of aggression are particularly valuable to would-be aggressors in work settings, for they permit such persons to achieve their primary goal—harming intended victims—while minimizing the likelihood that they will be identified and become targets of retaliation. Previous research indicates that such *covert* forms of aggression are common and are often preferred by would-be aggressors to more direct, *overt* forms of aggression (Björkqvist, Österman, & Lagerspetz, 1994).

Instances of intentional harm-doing have often been described by the terms *organizational politics*, or "dirty tricks." Because they are designed to harm intended victims in some manner, however, we feel that it is appropriate—perhaps even preferable—to view them as subtle forms of workplace aggression. Certainly, the harmful effects they produce can have serious consequences for intended victims, so in this sense, such actions meet the requirements of our basic definition of aggression: actions designed to inflict some kind of harm on others.

In our view, workplace aggression wastes a tremendous amount of precious resources—human and financial. Even minor forms of aggression may be extremely counterproductive. Individuals engaged in these activities waste time that might be utilized in more profitable, job-related pursuits and distract others from their work. It is our belief that if even a fraction of the energy currently expended on "harm-doing" could be redirected toward more prosocial behavior, the gains in organizational efficiency and effectiveness would be enormous. For this reason alone, we believe that the time is ripe for a concerted effort to understand better the causes and nature of all forms of aggression in the workplace. The potential benefits of acquiring such knowledge are, we feel, substantial, and the costs of continuing to focus on dramatic, but relatively rare, instances of workplace violence are far too high to pay.

References

American Management Association. (1994, April). *Workplace violence: Policies, procedures, and incidents.* New York: Author.

American Management Association. (1995, May). Executives rank people-related issues far below other business priorities. *Management Review, 84* (Human Resources Forum Suppl.), 1.

Anderson, C. A., Deuser, W. E., & DeNeve, K. M. (1995). Hot temperatures, hostile affect, hostile cognition, and arousal: Tests of a general model of affective aggression. *Personality and Social Psychology Bulletin, 21,* 434-448.

Anfuso, D. (1994, October). Deflecting workplace violence. *Personnel Journal, 73,* 66, 68, 70-71, 73-77.

Ash, P. (1991). A history of honesty testing. In J. W. Jones (Ed.), *Preemployment honesty testing: Current research and future directions* (pp. 3-19). Westport, CT: Quorum.

Baron, R. A. (1973). Threatened retaliation from the victim as an inhibitor of physical aggression. *Journal of Research in Personality, 7,* 103-115.

Baron, R. A. (1993). Reducing aggression and conflict: The incompatible response approach. Or: Why people who feel good usually won't be bad. In G. G. Brannigan & M. R. Merrens (Eds.), *The undaunted psychologist* (pp. 203-218). New York: McGraw-Hill.

Baron, R. A., & Neuman, J. H. (1996). Workplace violence and workplace aggression: Evidence on their relative frequency and potential causes. *Aggressive Behavior, 22,* 161-173.

Baron, R. A., & Richardson, D. R. (1994). *Human aggression* (2nd ed.). New York: Plenum.
Baron, S. A. (1993). *Violence in the workplace: A prevention and management guide for business.* Ventura, CA: Pathfinder.
Berkowitz, L. (1962). *Aggression: A social psychological analysis.* New York: McGraw-Hill.
Berkowitz, L. (1974). Some determinants of impulsive aggression: The role of mediated associations with reinforcements for aggression. *Psychological Review, 81,* 165-176.
Berkowitz, L. (1981). The concept of aggression. In P. F. Brain & D. Benton (Eds.), *Multidisciplinary approaches to aggression research* (pp. 3-15). Amsterdam: Elsevier.
Berkowitz, L. (1989). Frustration-aggression hypothesis: Examination and reformulation. *Psychological Bulletin, 106,* 59-73.
Berkowitz, L. (1990). On the formation and regulation of anger and aggression: A cognitive-neoassociationistic analysis. *American Psychologist, 45,* 494-503.
Berkowitz, L. (1994). Is something missing? Some observations prompted by the cognitive-neoassociationist view of anger and emotional aggression. In L. R. Huesmann (Ed.), *Aggressive behavior: Current perspectives* (pp. 35-57). New York: Plenum.
Björkqvist, K., Österman, K., & Hjelt-Bäck, M. (1994). Aggression among university employees. *Aggressive Behavior, 20,* 173-184.
Björkqvist, K., Österman, K., & Lagerspetz, K. M. J. (1994). Sex differences in covert aggression among adults. *Aggressive Behavior, 20,* 27-33.
Blake, R. R., & Mouton, J. S. (1964). *The managerial grid.* Houston: Gulf.
Brockner, J. (1988). The effects of work layoffs on survivors: Research, theory, and practice. In B. M. Staw & L. L. Cummings (Eds.), *Research in organizational behavior* (Vol. 10, pp. 213-255). Greenwich, CT: JAI Press.
Brockner, J., Konovsky, M., Cooper-Schneider, R., Folger, R., Martin, C., & Bies, R. J. (1994). Interactive effects of procedural justice and outcome negativity on victims and survivors of job loss. *Academy of Management Journal, 37,* 397-409.
Bureau of Labor Statistics. (1992). *Census of fatal occupational injuries.* Washington, DC: Author.
Buss, A. H. (1961). *The psychology of aggression.* New York: John Wiley.
Camara, W. J., & Schneider, D. L. (1994). Integrity tests: Facts and unresolved issues. *American Psychologist, 49,* 112-119.
Cameron, K. S. (1994). Guest editor's note: Investigating organizational downsizing— fundamental issues. *Human Resource Management, 33,* 183-188.
Cameron, K. S., Freeman, S. J., & Mishra, A. K. (1991). Best practices in white-collar downsizing: Managing contradictions. *Academy of Management Executive, 5,* 58.
Carroll, S. J., Jr., & Schneier, C. E. (1982). *Performance appraisal and review systems: The identification, measurement, and development of performance in organizations.* Glenview, IL: Scott, Foresman.
Cascio, W. F. (1993). Downsizing: What do we know? What have we learned? *Academy of Management Executive, 7,* 95-104.
Cascio, W. F. (1995). *Managing human resources: Productivity, quality of work life, profits* (4th ed.). New York: McGraw-Hill.
Catalano, R., Dooley, D., Novaco, R. W., Wilson, G., & Hough, R. (1993). Using ECA survey data to examine the effect of job layoffs on violent behavior. *Hospital and Community Psychiatry, 44,* 874-879.
Centers for Disease Control. (1985). Fatal occupational injuries: Texas, 1982. *Morbidity and Mortality Weekly Report, 34,* 130-139.
Centers for Disease Control. (1993). *Homicide in the workplace* (National Institute of Occupational Safety and Health Doc. No. 705003). Washington, DC: Author.

Chen, P. Y., & Spector, P. E. (1992). Relationship of work stressors with aggression, withdrawal, theft and substance use: An exploratory study. *Journal of Occupational and Organizational Psychology, 65*, 177-184.

Cialdini, R. B., & Kenrick, D. T. (1976). Altruism as hedonism: A social development perspective on the relationship of negative mood state and helping. *Journal of Personality and Social Psychology, 34*, 907-914.

Dalton, D. R., Metzger, M. B., & Wimbush, J. C. (1994). Integrity testing for personnel selection: A review and research agenda. In G. Ferris (Ed.), *Research in personnel and human resources management* (Vol. 12, pp. 125-160). Greenwich, CT: JAI Press.

Delaney, J. (1993). Handcuffing employee theft. *Small Business Report, 18*, 29-38.

DiBattista, R. A. (1991). Creating new approaches to recognize and deter sabotage. *Public Personnel Management, 20*, 347-352.

Dodge, K. A., & Coie, J. D. (1987). Social information-processing factors in reactive and proactive aggression in children's peer groups. *Journal of Personality and Social Psychology, 53*, 1146-1158.

Dodge, K. A., Pettit, G. S., McClaskey, C. L., & Brown, M. M. (1986). Social competence in children. *Monographs of the Society for Research in Child Development, 51*, 1-85.

Dollard, J., Doob, L., Miller, N., Mowrer, O. H., & Sears, R. R. (1939). *Frustration and aggression.* New Haven, CT: Yale University Press.

Donnerstein, E. J., & Donnerstein, M. (1976). Research in the control of interracial aggression. In R. G. Geen & E. C. O'Neal (Eds.), *Perspectives on aggression* (pp. 133-168). New York: Academic Press.

Drory, A., & Romm, T. (1990). The definition of organizational politics: A review. *Human Relations, 43*, 1133-1154.

Feldman, S. P. (1988). Secrecy, information, and politics: An essay in organizational decision making. *Human Relations, 41*, 73-90.

Felsenthal, E. (1995, April 5). Potentially violent employees present bosses with a Catch-22. *Wall Street Journal*, pp. B1, B5.

Ferris, G. R., & Kacmar, K. M. (1992). Perceptions of organizational politics. *Journal of Management, 18*, 93-116.

Ferris, G. R., & King, T. R. (1991). Politics in human resources decisions: A walk on the dark side. *Organizational Dynamics, 20*, 59-71.

Feshbach, S. (1964). The function of aggression and the regulation of aggressive drive. *Psychological Review, 71*, 257-272.

Feshbach, S. (1970). Aggression. In P. H. Mussen (Ed.), *Carmichael's manual of child psychology* (pp. 159-259). New York: John Wiley.

Feshbach, S. (1984). The catharsis hypothesis, aggressive drive, and the reduction of aggression. *Aggressive Behavior, 10*, 91-101.

Fierman, J. (1994a, March 21). Are companies less family-friendly? *Fortune*, pp. 64-67.

Fierman, J. (1994b, January 24). The contingency workforce. *Fortune*, pp. 30-34, 35.

Fisher, A. B. (1993, August 23). Sexual harassment: What to do. *Fortune*, pp. 84-88.

Folger, R., & Skarlicki, D. (1995, August). *A popcorn model of workplace violence.* Paper presented at the meeting of the Academy of Management, Vancouver, British Columbia, Canada.

Geen, R. G. (1991). *Human aggression.* Pacific Grove, CA: Brooks/Cole.

Glass, D. C. (1977). *Behavior patterns, stress, and coronary disease.* Hillsdale, NJ: Lawrence Erlbaum.

Goldstein, A. P. (1981). Social skills training. In A. P. Goldstein, E. G. Carr, W. S. Davidson II, & P. Wehr (Eds.), *In response to aggression: Methods of control and prosocial alternatives* (pp. 159-218). New York: Pergamon.

Govoni, S. J. (1992, February). To catch a thief. *CFO*, pp. 24-32.

Greenberg, J. (1990). Employee theft as a reaction to underpayment inequity: The hidden cost of pay cuts. *Journal of Applied Psychology, 75,* 561-568.

Greenberg, J. (1993a). The social side of fairness: Interpersonal and informational classes of justice. In R. Cropanzano (Ed.), *Justice in the workplace: Approaching fairness in human resource management* (pp. 79-103). Hillsdale, NJ: Lawrence Erlbaum.

Greenberg, J. (1993b). Stealing in the name of justice: Informational and interpersonal moderators of theft reactions to underpayment inequity. *Organizational Behavior and Human Decision Processes, 54,* 81-103.

Greenberg, J. (1994a). *Restitution and retaliation as motives for inequity-induced pilferage.* Unpublished manuscript, Ohio State University.

Greenberg, J. (1994b). Using social fair treatment to promote acceptance of a work site smoking ban. *Journal of Applied Psychology, 79,* 288-297.

Greenberg, J., & Scott, K. S. (1996). Why do workers bite the hands that feed them? Employee theft as a social exchange process. In B. M. Staw, & L. L. Cummings (Eds.), *Research in organizational behavior* (Vol. 18, pp. 111-156). Greenwich, CT: JAI Press.

Grote, R. C., & Harvey, E. L. (1983). *Discipline with punishment.* New York: McGraw-Hill.

Hammer, M., & Champy, J. (1993). *Reengineering the corporation: A manifesto for business revolution.* New York: Harper Business.

Hartup, W. W. (1974). Aggression in childhood: Developmental perspectives. *American Psychologist, 29,* 336-341.

Hendricks, C. F. (1992). *The rightsizing remedy: How managers can respond to the downsizing dilemma.* Homewood, IL: Business One Irwin.

Hogan, J., & Hogan, R. (1986). *Hogan personnel selection series manual.* Minneapolis: National Computer Systems.

Hogan, J., & Hogan, R. (1989). How to measure employee reliability. *Journal of Applied Psychology, 74,* 273-279.

Hollinger, R. D., & Clark, J. P. (1983). *Theft by employees.* Lexington, MA: Lexington.

Huesmann, L. R. (Ed.). (1994). *Aggression: Current perspectives.* New York: Plenum.

Jenkins, E. L., Layne, L. A., & Kisner, S. M. (1992). Homicide in the workplace: The U.S. experience, 1980-1988. *AAOHN Journal, 40,* 215-218.

Johnson, E. H. (1978). *Crime, correction, and society.* Homewood, IL: Dorsey.

Kilborn, P. T. (1993, May 17). Inside post offices, the mail is only part of the pressure. *New York Times,* pp. 1, 15.

Larson, E. (1994, October 13). A false crisis: How workplace violence became a hot issue. *Wall Street Journal,* pp. A1, A10.

Lazarus, R. S., & Folkman, S. (1984). *Stress, appraisal and coping.* New York: Springer-Verlag.

Lilienfeld, S. O., Alliger, G., & Mitchell, K. (1995). Why integrity testing remains controversial. *American Psychologist, 50,* 457-458.

London House. (1980). *Personnel Selection Inventory.* Park Ridge, IL: Author.

Mantell, M. (1994). *Ticking bombs: Defusing violence in the workplace.* Burr Ridge, IL: Irwin.

McDaniel, M. A. (1989). Biographical constructs for predicting employee suitability. *Journal of Applied Psychology, 74,* 964-970.

McGurn, T. (1988, March 7). Spotting the thieves who work among us. *Wall Street Journal,* p. 16A.

McKinley, W., Sanchez, C. M., & Schick, A. G. (1995). Organizational downsizing: Constraining, cloning, learning. *Academy of Management Executive, 9*, 32-42.

Muchinsky, P. M. (1979). The use of reference reports in personnel selection: A review and evaluation. *Journal of Occupational Psychology, 52*, 287-297.

Murphy, K. R. (1993). *Honesty in the workplace.* Pacific Grove, CA: Brooks/Cole.

New York Committee for Occupational Safety and Health. (1995, March). *Violence in the workplace: The New York experience.* New York: Civil Service Employees Association.

Northwest National Life. (1993, October). *Fear and violence in the workplace: A survey documenting the experience of American workers.* Minneapolis, MN: Author.

Ones, D. S., Viswesvaran, C., & Schmidt, F. L. (1995). Integrity tests: Overlooked facts, resolved issues, and remaining questions. *American Psychologist, 50*, 456-457.

O'Reilly, B. (1994, June 13). The new deal: What companies and employees owe one another. *Fortune,* pp. 44-47, 50, 52.

Owens, W. A. (1976). Background data. In M. D. Dunnette (Ed.), *Handbook of industrial and organizational psychology* (pp. 609-644). Chicago: Rand McNally.

Peres, S. H., & Garcia, J. R. (1962). Validity and dimensions of descriptive adjectives used in reference letters for engineering applicants. *Personnel Psychology, 15*, 279-286.

Personnel Decisions Incorporated. (1985). *Development and validation of the PDI Employment Inventory.* Minneapolis, MN: Author.

A postal employee, 22 years on the job, kills his supervisor. (1995, July 10). *New York Times,* p. A10.

Rahim, M. A. (1992). *Managing conflict in organizations* (2nd ed.). Westport, CT: Praeger.

Robinson, S. L., & Bennett, R. J. (1995). A typology of deviant workplace behaviors: A multidimensional scaling study. *Academy of Management Journal, 38*, 555-572.

Rogers, R. W. (1980). Expressions of aggression: Aggression-inhibiting effects of anonymity to authority and threatened retaliation. *Personality and Social Psychology Bulletin, 6*, 315-320.

Ryan, A. M., & Lasek, M. (1991). Negligent hiring and defamation: Areas of liability related to pre-employment inquiries. *Personnel Psychology, 44*, 293-319.

Sackett, P. R., Burris, L. R., & Callahan, C. (1989). Integrity testing for personnel selection: An update. *Personnel Psychology, 42*, 491-529.

Sancilio, M. F. M., Plumert, J. M., & Hartup, W. W. (1989). Friendship and aggressiveness as determinants of conflict outcomes in middle childhood. *Developmental Psychology, 25*, 812-819.

Schneider, B. H. (1991). A comparison of skill-building and desensitization strategies for intervention with aggressive children. *Aggressive Behavior, 17*, 301-311.

Schneider, B. H., & Byrne, B. M. (1987). Individualizing social skills training for behaviorally distorted children. *Journal of Consulting and Clinical Psychology, 55*, 444-445.

Service Employees International Union, AFL-CIO, CLC. (1995). *Assault on the job: What can we do about workplace violence* (2nd ed.). Washington, DC: Author.

Shellenbarger, S. (1993, September 3). Work-force study finds loyalty is weak, divisions of race and gender run deep. *Wall Street Journal,* pp. B1, B8.

Sleight, R. B., & Bell, G. D. (1954). Desirable content of letters of recommendation. *Personnel Journal, 32*, 421-422.

Slora, K. B., Joy, D. S., Jones, J. W., & Terris, W. (1991). The prediction of on-the-job violence. In J. W. Jones (Ed.), *Preemployment honesty testing: Current research and future directions* (pp. 171-183). Westport, CT: Quorum.

Sniezek, J. E., & Horiagon, T. M. (1989). Medical-examiner-reported fatal occupational injuries, North Carolina, 1978-1984. *American Journal of Industrial Medicine, 15,* 669-678.

Society for Human Resource Management. (1993, December). *Violence in the workplace survey.* Alexandria, VA: Author.

Solomon, M. (1990). *Working with difficult people.* Englewood Cliffs, NJ: Prentice Hall.

Spector, P. E. (1975). Relationships of organizational frustration with reported behavioral reactions of employees. *Journal of Applied Psychology, 60,* 635-637.

Spector, P. E. (1978). Organizational frustration: A model and review of the literature. *Personnel Psychology, 31,* 815-829.

Storms, P. L., & Spector, P. E. (1987). Relationships of organizational frustration with reported behavioural reaction: The moderating effect of locus of control. *Journal of Occupational Psychology, 60,* 227-234.

Strube, M. J. (1989). Evidence for the Type A behavior: A taxonomic analysis. *Journal of Personality and Social Psychology, 56,* 972-987.

Strunk, D. L. (1993). Bureau of Labor Statistics releases occupational injuries and illnesses survey. *Job Safety and Health Quarterly, 4,* 12-14.

Toch, H. (1992). *Violent men: An inquiry into the psychology of violence* (Rev. ed.). Washington, DC: American Psychological Association.

Tomasko, R. M. (1990). *Downsizing: Reshaping the corporation for the future.* New York: AMACOM.

Tomasko, R. M. (1993). *Rethinking the corporation: The architecture of change.* New York: AMACOM.

Torestad, B. (1990). What is anger provoking: A psychophysical study of perceived causes of anger. *Aggressive Behavior, 16,* 9-26.

Velasques, M., Moberg, D. J., & Cavanaugh, G. F. (1983). Organizational statesmanship and dirty politics: Ethical guidelines for the organizational politician. *Organizational Dynamics, 11,* 65-79.

Watson, D., & Clark, L. A. (1984). Negative affectivity: The disposition to experience aversive emotional states. *Psychological Bulletin, 96,* 465-490.

Weyant, J. M. (1978). Effects of mood states, costs, and benefits of helping. *Journal of Personality and Social Psychology, 36,* 1169-1176.

Williams, L. C. (1994). *Organizational violence: Creating a prescription for change.* Westport, CT: Quorum.

Zillmann, D. (1979). *Hostility and aggression.* Hillsdale, NJ: Lawrence Erlbaum.

4

Lying in Organizations

Theory, Research, and Future Directions

Steven L. Grover

Pundits, practitioners, and policy makers have trumpeted the importance of ethical business behavior. To the general public, "business ethics" conjures up images of the major, publicized catastrophes, such as the gas leak at Union Carbide's Bhopal plant and the Exxon Valdez oil spill. Closer inspection of highly publicized unethical activity, however, often reveals a constellation of much smaller behaviors that allow catastrophes or gross misconduct to occur (Guy, 1990). Business ethics theory can be enhanced by examining the underlying behaviors that contribute to major wrongdoing. This chapter analyzes one such behavior: lying. In this chapter, I demonstrate the need to examine lying, review the extant literature on lying, and suggest future directions for lying research.

"A false statement made with the intent to deceive" is the definition of *lying* given by the *Oxford English Dictionary*, and it matches the definition adopted by social psychologists (DePaulo & DePaulo, 1989; DePaulo, Stone, & Lassiter, 1985; Ekman, 1985). The essential aspects of this definition are that the perpetrator *knows* the information is false, *wants* to mislead another person, and engages in the behavior proactively (Bok, 1978). Other than by lying, people can deceive by omitting facts or information, by presenting information in a certain order, or by framing statements to guide the listener away from the truth. Ekman (1985) categorized these methods of deceit as *concealment*, and Bok (1982) called them *secrets*. In either taxonomy, these methods are distinct from lying because they do not involve giving false information. For the purposes of this chapter and the study of lying in organizations, a definition restricted to attempts to deceive by giving information one knows to be false is beneficial for two reasons. First, it is an unambiguous conceptualization based on facts and thus facilitates studying the behavior and making comparisons across studies. Second, it is a precise definition that differentiates lying from other ethical and unethical behaviors.

Why Study Lying in Organizations?

Lying is a key form of antisocial behavior. For people to form and maintain social units, some level of truthful information is required. Conversely, untruthful information transferral undermines the bonds of the social unit.

Lying and its converse are critical elements of behavior in organizations due to their relation to information. Organization theorists have long established that information flow has important implications for organizations (Fayol, 1949; Galbraith, 1973; Lawrence & Lorsch, 1964). Information flow between organization units engenders coordination of the those units toward the overarching goals of the organization. Not only is the amount of information transferred among units important to organizational effectiveness, but the quality is clearly an essential ingredient to integration.

Lying jeopardizes information quality and therefore the integrity of organizations. When the plans and actions of one unit of an organization are predicated on information gleaned from another unit, those plans and actions are only as good as that information. If the person delivering information lies, then that information is flawed, and therefore the resulting actions will be flawed or misguided. Lying therefore has potentially detrimental effects on how organizations function.

Lying threatens the foundation of trust that underlies cross-level and peer relationships in organizations. Trust plays a potential role in an array of organization outcomes because it is a precursor to cooperation (Mayer, Davis, & Schoorman, 1995; McAllister, 1995). Although somewhat speculative, an emerging literature on organizational trust suggests that the lack of trust generated by lying may make people less committed to their organization (Cook & Wall, 1980; Gambetta, 1988). The resulting reduction in loyalty may have an impact on organizational turnover (Allen & Meyer, 1990; Mowday, Porter, & Steers, 1982), and hence hiring and training costs.

Lying has serious consequences to organizational life that warrant further attention. Because lying may negatively influence information quality, trust, and cooperation, too much lying has potentially deleterious effects on overall organization functioning. At this point, we should explore what is known about human lying.

Review of Psychological Literature

The psychology of lying is a rich and varied literature, having been studied by researchers of nonverbal communication, clinical psychology, forensic psychology, applied psychology, and social psychology.

Nonverbal communication researchers have examined the nonverbal displays associated with lying as well as people's accuracy in detecting these displays (for a review, see Ekman, 1988). The body of research demonstrates a pattern of nonverbal behavior displayed while lying. Liars tend to have dilated pupils, exhibit frequent self-regulators (touching or grooming the self), blink more frequently, and speak with a higher vocal pitch (DePaulo et al., 1985; Ekman, 1985, 1988; Streeter, Krauss, Geller, Olson, & Apple, 1977). In addition, people's facial cues leak the emotion that they are truly feeling when they attempt to communicate falsely a different emotion (Ekman, 1985). For example, Ekman (1988) conducted studies in which he asked student nurses to lie about how they felt while observing films of grotesque medical procedures. Many of the subjects showed their true emotions through identifiable facial expressions. Notably, disguising emotions seemed to be a useful job skill because the nurses who more skillfully hid their true emotions were also more likely to complete their nursing program successfully (Ekman, 1988).

A paradox of the nonverbal behavior literature is that even though research has identified patterns of nonverbal cues to lying, few people can accurately detect lying (DePaulo et al., 1985). One reason people cannot detect lying is that they attend to the wrong cues. People typically interpret shifty eyes and stammering as evidence of lying, when body movement, pupil dilation, and vocal pitch are much better indicators of intentional deception (Ekman & O'Sullivan, 1991). Studies of lying detection that have naive subjects view nonverbal cues from videotape find that typical detection rates are in the 55% to 60% range (Bond & Fahey, 1987; Zuckerman, DePaulo, & Rosenthal, 1981). Even people in professions that may hone detection skills, such as police interrogators and psychologists, are not very good at detection, although they have much greater confidence in their error-prone judgments (DePaulo & Pfeifer, 1986; Ekman & O'Sullivan, 1991; Vrij, 1993).

Clinical psychologists research pathological liars and the pathologies of which lying is symptomatic. Lying, especially lying for no apparent reason, is a symptom of a host of psychological disorders, including antisocial, histrionic, narcissistic, borderline, and compulsive personality disorders (Ford, King, & Hollender, 1988). People with brain pathologies lie incoherently (Modell, Mountz, & Ford, 1992), and there is controversy over whether pathological liars can be psychoanalyzed (O'Shaughnessy, 1990). Lying is also a key symptom of antisocial personality disorder (Cacciola, Rutherford, Alterman, & Snider, 1994).

Applied psychologists have developed and debated technologies for detecting lies and liars, including the polygraph and paper-and-pencil integrity tests. In a recent review of paper-and-pencil integrity and polygraph tests, Saxe (1991) commented on the difficulty of predicting when people will lie or steal. The tests have limited utility because they have accuracy rates with high false positives (Sackett, Burris, & Callahan, 1989) and fall far short of a reasonable-doubt measure (Murphy, 1987). Saxe (1991) concluded that to inform theory and to have practical significance for detecting and avoiding lies in the workplace, studies should focus on the reasons people lie.

Individual Differences

It seems reasonable that people vary in their propensity to lie or to tell the truth. In fact, attempts to identify an honesty trait are renowned in early social psychology. Hartshorne and May (1928) reported a series of experiments conducted in their quest to validate a personality type of honesty. However, their summary findings of their studies did not support the contention that individuals systematically varied on this dimension. Hartshorne and May's (1928) conclusion was that people's ethical behavior was more influenced by situational variables than by individual differences.

The interactionist perspective on personality, which portrays behavior as resulting from an interaction of individual personality differences and situational variables, may provide a fruitful approach to individual differences and lying. Trevino (1986) presented a thorough analysis of unethical behavior from the interactionist perspective and has empirically supported the notion that individual locus of control interacts with situations to inform a host of ethical behaviors (Trevino & Youngblood, 1990). Another of Trevino's (1986) key propositions was that ethical behavior results from an interaction of moral maturity and "pressureful situations." Grover (1993b) tested this proposition with lying behavior as the specific behavior of interest. As predicted, people closer to the conventional level of moral development were more likely to lie as a function of role conflict in the situation. More principled people were not influenced by the situation. The explanation was that more conventional (less principled) people are likely to look to rules and norms or laws or behavior of others to inform their moral choices. In contrast, people who are more principled in their moral decision making are less concerned with formal rules or laws and look to a set of ethical principles that may not correspond with majority opinion.

The Machiavellianism personality construct may predict lying. The dimension, based on Machiavelli's *Prince*, assesses one's way of dealing with people, specifically the degree to which one feels other people can be manipulated (Christie & Geis, 1970). Wrightsman (1974) argued that highly Machiavellian individuals are not particularly hostile or vicious. Rather, the construct taps a manner of dealing with people that represents a cool detachment or a lower emotional response to sensitive situations involving other people. The idea is that highly Machiavellian individuals manipulate others with less emotional response than do people lower on this dimension. As one would expect from cool detachment, studies have shown that high Machs are better liars in the sense that they can maintain eye contact while lying (Exline, Thibaut, Hickey,

& Gumpert, 1970) and that their lies are less likely to be detected (DePaulo & Rosenthal, 1979). In addition, high Machs are more likely than low Machs to lie when placed in a conflictual situation (Grover & Enz, 1996).

It is apparent from the research reviewed that lying is arousing and that the arousal is displayed but is difficult to identify. Consequently people can get away with lying. In addition, lying occurs in a range of professions. Corporate presidents lie in their reports to shareholders (Abrahamson & Park, 1994), nurses lie in documentation and to physicians, and police officers lie or "fluff" evidence in crime reports (Barker & Carter, 1990). With all this lying in organizations, it should be fruitful to create theory that explains why people lie and under what conditions they are more likely to lie.

Causes of Lying

Few theorists have speculated on the reasons for, and hence causes of, lying. In this section, I will develop two dominant explanations. The first is grounded in the notion of self-interest, which is a common element from a number of different literatures. The second potential cause is role conflict, or an inability to meet conflicting expectations.

Self-Interest

Several different theories explain lying under the rubric of self-interest. The rudimentary claim of the self-interest paradigm is that people will behave in their own best interest, a notion found in exchange theories (Kelley & Thibaut, 1978), agency theory (Eisenhardt, 1989; Holstrom, 1979; Jensen & Meckling, 1976), and reinforcement-learning theories (Bandura, 1969; Skinner, 1969). Applied to lying, self-interest theories imply that people will lie when it benefits them to do so. For example, Lewicki (1983) postulated that lying was an explicit negotiation tactic used for the benefit of its wielder.

A rival of self-interest theory, Etzioni's (1988) socioeconomics theory makes the case that people owe moral allegiance to, and behave consistently with, their identification group's requirements. Furthermore, behaviors such as lying have ethical components that are governed by cultures and taboos. People who believe that lying is immoral may not lie even when it benefits them to do so. Consequently self-interest is a dominant theory that has potential pitfalls in explaining lying.

Role Conflict

In previous work, I have chronicled the problems with self-interest theory, and from those problems I have drawn a theory that makes predictions about the likelihood of lying in a variety of situations (Grover, 1993a). This theory of lying is driven by role theory (Gross, Mason, & McEachern, 1958), which states that people assume many different roles in their lives. Each of these roles has certain requirements or expectations attached to it, and sometimes our various role expectations conflict. When roles conflict, people become distressed and attempt to alleviate the role conflict in some way. Of the many different ways to resolve role conflict, one is to lie.

Lying as a response to role conflict occurs when people behave according to one role and report having behaved differently to the sender of the other role. An example of a simple role conflict occurs when one boss tells a secretary to spend the afternoon working on one project, whereas another boss tells the secretary to do another project. Although many alternative responses exist, one response to this role conflict for the secretary is to complete the work of one boss and lie to the other boss.

The strength of a person's allegiance to a particular role may affect lying (Grover, 1993a). Some roles have a stronger impact than others because we deem them more powerful or of greater consequence. When roles conflict, people are more likely to meet the demands of the stronger role. Therefore a person strongly committed to one role is unlikely to lie to the sender of that role but may lie to the sender of another role.

In summary, self-interest is the dominant theoretical explanation of dishonesty, but this explanation has been criticized (Etzioni, 1988). The second, more recent, contending theory is the role conflict theory.

Empirical Testing of Major Explanations

My colleagues and I have conducted three studies that examine the antecedents of lying in the context of role theory and self-interest theory.

The first study (Grover, 1993b) of role-conflict-induced lying examined professional role conflict—the conflict between what an organization expects from an employee and what the norms of the employee's profession demand. The study examined professional registered nurses, testing the hypothesis that nurses would be more likely to lie about their behavior when role conflict was present than when it was absent. Practicing nurses read scenarios of nursing situations and then were asked how likely they were to report a specific behavior from the scenario in a chart, to supervisors, and to peers. An example of a scenario with a high degree of professional role conflict is one in which a nurse is instructed to administer a certain drug level that will make the patient uncomfortable. The nursing demands to make patients comfortable conflict with institution demands to follow orders. The lying resolution to the conflict is to give a dose the nurse deems appropriate and to report giving the amount ordered. This first study supported role conflict theory: Nurses were more likely to lie when placed under role conflict than when they faced no role conflict.

Although the nursing study provided support for role conflict theory, it said little about the dominant self-interest effect on lying. One could argue that there is some element of self-interest inherent in professional role conflict that led these nurses to lie. For example, one might have lied in those scenarios to avoid an interpersonal confrontation. In addition, the nursing study examined only professional role conflict. If role conflict theory is truly a robust, parsimonious theory, then the other types of role conflict also should explain lying. To close these gaps, Hui and I (Grover & Hui, 1994a) conducted a study that examined a different type of role conflict and compared its effects to a self-interest effect.

To examine the differential influence of role conflict and self-benefit on lying, we independently manipulated these two variables in a scenario-based experiment (Grover & Hui, 1994a). Following the two dominant theories of role conflict and self-interest, our hypotheses were that people lie when they benefit from doing so (self-interest) and when role conflict is present. The results supported both of these hypotheses: People were indeed more likely to lie in either condition compared to its control condition. More striking, however, was that these two causes of lying in combination promoted lying far beyond the impact of either the reward or role conflict effects separately. When both role conflict and some reward for lying were present, people were the most likely to lie. The study therefore supported both theories but did not favor either one. That is, neither role conflict nor self-interest theory alone fully explained lying.

A methodological problem with the first two studies was their reliance on self-reported assessments of lying. We well know that people may be unable to state what their behavior will be in certain situations (Nisbett & Wilson, 1977). The next study in the stream of research therefore examined similar conceptual issues, bolstering the methodological rigor by examining actual behaviors.

Our third empirical study compared self-interest to role conflict, independently manipulating these two variables in a laboratory experiment measuring real behavior (Grover & Hui, 1994b). Students were asked to complete a proofreading exercise in which they compared a hard-copy written document to one appearing on a computer screen. At the end of the session, time and error data were displayed on the computer screen and then recorded by the subject. Unknown to the subject, the information also was recorded by the computer in a way that could later be checked by the experimenter, who would compare the reported to actual performance to test for truthful reporting. Hence the experiment created an unobtrusive, observable opportunity to lie.

Reward was manipulated by comparing a reward condition in which participants could earn $3 or $5 if they fell within certain bounds to a control condition that had no monetary rewards associated with performance. Performance pressure was manipulated by qualitatively labeling zones of performance on the report completed by the subject. Time pressure role conflict was produced by adjusting those labels such that it was difficult to perform at a high level.

The results of the study replicated the results of the earlier study: Role conflict, operationalized as performance pressure, and reward predicted lying independently and interactively. The strength of the study lies in its use of observable behavior as the operationalization of the dependent variable.

Reconciliation of Role Conflict and Self-Interest Theories

That two studies indicate lying is most likely when both role conflict and reward for lying are present prompts a reconsideration of how the two mechanisms operate. In light of the data, it appears that role conflict acts as a stimulus for lying and that the reward reinforces or further encourages the act of lying. It is perhaps clearer to think of role conflict and reward as stimulus and encourager, respectively. Role conflict alone gives a reason for a lie, provides a situation for a lie, and is a stimulus and provides impetus for a lie. However, most people are likely to require more than the stimulus of role conflict to lie. Even when conflicting roles create a context inviting lying, people apparently are unlikely to lie in the absence of sanctions for not lying or rewards for doing so. This intuitive finding suggests that role obligations provide opportunity but not motivation to lie, which comes from the reward. Reward occurs with role conflict in many real situations. For example, the nursing study engendered clear role conflicts, but consequences were attached to either side of the role conflict. If the nurse gives a patient a prescribed dose that the nurse knows will make the patient uncomfortable, then observing that discomfort is a sanction of not lying. In summary, role conflict acts as the stimulus to lie, lying usually requires some reward or sanction to promote lying, and sometimes the reward is part of the role conflict.

Just as role conflict acts as a stimulus but cannot engender lying behavior, reward alone is not strong enough for most people to engage in the moral transgression of lying. Reward may bring people to the point of considering whether to lie but cannot push many people over the brink of lying. We have a common moral code against lying, and most adults do not use simple reward as the criterion for moral decisions (Kohlberg, 1969). Therefore the combination of role conflict and reward works to engender lying, with reward providing motivation and role conflict providing the impetus to puncture the moral boundary. In one sense, we can view these two forces as two reasons to lie: When combined, they provide the motivation for and disintegrate the barriers to engaging in lying behavior. My speculation that role conflict provides the impetus to break the moral boundary requires empirical testing. Future research examining that very issue will enrich the theory on this topic.

Future Directions of Lying Research

The causes of lying are not yet unraveled. Empirical research shows that lying is caused by a combination of self-interest and conflicting pressures. Future research should investigate more precisely how self-interest and role conflict interact. The speculation that role conflict serves as the impetus for lying and is supported by reward needs to be tested. As it stands, we know only that lying is more likely when both role conflict and reward are present. Perhaps the biggest leap that this area can make is to delineate the psychological mechanism that makes role conflict and self-interest work together. Some of this exacting psychological work needs to be done in the laboratory so as to finely manipulate variables that will yield insight into the lying mechanism, or the mental processes of lying.

Outcomes

An intriguing, multifaceted question asks, What are the outcomes of lying in organizations? This question should be addressed empirically because we have largely assumed that lying is bad for organizations. The question relates to different levels of analysis: That is, what are the outcomes to individuals who lie, to organizations in which lying occurs, and to peer relationships? Lying presumably diminishes a person's credibility and probably reduces cooperation in social and work groups. Studies need to be conducted at the organizational level of analysis to assess the outcomes of many people lying within the organization.

Macro-Organization

The influence of organization-level variables on individual honesty or lying is fascinating, yet unexplored. One question is, In what ways do the structure, norms, and culture of an organization affect ethical behavior within that organization? This question is important because documented differences among organizations would suggest that organizations may be able to influence the lying that occurs within them.

One approach to this problem is to use Enz's (1986, 1988) value-based approach to understanding culture in organizations. In her paradigm, the values represent core beliefs about what is important in the organization and how it should function. A set of core values may influence ethical behavior, specifically lying. Some dimension of values may be oriented toward ethics. That is, an "honesty" value dimension may make some companies emphasize veracity. Moreover, the honesty value may lie in opposition to others in the value constellation, such as profitability or productivity. Therefore one question concerns whether a value exists that encourages or discourages truthtelling in organizations. A second question concerns how this value forms and to what it is related. If values are largely based on upper management actions or the goals set for people in the organization, then managers may influence the level of honesty in organizations.

Victor and Cullen's (1988) ethical climate construct provides a second approach to the macro-organization influence on lying. Their five ethical climates vary by the criteria that people in the company generally use to make ethical decisions. The criteria include making decisions based on relationships with others, laws and professional codes, company rules, and company or individual moral codes. Shepard and Hartenian (1991) have shown that ethical climates are related to lying, cheating, and stealing. The causes of lying may vary among ethical climates: For example, lying when it is rewarded may be more common in self-interested (called *instrumental*) ethical climates. Conversely, lying to protect a person may be more common in organizations holding the caring ethical climate, which makes moral decisions based on relationships. These propositions beg empirical testing, and tests would strengthen the nomological net by linking organization theory, organizational behavior, and the specific lying theories.

National Culture

The research cited in this chapter is largely culture bound to the United States. People across cultures may have different norms for honesty, which may affect lying. Perhaps more interesting than the absolute comparative occurrence of lying in different cultures is an analysis of what causes lying in different cultures. Hofstede's (1980) taxonomy of national cultures might be useful in this regard. Two of Hofstede's dimensions may influence lying. Cultures vary on collectivism/individualism, or the degree to which people value being members of groups and the allegiance they feel toward these groups. Research has shown that more collectivistic cultures do not experience social loafing in group work and that people in individualistic cultures perform at higher levels when their work is individually accountable (Earley, 1989, 1993; Wagner, 1995). Collectivists hold more responsibility toward fellow group members and therefore should be less likely than individualists, who have a weaker group connection, to lie to fellow group members. Moreover, collectivists may be more likely to lie to an out-group when doing so benefits the in-group. Impact of the collectivist construct on lying warrants empirical exploration.

Power distance is another of Hofstede's (1980) national culture elements that may influence lying behavior. Power distance refers to the magnitude of status differences, or the degree to which people defer to those of higher status. Power distance may have an interesting influence on the truthfulness of communication among people of different status levels. However, the direction of the effect arguably may be in either direction. In high-power-distance contexts, subordinates may lie to superiors to tell them what they want to hear. In a culture that reveres authority, subordinates may withhold information due to a reluctance to communicate excessively with superiors. On the other hand, more powerful individuals in high-power-distance societies may feel they have license to lie to subordinates for any number of reasons, such as to protect the subordinate, to make themselves look good, or to protect the sanctity of the upper echelon. In sum, the power distance effect on lying is difficult to predict, and it could be served well with empirical testing.

Summary

The intention of this section was to suggest some immediate research needs to inform or fill the gaps left by our current state of knowledge on lying in organizations. I have articulated the need to study the psychological mechanism of role conflict and reward, the outcomes of lies, the influence of macro-organization elements, and national cultures. These issues are gaps in our knowledge that are potentially informed by extant theory from related topics. Our understanding of lying in the context of organizational behavior can advance best by integrating lying theory with other established theories.

Practical Implications

Practitioners interested in honesty, including truthtelling, have reason to be concerned by the issues and research presented in this chapter:

1. It is difficult to tell when people are lying because few people can decipher the nonverbal cues.
2. No discernible personality type dictates who will lie and who will not. The circumstances in which people find themselves strongly influence their truthtelling.
3. Professionals in whom we place our trust, such as nurses, police officers, and presidents, lie.

The picture is not completely dismal, however, for practitioners and seekers of truth. The situational factors that lead people to lie are controllable, and therefore lying may be controllable. Both rewards for lying and role conflicts are situational factors that managers can influence. Reward, or self-interest, has a social-learning component. When people are punished for dishonesty and rewarded for honesty, other people in the organization observe that and modify their own behavior to mirror the rewarded behavior. In addition, the very essence of the role conflict model of lying engenders the sense that many conflicts in work life are directly or indirectly caused by managers or supervisors. Hard-driving managers with high expectations may create conflict strong enough for some employees to lie when they cannot meet the expectations. The implication is that managers and those in power may have considerable influence over the level of honesty in an organization. Interestingly, administrators may feel powerless against illicit, dishonest behavior when in fact they can have profound effects on it.

Conclusion

Researchers have only recently begun studying lying in organizations; hence we currently know relatively little about how often people lie, why people lie, and the consequences of their lies. I have attempted to draw from various social science disciplines to illuminate the present state of knowledge on lying. From this background, I have identified the practical and theoretical need to focus attention on the situational causes of lying. The empirical work on lies' causes has primarily tested the self-interest and role conflict theories. Because both these theories have merit, I have identified paths for future research on lying, including additional work on the mechanism of lying, macro-organizational influences on lying, and international cultural effects on lying. Although there is little cause to be overly optimistic, some evidence suggests that practitioners may have some control over lying through their influence on jobs. Despite our limited knowledge and the rather dismal practical projection, what could be more interesting than studying lying in organizations as an antisocial behavior?

References

Abrahamson, E., & Park, C. (1994). Concealment of negative organizational outcomes: An agency theory perspective. *Academy of Management Journal, 37,* 1302-1334.

Allen, N. J., & Meyer, J. P. (1990). The measurement and antecedents of affective, continuance, and normative commitment to the organization. *Journal of Occupational Psychology, 63,* 1-19.

Bandura, A. (1969). *Principles of behavior modification.* New York: Holt, Rinehart & Winston.

Barker, T., & Carter, D. (1990). Fluffing up the evidence and covering your ass: Some conceptual notes on police lying. *Deviant Behavior, 11,* 61-73.

Bok, S. (1978). *Lying: Moral choice in public and private life.* New York: Random House.

Bok, S. (1982). *Secrets.* New York: Pantheon.

Bond, C. F., & Fahey, W. E. (1987). False suspicion and the misperception of deceit. *British Journal of Social Psychology, 26,* 41-46.

Cacciola, J. S., Rutherford, M. J., Alterman, A. I., & Snider, E. C. (1994). An examination of the diagnostic criteria for antisocial personality disorder in substance abusers. *Journal of Nervous and Mental Disease, 182,* 517-523.

Christie, R., & Geis, F. L. (1970). *Studies in Machiavellianism.* New York: Academic Press.

Cook, J., & Wall, T. (1980). New work attitude measures of trust, organizational commitment, and personal need nonfulfilment. *Journal of Occupational Psychology, 53,* 39-52.

DePaulo, B. M., & Pfeifer, R. L. (1986). On-the-job experience and skill at detecting deception. *Journal of Applied Social Psychology, 16,* 249-267.

DePaulo, B. M., & Rosenthal, R. (1979). Telling lies. *Journal of Personality and Social Psychology, 37,* 1713-1722.

DePaulo, B. M., Stone, J. I., & Lassiter, G. D. (1985). Deceiving and detecting deceit. In B. R. Schlenker (Ed.), *The self and social life* (pp. 323-370). New York: McGraw-Hill.

DePaulo, P. J., & DePaulo, B. M. (1989). Can deception by salespersons and customers be detected through nonverbal behavioral cues? *Journal of Applied Social Psychology, 19,* 1552-1577.

Earley, P. C. (1989). Social loafing and collectivism: A comparison of the United States and the People's Republic of China. *Administrative Science Quarterly, 34,* 565-581.

Earley, P. C. (1993). East meets West meets Mideast: Further explorations of collectivistic and individualistic work groups. *Academy of Management Journal, 36,* 319-348.

Eisenhardt, K. (1989). Agency theory: An assessment and review. *Academy of Management Review, 14,* 57-74.

Ekman, P. (1985). *Telling lies: Clues to deceit in the marketplace, politics, and marriage.* New York: Norton.

Ekman, P. (1988). Lying and nonverbal behavior: Theoretical issues and new findings. *Journal of Nonverbal Behavior, 12,* 163-175.

Ekman, P., & O'Sullivan, M. (1991). Who can catch a liar? *American Psychologist, 46,* 913-920.

Enz, C. A. (1986). *Power and shared values in the corporate culture.* Ann Arbor, MI: UMI Research Press.

Enz, C. A. (1988). The role of value congruity in intra-organizational power. *Administrative Science Quarterly, 33,* 284-304.

Etzioni, A. (1988). *The moral dimension.* New York: Free Press.

Exline, R., Thibaut, J., Hickey, C., & Gumpert, P. (1970). Visual interaction in relation to machiavellianism and an unethical act. In R. Christie & F. Geis (Eds.), *Studies in Machiavellianism* (pp. 53-75). New York: Academic Press.

Fayol, H. (1949). *General and industrial management.* London: Pitman.

Ford, C. V., King, B. H., & Hollender, M. H. (1988). Lies and liars: Psychiatric aspects of prevarication. *American Journal of Psychiatry, 145,* 554-562.

Galbraith, J. R. (1973). *Organizational design.* Reading, MA: Addison-Wesley.

Gambetta, D. G. (1988). *Trust.* New York: Basil Blackwell.

Gross, N., Mason, W. S., & McEachern, A. W. (1958). *Explorations in role analysis.* New York: John Wiley.

Grover, S. L. (1993a). Lying, subterfuge, and deceit: A model of dishonesty in the workplace. *Organization Science, 4,* 478-495.

Grover, S. L. (1993b). Why professionals lie: The impact of professional role conflict on reporting accuracy. *Organizational Behavior and Human Decision Processes, 55,* 251-272.

Grover, S. L., & Enz, C. A. (1996). *Macro-organization influences on lying behavior.* Manuscript submitted for publication.

Grover, S. L., & Hui, C. (1994a). The influence of role conflict, role strength, and reward contingencies on lying behavior. *Journal of Business Ethics, 13,* 295-303.

Grover, S. L., & Hui, C. (1994b). *Moving toward theoretical consensus on a specific unethical behavior: The case of lying in organizations.* Paper presented at the national meeting of the Academy of Management, Dallas, TX.

Guy, M. E. (1990). *Ethical decision making in everyday work situations.* Westport, CT: Quorum.

Hartshorne, H., & May, M. A. (1928). *Studies in the nature of character.* New York: Macmillan.

Hofstede, G. H. (1980). *Culture's consequences: International differences in work related values.* Beverly Hills, CA: Sage.

Holstrom, B. (1979). Moral hazard and observability. *Bell Journal of Economics, 10,* 74-91.

Jensen, M., & Meckling, W. (1976). Theory of the firm: Managerial behavior, agency costs, and ownership structure. *Journal of Financial Economics, 3,* 305-360.

Kelley, H. H., & Thibaut, J. W. (1978). *Interpersonal relations: A theory of interdependence.* New York: John Wiley.

Kohlberg, L. (1969). Stage and sequence: The cognitive-developmental approach to socialization. In D. A. Goslin (Ed.), *Handbook of socialization theory and research* (pp. 347-480). Chicago: Rand McNally.

Lawrence, P. R., & Lorsch, J. W. (1964). *Organizations and environments.* Homewood, IL: Irwin.

Lewicki, R. J. (1983). Lying and deception: A behavior model. In M. H. Bazerman & R. J. Lewicki (Eds.), *Negotiating in organizations* (pp. 68-90). Beverly Hills, CA: Sage.

Mayer, R. C., Davis, J. H., & Schoorman, F. D. (1995). An integrative model of organizational trust. *Academy of Management Review, 20*, 709-734.

McAllister, D. J. (1995). Affect- and cognition-based trust as foundations for interpersonal cooperation in organizations. *Academy of Management Journal, 38*, 24-59.

Modell, J. G., Mountz, J. M., & Ford, C. V. (1992). Pathological lying associated with thalamic dysfunction demonstrated by (-super(99m)Tc) HMPAO SPECT. *Journal of Neuropsychiatry and Clinical Neurosciences, 4*, 442-446.

Mowday, R., Porter, L., & Steers, R. (1982). *Employee-organization linkages: The psychology of commitment, absenteeism, and turnover.* New York: Academic Press.

Murphy, K. R. (1987). Detecting infrequent deception. *Journal of Applied Psychology, 72*, 611-614.

Nisbett, R. E., & Wilson, T. D. (1977). Telling more than we can know: Verbal reports on mental processes. *Psychological Review, 84*, 231-259.

O'Shaughnessy, E. (1990). Can a liar be psychoanalysed? *International Journal of Psychoanalysis, 71*, 187-195.

Sackett, P. R., Burris, L. R., & Callahan, C. (1989). Integrity testing for personnel selection: An update. *Personnel Psychology, 42*, 491-529.

Saxe, L. (1991). Lying: Thoughts of an applied social psychologist. *American Psychologist, 46*, 409-415.

Shepard, J. M., & Hartenian, L. S. (1991). Egoistic and ethical orientations of university students toward work-related decisions. *Journal of Business Ethics, 10*, 303.

Skinner, B. F. (1969). *Contingencies of reinforcement.* New York: Appleton-Century-Crofts.

Streeter, L. A., Krauss, R. M., Geller, V., Olson, C., & Apple, W. (1977). Pitch changes during attempted deception. *Journal of Personality and Social Psychology, 35*, 354-350.

Trevino, L. K. (1986). Ethical decision-making in organizations: A person-situation interactionist model. *Academy of Management Review, 11*, 601-617.

Trevino, L. K., & Youngblood, S. A. (1990). Bad apples in bad barrels: A causal analysis of ethical decision-making behavior. *Journal of Applied Psychology, 75*, 378-385.

Victor, B., & Cullen, J. B. (1988). The organizational bases of ethical work climates. *Administrative Science Quarterly, 33*, 101-125.

Vrij, A. (1993). Credibility judgments of detectives: The impact of nonverbal behavior, social skills, and physical characteristics on impression formation. *Journal of Social Psychology, 133*, 601-610.

Wagner, J. A. (1995). Studies of individualism-collectivism: Effects on cooperation in groups. *Academy of Management Journal, 38*, 152-172.

Wrightsman, L. W. (1974). *Assumptions about human nature: A social-psychological analysis.* Monterey, CA: Brooks/Cole.

Zuckerman, M., DePaulo, B. M., & Rosenthal, R. (1981). Verbal and nonverbal communication of deception. In L. Berkowitz (Ed.), *Advances in experimental social psychology* (Vol. 14, pp. 1-59). New York: Academic Press.

5

The STEAL Motive

Managing the Social Determinants of Employee Theft

Jerald Greenberg

Theft by employees is one of the most prevalent and costly problems confronted by today's organizations. Although questions can be raised about the accuracy of the exact figures reported (Murphy, 1993), the statistics paint an unsettling picture. Notably, it has been estimated that American businesses bear costs of employee theft rapidly approaching $200 billion (Govoni, 1992; Snyder, Blair, & Arndt, 1990). As such, employee theft has been reported to be 10 times more costly than all the nation's street crime and has been blamed for 30% to 50% of all business failures (Bullard & Resnik, 1983; Snyder & Blair, 1989). Further statistics reveal that these figures do not stem primarily from a few isolated cases of grand theft that grab headlines (e.g., Emshwiller, 1993) but rather

Author's Note: Preparation of this chapter was supported by National Science Foundation Grant No. SBR-9224169. I thank Robert Bies and Robert Giacalone for their helpful comments on an earlier draft of this chapter.

from repeated instances of minor theft whose effects insidiously accumulate over time (Lipman & McGraw, 1988). In fact, it has been reported
that approximately 75% of all employees steal from their employers on
at least one occasion (McGurn, 1988) and that many engage in theft as
a regular part of their lives on the job (Delaney, 1993; London House &
Food Marketing Institute, 1993).

Before proceeding, a formal definition is in order. Writing elsewhere, I defined *employee theft* as "any unauthorized appropriation of
company property by employees either for one's own use or for sale to
another. It includes, but is not limited to, the removal of products,
supplies, materials, funds, data, information, or intellectual property"
(Greenberg, 1995, p. 154). Importantly, as I use the term, employee theft
does not include taking property belonging to one's coworkers. Although employee theft can take many forms, incidents of theft typically
are distinguished with respect to their magnitude: Misappropriation of
items of limited value is referred to as *pilferage* or *petty theft*, and
misappropriation of items of considerable value is referred to as *grand
theft* (Merriam, 1977; Smigel & Ross, 1970).

Given the considerable scope of the problem, it is not surprising
that employee theft has received a great deal of attention from a variety
of social scientists. In this chapter, I identify these traditional approaches
to employee theft and then present an alternative. In so doing, I address
a basic set of parallel questions: Why do employees steal, and what can
be done to deter it?

Traditional, Nonsocial Approaches to Employee Theft: Setting the Stage for a Social Psychological Alternative

Over the years, the question of why people steal from their employers has been answered in several different ways, each of which is
associated with specific techniques for preventing theft (Hollinger &
Clark, 1983; Murphy, 1993). For example, one major approach, ad-
vanced primarily by security experts (e.g., Jaspan, 1974), has focused on
the contextual variables responsible for employee theft. The security
orientation is based on the premise that people steal because they have
opportunities to do so, and it assumes that theft can be controlled by
limiting these opportunities (e.g., by installing security cameras and by

using internal accounting control systems). As such, the focus is primarily on deterring thieves and catching them if the deterrents fail. I agree with Murphy's (1993) assessment that this approach is limited by its assumption that all individuals will engage in theft when given opportunities to do so. The reality is that some individuals will not steal despite opportunities to do so and that others will attempt to steal despite security precautions. Although security measures certainly can be effective deterrents (Bintliff, 1994), the failure to recognize individual differences limits the value of this approach.

In contrast, a second traditional approach to employee theft—one favored by criminologists (e.g., Robin, 1969)—embraces the possibility of individual differences. By examining the *personal determinants* of theft, criminologists have disclosed a profile of individuals who are inclined to steal. Specifically, it has been found that employees prone to engage in theft are young, face economic pressures, and are emotionally unstable (Hollinger & Clark, 1983). In keeping with this approach, industrial psychologists have sought to control employee theft by systematically testing prospective employees and rejecting those who are most highly predisposed to engage in theft (Murphy, 1993; Sackett, 1994). Although such integrity testing, as it is known, has proven to be valuable in many ways, two recent comprehensive reviews of the literature have shown that the ability to predict theft behavior on the basis of various personal variables is rather limited (e.g., Dalton, Metzger, & Wimbush, 1994; Ones, Viswesvaran, & Schmidt, 1993). Thus, although the idea of weeding out of the workplace those individuals most predisposed to steal is quite reasonable, the full potential of this approach has not been realized. Although some have blamed such shortcomings on the psychometric limitations associated with measuring the variables of interest (e.g., Ones et al., 1993), others have recognized that complex social dynamics in the workplace preclude the possibility of accurately predicting employee theft (Greenberg & Scott, 1996; Murphy, 1993).

I consider both the security/contextual approach and the individual differences/criminology approach to be *nonsocial* insofar as they focus on the situational and individual determinants of theft while ignoring the interpersonal forces acting on employees. As such, they approach employee theft as a law enforcement problem: the act of someone with a "dishonest personality" who will be likely to steal when the opportunity presents itself. Although these two orientations are very different, they share the common underlying assumption that employee theft is a criminal activity that can be managed by controlling access to jobs and opportunities for theft. Despite advances among advocates of these approaches, organizations remain largely unsuccessful in controlling theft—a reality that leaves the door open for considering other orientations.

Traditionally, by fatalistically pointing to a decline in moral standards, organizational scientists have had little incentive to do anything about employee theft but direct their energies toward improving security precautions (Jones & Gautschi, 1988). And by conceiving of employee theft as a law enforcement problem instead of a management problem, organizational scientists have paid little attention to the social dynamics of employee theft. As a result, the determinants of theft that emanate from social interaction with superiors and coworkers represent an untapped potential source of insight. Acknowledging this lack of attention to the social psychology of employee theft, Murphy (1993) referred to this void as "a major roadblock to understanding and controlling dishonesty in the workplace" (p. 35).

In this chapter, I draw on social psychological research to propose an approach that sheds light on the *social determinants* of employee theft. Specifically, I argue that much employee theft can be thought of as the result of a variety of social motives. In the sections that follow, I present these motives in a taxonomic fashion and then consider ways in which they may be drawn on to help manage employee theft.

Introducing the STEAL Motive: Categorizing the Social Determinants of Employee Theft

In the process of reviewing and analyzing the literature on employee theft, I noted that the motives underlying theft were more complex than generally conceived (Greenberg & Scott, 1996). Typically, we think of theft as a form of deviant, or *antisocial*, behavior designed to bring harm. For example, employees may wish to strike back at an organization, or disrupt a work group that did them wrong. Indeed, theft may be a useful vehicle in bringing to fruition these antisocial intentions. At the same time, I found that employee theft is a behavior that is carefully regulated by organizational norms and work group

Table 5.1 The STEAL Motive: Four Components

	Target	
Actor's Intention	*Employer*	*Coworkers*
Prosocial	*ApprovaL* Adherence to supervisory norms condoning theft	*Support* Adherence to work group norms condoning theft
Antisocial	*Even the score* Desire to harm, strike back at employer	*Thwart* Violating work group norms regulating theft

norms and that stealing is an effective way of supporting these norms. Thus, although the conclusion is counterintuitive, employee theft also may be thought of as a *prosocial* behavior designed to promote organizational and work group norms.

Underlying these observations is a pair of basic distinctions revealing much richness in the social motives underlying employee theft. First, social motives for theft may be distinguished with respect to an actor's *intention:* that is, whether the act was guided by an interest in being helpful (i.e., a *prosocial* motive) or harmful (i.e., an *antisocial* motive). Second, these motives may be directed toward either of two *targets:* one's *employer* or one's *coworkers.* By crosscutting these two dimensions, we may identify four distinct social motives (see Table 5.1). I refer to the overall set of resulting motives as the *STEAL motive*—an acronym for the four social motives identified by combining prosocial and antisocial intentions with employers and coworkers as targets: *Support, Thwart, Even the score,* and *ApprovaL.* I will now explain the interpersonal dynamics underlying employee theft by describing each of the four components of the STEAL motive.

The ApprovaL Motive: Adhering to Supervisory Norms Condoning Theft

Traditionally, organizational officials are expected to prevent theft by employees insofar as it is both morally inappropriate and fiscally irresponsible. However, it has been reported that informal norms widely condone, and often encourage, employee theft (Dalton, 1959). In other words, an *approval* motive appears to be operating. Careful examination of the processes underlying supervisory support of theft from one's organization suggests that it stems from the tendency for supervisors to encourage theft actively as a legitimate mechanism of behavior control (Greenberg & Scott, 1996; Zeitlin, 1971).

To some extent, a case can be made that supervisors tacitly encourage employee theft when they engage in theft themselves. That is, unless superiors "walk the talk" when it comes to theft, subordinates are likely to perceive that it is legitimate for them to engage in theft as well (Adams, 1981; Cherrington & Cherrington, 1985; Hollinger, 1989; Snyder, Broome, Kehoe, McIntyre, & Blair, 1991). However, the evidence is overwhelming that supervisory approval of employee theft goes beyond the modeling of deviant behavior (Kemper, 1966). Indeed, many supervisors actively encourage employee theft, at least in a controlled manner. For example, among the gypsum factory workers studied by Gouldner (1954), an "indulgency pattern" was widespread: Supervisors allowed employees to take home company-owned tools and raw materials for their personal use. Similarly, Sieh (1987) found that foremen routinely permitted garment workers to take home small items, such as pins, thread, and old fabric scraps. In an extreme case, Altheide, Adler, Adler, and Altheide (1978) found that a supervisor acted as an accomplice to one employee's theft. In exchange for doing a particularly good job of cleaning up the stock room, the supervisor allowed the employee to take home a bagful of diapers for only 10 cents. According to the informant interviewed in the study, "Now that went on in managing all the time" (Altheide et al., 1978, p. 111).

In some cases, supervisors go well beyond merely helping their subordinates steal from the company by proactively making arrangements for it. A good example may be seen in Ditton's (1977a) study of British bread bakers. So extreme was the theft in one bakery, and so widely accepted was the practice, that supervisors had to plan for extra loaves to be baked each day just to avoid running short. Some supervisors have gone so far as to have their companies intentionally prepare to order specific items to be stolen. This was observed, for example, among retail store managers who intentionally allowed some items to gather dust so they could be purchased at reduced prices by clerks (Altheide et al., 1978) and among manufacturing plant foremen who arranged for custom products to be fabricated just so they could be taken by some employees (Dalton, 1959). Although it is impossible to tell how widespread such practices are, the wide variety of sociological evidence pointing to superiors' involvement in their subordinates' theft suggests that this phenomenon should not be dismissed casually.

Typically, when supervisors are partners to the theft enterprise, there exist specific limits with respect to the exact nature and degree of theft that will be tolerated. Thus, rather than declaring open season on all company property, supervisors maintain what Zeitlin (1971) has called a "system of controlled larceny." For example, whereas Sieh's (1987) garment workers were permitted to steal small supplies from their shop, theft of materials needed to make items to be sold privately was strictly prohibited. Similarly, the bakery workers interviewed by Ditton (1977a), who routinely took home loaves of bread, faced strong pressures against stealing cash. Hence, although many cases in which supervisors approve of theft have been documented, these instances are often accompanied by the clear imposition of limits.

This suggests that supervisors may be using theft instrumentally, as an extralegal adjunct to an organization's official reward structure— what Ditton (1977b) has referred to as the *invisible wage structure.* Extending this point, Henry (1981) has argued that wages may be regarded as emanating from two sources: legal sources, both formal (e.g., wages and salaries) and informal (e.g., perks and tips), and illegal sources, "hidden economic rewards" (e.g., pilfered items). As one British waiter put it, "Fiddles are a part of wages. The whole issue runs on fiddles; it wouldn't work otherwise" (Mars, 1973, p. 202).

Several studies have shown that managers rely on the rewards gained through the theft of company property as a supplement to workers' overall rewards (e.g., Altheide et al., 1978; Bradford, 1976). For example, Altheide et al. (1978) found that supervisors expected employees scheduled to work late-night shifts in retail stores to engage in theft. Not only are opportunities to steal without detection greater at such hours, but also theft was used as a bonus for those working undesirable shifts: "Working the late hour entitles them to a few more privileges than the day shift" (Altheide et al., 1978, p. 112).

The impact of supervisory approval of employee theft can be great. This is in part because the value of theft-based rewards can be considerable, especially when theft occurs regularly. Moreover, the practice of permitting theft as "side payments" is often considered "quicker and more convenient to dispense than promotions" (Altheide et al., 1978, p. 97) and frequently is far less cumbersome (Dalton, 1959). At the same time, it should be cautioned that managerial acceptance of employee theft is almost always informal and unspoken. Understandably, organizations cannot publicly condone a practice that is strictly illegal and unethical, although they may condone it privately. Liebow (1967) nicely articulated this duplicity when he said, "The employer knowingly provides the conditions which entice (force) the employee to steal the unpaid value of his labor, but at the same time, he punishes him for theft if he catches him doing it" (pp. 38-39).

The Support Motive: Adhering to Work Group Norms Condoning Theft

Although organizational scientists have paid little attention to the way groups develop norms of deviant behavior in the workplace, it is clear that employees become socialized with respect to deviant norms and that these have strong effects on theft behavior. Indeed, Jaspan (1974) has called organizations "schools for dishonesty" (p. 17). According to Altheide et al. (1978), "Not only does one learn how and what to steal, but one is also expected to participate in the theft directly" (p. 109), adding that employee theft is "ritualistically and symbolically tied to becoming a successful employee, one who gets along well" (p. 101). The idea is that some theft occurs as a result of employees' prosocial interest in their coworkers—here referred to as the *support* motive.

Interestingly research has shown that employees are implicitly aware of the strong pressures they face to support work group norms condoning theft. In a large-scale questionnaire study, Hollinger and Clark (1982) compared perceptions of the importance of both formal and informal norms as deterrents to theft. The employees surveyed reported that their theft would be more strongly restrained by concerns about adverse reactions from their coworkers (e.g., social ostracism) than by threats of formal sanctions imposed by management (e.g., dismissal).

Several investigators have found that the majority of employee theft occurs by individuals acting completely on their own (Hawkins, 1984; Horning, 1970; Robin, 1969). In such cases, support for group norms condoning theft takes the form of turning a blind eye to those caught in the act of stealing—that is, not "blowing the whistle" on them (Miceli & Near, Chapter 7 of this volume). By contrast, workers on some types of jobs, such as members of mining teams, trash collection crews, and airline flight crews, have been referred to as "wolves," who tend to "steal in packs" (Mars, 1982, p. 32). The high degree of coordination required to perform these jobs legitimately appears to generalize to the behavior required to steal. As a case in point, consider the high degree of cooperation and task specialization needed to steal among the dock workers observed by Mars (1982): There were "checkers" who falsified paperwork, forklift drivers who stacked cargo into piles high enough to create visual barriers, and "signalers" who stood watch. These roles were so central to the enterprise that new members of the dock crew were thoroughly socialized into understanding the carefully coordinated rituals that made support of theft activities possible.

Support for coworkers engaging in theft takes the form not only of cooperation but of reciprocation as well. In its simplest form, reciprocation involves sharing suggestions about effective ways of stealing, a widespread practice in the department store studied by Altheide et al. (1978). Reciprocation also may take a longer-term form: sowing the seeds of obligation to reciprocate for harvest at a later date. For example, by helping a coworker steal, one may be paving the way for his or her assistance in helping oneself steal in the future. Demonstrating precisely this, Altheide et al. (1978) reported an incident in which a music store clerk gave a fellow employee large, unauthorized discounts on equipment he purchased, explicitly mentioning, "I might need your help later in getting something for myself" (p. 113).

It is important to note that evoking the reciprocity norm is effective in large part because of the social rewards it provides. The act of stealing demonstrates conformity to a valued group norm, enhancing one's status within one's work group. Thus employees who steal company property may be praised by their peers for supporting group standards. In so doing, they simultaneously raise the thief's status and legitimize their own thievery (Jaspan, 1974). As such, it makes good sense to consider employee theft as driven not purely by material motives of profit maximization but by social motives as well.

By supporting one's fellow group members in theft activities, a consensually held reality is established in which theft is considered acceptable. This social approval precludes the need for employees to reconstruct their private selves by acknowledging that they are thieves (Ditton, 1977a). By supporting the legitimacy of employee theft, groups enable those who steal to continue to think of themselves as good people who have not done anything wrong (Payne, 1989). This self-reinforcing function makes norms supporting employee theft especially potent within groups.

The Motive to Even the Score: Striking Back at Deviant Organizations

Thus far, I have conceived of employee thefts as prosocial acts designed to enhance relationships with one's employers and coworkers. However, it is also widely recognized that employee theft may be considered antisocial in intent, designed to bring harm—especially to employers believed to have harmed oneself (Hopkins, 1978; Tucker, 1989). This social motive, to *even the score* by striking back at an employer against whom one is aggrieved, is a potent determinant of employee theft (Greenberg & Scott, 1996).

From the perspective of distributive justice (Homans, 1961), stealing company property can be understood as an attempt to reestablish equity between the parties involved in a social exchange relationship. Specifically, in equity theory (Adams, 1965) terms, employees who believe they are receiving insufficient outcomes (e.g., pay) in exchange for their work contributions may effectively raise these outcomes by stealing, thereby redressing the perceived inequity with their employer. Respondents in interview studies have expressed this motive explicitly. For example, a clothing store employee interviewed by Zeitlin (1971) said, "I feel I deserved to get something additional for my work since I was not getting paid enough" (p. 26). Similarly, among the bread delivery drivers interviewed by Altheide et al. (1978), stealing was widely considered a necessary way of compensating for a pay system that penalized them for making mistakes: "When it really hits you hard . . . is when you come up $8 short. . . . That's when you start saying, 'Well shit, I've got to make this up' " (p. 101). Such statements suggest that employee theft may be an attempt to raise levels of payment perceived to be inequitably low.

I have empirically demonstrated this phenomenon in a recent series of studies. In the first, a quasi-experiment conducted in an organization

(Greenberg, 1990a), I compared the theft rates within three manufacturing plants belonging to the same company. In two of these factories (comprising the experimental groups), all employees encountered a pay cut of 15% over a 10-week period (as the company's response to a financial crisis). A third plant, with demographically similar employees, in which there were no pay cuts served as the control group. Insofar as employees in the first two plants received lower pay than they had in the past, they were considered to have suffered underpayment inequity. To assess theft, standard measures of shrinkage were taken by agents unaware of the study. Consistent with equity theory (Adams, 1965), I found that theft rates were significantly higher within the plants in which employees' pay was cut than in the control group. These differences are particularly dramatic when one considers that theft rates were consistently low in all three plants both before the pay cut and after regular rates of pay were reinstated.

Going beyond this straightforward test of equity theory, this investigation also considered the social determinants of justice (Greenberg, 1993a) by examining the manner in which the pay cut was explained to the workers in the two experimental groups. Employees at one plant, selected at random, were given an elaborate and caring explanation of the need for pay to be cut (the adequate explanation condition). By contrast, workers in the other experimental plant were given limited information about the need for the pay cut, accompanied by only superficial expressions of remorse (the inadequate explanation condition). The differences between these two plants was striking: Over twice as much theft occurred in the plant whose employees received the inadequate explanation compared to the plant whose employees received the adequate explanation.

These dramatic findings are limited by the confounding of two key variables—the amount of information presented about the reason for the pay cut and the amount of sensitivity shown regarding the impact of the pay cut. To eliminate this confounding, I independently manipulated these variables in a follow-up experiment conducted in a laboratory setting (Greenberg, 1993b). In this investigation, undergraduates were hired to perform a clerical task in exchange for $5 per hour, a rate shown in pretesting to be perceived as fair. After performing the task, a random half of the participants (the underpaid group) were told that they would be paid only $3. The other half of the participants (the equitably paid group) were told they would be paid the $5 promised.

As I announced the pay rate, I systematically manipulated the quality of the information used as the basis for establishing the pay rate, giving an explanation that was either extremely thorough and based on ostensibly verified facts (the high valid information condition) or one that was extremely incomplete and based on questionable facts (the low valid information condition). I also manipulated via my remarks the amount of remorse and concern shown for having caused the underpayment, demonstrating either great amounts (the high social sensitivity condition) or very limited amounts (the low social sensitivity condition). After treating the subjects in these manners, I left them alone in a room with a seemingly unknown sum of money and invited them to take the amount they were supposed to take. However, because I knew the exact amount of money left on the desk, I was able to determine precisely how much was taken. Amounts in excess of the stated wages ($3 in the underpayment group and $5 in the equitable payment group) were considered to be theft.

Consistent with equity theory and my earlier field experiment (Greenberg, 1990a), subjects who were equitably paid did not steal, whereas those who were underpaid did steal. Further, the amount they stole was dependent on the way they were treated. Subjects receiving high amounts of information stole less than those receiving low amounts. Similarly, subjects treated with high levels of social sensitivity stole less than those receiving low levels. These effects combined in an additive fashion: Subjects receiving high amounts of both variables stole the least, whereas those receiving low amounts of both stole the most.

These findings suggest not only that pay inequity induces theft but also that the amount of theft in which people engage depends on the nature of the interpersonal treatment they receive: Positive treatment (i.e., thorough information presented in a socially sensitive manner) at the hands of an authority figure lowers theft. People are interested in evening the score with those who have treated them inequitably and use theft as a device for doing so, particularly when the source of the inequity shows little concern and remorse. Apparently, one's interest in evening the score by stealing is triggered by the injury of underpayment inequity magnified by the insult of insensitive treatment.

The Thwart Motive:
Violating Group Norms Regulating Theft

The final cell in the STEAL taxonomy describes conditions under which the motive to steal from one's employer is based on the desire to harm one's coworkers. Specifically, what I refer to as the *thwart* motive involves violating work group norms regulating theft: harming one's employer for purposes of striking out at members of one's work group. In this connection, theft may be considered a vehicle for thwarting the group's attempts at control and sending the message that this will not be tolerated.

To the extent that groups attempt to regulate carefully the behavior of members when it comes to theft (Mars, 1982), situations are likely to arise in which uncertainties exist about the degree and form of wage pilferage to which one is entitled. And in such cases, conflict may result: disagreements in which theft against one's organization is used as a weapon, a means of challenging group norms. For example, Horning (1970) recounted an incident in which a worker at a manufacturing plant was chastised by his peers for exceeding the normatively accepted limits of theft established in the work group. The employee disagreed with these limits and regularly exceeded them by stealing more company property than his cohorts. By these actions, he intended to send the message to his coworkers that he would not be controlled by their norms. Not surprisingly, he was chastised for violating these limits.

Challenges to a group's efforts to control theft are likely to face strong opposition among one's coworkers insofar as they threaten the social system by which theft is regulated. For this reason, those who "push the envelope" are likely to face severe informal sanctions. Examples may be seen in interview studies of dock workers (Mars, 1974), factory workers (Horning, 1970), and garment workers (Sieh, 1987), in which employees who stole more than expected, or who stole the "wrong" items, were routinely chastised. In fact, among the dock workers interviewed by Mars (1974), those who resisted group control by taking too much were so severely mistreated that they regularly quit their jobs. It is this strong resistance that makes excessive levels of inappropriate forms of employee theft so effective as tools among those who wish to harm their work groups.

My examples thus far have involved stealing as a mechanism of thwarting group interests with respect to theft itself. However, this is not to say that disgruntled group members may not purposely violate group norms regulating theft as a means of striking back at one's group over other matters. For example, in team-oriented organizations, members of self-regulated work teams often resent the lack of individual recognition they receive (Katzenbach & Smith, 1993). Employee theft may be recognized as an effective way of compensating for recognition not received in such cases. Although such a practice may not directly reestablish equity with the perceived cause of one's perceived inequity, it may be recognized as a "safer" means of expressing discontent than directly confronting one's coworkers, particularly when the theft is believed to go undetected.

Managing The STEAL Motive: Practical Implications for Deterring Employee Theft

When employee theft is conceptualized in terms of social motives, the problem of deterrence becomes a matter of considering how to weaken these motives. In essence, the question can be framed with respect to identifying actions that may weaken the motives for approval, supporting, evening the score, and thwarting. Given that the STEAL motive is complex and multiply determined, and given that more than one component of the motive may be operating at a given time, it makes sense to consider the value of using several different approaches. I will now discuss some of the key deterrents suggested by the model.

Rotate Group Membership

To the extent that employee theft results from proactive attempts to conform to work group norms condoning theft (i.e., the support motive), it may be argued that attempts to weaken group influences on antisocial behavior would help reduce theft stemming from this motive. In other words, thefts triggered by the support motive are unlikely to occur when informal work group norms are either weak or nonexistent. Although it is impossible to interfere completely with the development of informal group norms, one practice that has been shown to inhibit this process is the frequent reassignment of group members, such as by deliberately rotating employees into and out of work groups. The rationale for this practice is straightforward: It is difficult for group norms to develop when group membership is unstable (Feldman, 1984).

It is in large part with this rationale in mind that the practice of scheduling airline cockpit crews on a rotating basis has been used (Ginnett, 1993). The basic idea is that as crew members become familiar with each other, sloppiness in their communication may become the norm (Kanki & Palmer, 1993). In contrast, crew members who do not regularly work together must maintain a high degree of clarity and vigilance in communication, thereby promoting safe operating practices. In fact, it has been reported that it is not unusual for members of commercial aircraft crews to work with two or three different crews in a given day (Hackman, 1993). Under such conditions, local norms promoting less than explicit communications are unlikely to develop. Analogously, local norms promoting theft are unlikely to develop in work groups whose membership is unstable.

The down side of this practice, of course, is that it interferes with the coordination of effort that is demanded on many jobs, thereby lowering performance. For example, research has shown that airline crew members who have had experience flying together tend to make fewer errors than those who have not done so (Foushee, Lauber, Baetge, & Acomb, 1986). Furthermore, it is admittedly sometimes difficult to rotate employees into and out of groups insofar as people do not always have interchangeable skills. Another barrier is that employees may resist group rotation precisely because it prohibits them from forming close relationships with their coworkers. To the extent that these barriers prove formidable, it may be impractical to rotate work group membership as a means of combating employee theft. However, to the extent that group norms strongly encourage theft, as has been demonstrated, efforts to disrupt these norms may be an effective theft prevention measure. Creating unstable membership may be helpful in this regard.

It should be cautioned that group norms supporting behaviors that benefit individual members may persist within groups even after the members who were initially responsible for encouraging those behaviors have departed (Cartwright & Zander, 1968). Insofar as employees believe that they stand to benefit by stealing from their organization, new members may be readily socialized into accepting this norm. However, work group rotation may help disrupt these norms in two ways. First, to the extent that a work group is completely disbanded and replaced by an entirely new members, the social foundations supporting theft will have been eliminated. Second, it may take the removal of only a single highly disaffected employee, one who encourages theft, and his or her replacement by a highly regarded individual who is reluctant to steal, to turn around the group's behavior. In conclusion, although it is not possible to stipulate the exact formula for eliminating group-based support for employee theft, there is good reason to believe that the rotation of group members will, at least to some degree, be an effective means of attenuating this motive.

Explain the Personal Costs of Stealing

Part of the reason that group norms promote employee theft is that employees believe they will benefit from these activities. Indeed, although employees certainly do stand to gain from theft in the short term, they stand to lose from actions that harm their organizations over the long run. For the most part, employees (particularly those who work in large organizations) do not readily appreciate the fact that by stealing from their organizations they are bringing harm that could eventually cost them their jobs. A single incident of theft may be thought of as being just a "drop in the bucket" when it comes to the costs incurred by a large organization. However, employees who recognize that the cumulative effects of many such acts by many employees may be quite harmful may think twice before engaging in theft.

Although this possibility may sound far-fetched, it should be noted that analogous pleas to adhere to another behavior with long-term societal benefits and short-term personal costs—saving the earth's environment by recycling newspapers—have been quite successful (Boldero, 1995). When environmentalists explained the benefits of recycling, people were willing to behave more responsibly toward their planet. Analogously, it may be argued that when the benefits of refraining from employee theft are explained, workers may behave more responsibly toward their organizations. As Hollinger (1989) put it, "The social prevention of employee theft involves convincing employees that stealing from the company is against their own best interests . . . . Employees must be helped to recognize the personal benefits derived by protecting the property and assets of their employers" (p. 40).

How exactly can this be accomplished? Research has shown that one effective means is *public posting:* the practice of providing explicit open feedback about some target behavior. For example, in a study conducted at a Swedish grocery store, Carter, Holström, Simpanen, and Melin (1988) displayed in the company lunchroom signs graphing the rates at which various items were stolen by employees. They found that presenting this information led to significant reductions in the rates of employee theft encountered during the posting period compared to beforehand. Presumably, this practice increased employees' awareness of the impact of their actions on the company, information that opened their eyes to the magnitude of the problem. This information presumably created pressures to help the company, effectively countering any pressures to steal that may have been incorporated into local norms.

It would seem wise to make the practice of public posting part of a broader initiative in which company officials publish internally (e.g., in newsletters) information about the extent and costs of employee theft suffered by the company. The idea is that by this measure, employees may come to understand the cumulative effects of their behavior on the company. Such information may challenge widespread rationalizations such as "They'll never miss it" and "They can easily afford it." In fact, to the extent that specific organizational problems resulting from the widespread effects of theft can be identified, particularly problems affecting themselves (e.g., shortage of funds for yearly bonuses), employees may come to recognize the broader implications of their actions. This may be an important first step toward discouraging those actions.

One reason that this practice may work is simply that it publicly condemns theft. To the extent that theft occurs in large part because supervisors condone it (i.e., the approval motive), pronouncements designed to deter theft may send a clear signal that theft will not, in fact, be tolerated. Although this may have little impact, if any, on individuals who are determined to steal, it may have a great deterrent effect on those whose latitude of acceptable behavior has grown to unacceptable proportions. In particular, among supervisors who have come to accept theft as a legitimate form of side-payment, public prohibitions against theft are likely to make less ambiguous the acceptability of such actions. And to the extent that it is difficult to rationalize one's actions as justifiable, the possibility of behavioral change looms large.

Use Corporate Hotlines

Two themes that emerge clearly from our discussion are that employees steal from their employers because they desire to get even with them for underpaying them and because they are socialized into work groups in which theft is normatively appropriate. Fortunately, one practice appears to be effective in combating both these forces: the use of corporate hotlines. These are special telephone numbers that employees can use to voice their concerns about organizational issues and have their questions answered.

It is clear that the more employees believe they are fairly paid, the less they steal. It is those individuals who believe that they were denied something they had coming to them who are most likely to engage in theft (Altheide et al., 1978; Hollinger & Clark, 1983). To the extent that such perceptions can be challenged, theft is less likely to occur. With this in mind, corporate hotlines have proven to be effective devices for employees seeking answers to their questions about pay (Taft, 1985). Employees who phone in may receive explanations of the procedures used to determine pay, information that can help enhance their perceptions of pay fairness (Folger & Greenberg, 1985). This is effective in part because the information itself that is imparted may shed new light on the fairness of the organization's pay procedures. Likewise, it also may be effective simply because by introducing a hotline, an organization is making a statement about itself as a fair company, one that cares enough about its employees to make such a mechanism available (Greenberg, 1990b). In this regard, hotlines may enhance perceptions of fairness because of both the instrumental and the "value-expressive" functions they serve (see Tyler, 1987).

Hotlines also have been used to help combat employee theft by providing opportunities for employees to "blow the whistle" anonymously on theft by their coworkers (Addis, 1992). This mechanism effectively provides an "escape route" for individuals who would like to challenge the well-entrenched normative pressures that encourage theft. Although such an avenue may not eliminate all theft, it will help combat it by providing a tool for cracking the foundation of local norms embracing theft. Addis (1992) has reported that several companies have found hotlines to be extremely cost-effective ways of controlling theft (as well as other types of deviant behavior, such as sexual harassment). For example, Georgia-Pacific has used its "Business Conduct and Security Hotline" to keep employee theft under control for over two decades. To the extent that hotlines open avenues of communication between employers (who would like opportunities to explain the fairness of their pay policies) and employees (who would like to reduce group pressures to steal), they may be highly effective tactics for deterring employee theft.

Treat Employees With Dignity and Respect

The research reviewed here has shown that employees' antisocial motives are triggered by the insensitive treatment they receive at the hands of their employers. Indeed, to the extent that workers perceive that their superiors have not treated them with the care, dignity, and respect to which they feel entitled, they are unlikely to refrain from the temptation to engage in deviant behavior. This point goes beyond the idea of simply evening the score with those who have withheld deserved outcomes. Rather, it focuses on the willingness to strike back at those who have treated them in this manner. Demonstrating this point, in a recent study I found that participants in a laboratory experiment stole items of no value to themselves when their superiors treated them in an uncaring fashion (Greenberg, 1994). As I noted earlier, it is the injury of poor interpersonal treatment that triggers theft when added to the insult of underpayment. Thus, to the extent that perceptions of underpayment cannot be avoided, it would be useful at least to avoid encouraging theft by treating employees with dignity and respect (for insight into the processes underlying this phenomenon, see Brockner & Wiesenfeld, in press).

Security industry practitioners have been implicitly aware of the value of kind interpersonal treatment when it comes to reducing theft. As an example, Taylor (1986) has advised managers to "treat employees with dignity, respect and trust" and to "establish personal, caring, nonadversarial relationships with employees," noting that "it's more difficult to steal from a friend than from someone who doesn't care about you" (p. 24). Certainly, to the extent that "being nice" helps control theft, it may be considered one of the easiest and least expensive deterrents one can imagine.

Another form that interpersonal sensitivity can take involves giving employees a say in determining how theft will be defined in their workplace, clarifying exactly what may and may not be taken. Expressing this idea earlier, Snyder et al. (1991) have advised that "the process used to define theft should be participatory; that is, employees should be as involved in it as possible" (p. 46). This practice would be expected to be effective for three reasons. First, it acknowledges that taking some items (e.g., scrap material) is perfectly acceptable, thereby legitimizing this behavior. By clarifying the boundaries of theft and nontheft, it is hoped that employees will respect admonitions to refrain from stealing other, forbidden items (Ditton, 1977b). Second, it illustrates how very serious the company is about eliminating theft (therefore discouraging the approval motive). Third, and finally, this form of involvement enhances employees' commitment to reducing theft. Again, quoting Snyder et al. (1991), "The more involved [employees] are, the more committed they should be to the decisions made and the more likely they and their fellow employees will not steal from the company" (p. 46). This assertion is supported by research demonstrating the beneficial effects of "voice" on perceptions of procedural justice (Greenberg & Folger, 1983).

Conclusion

I have on these pages presented the STEAL motive as a conceptualization of employee theft that is deeply grounded in the social psychology of group dynamics. It is an approach that conceives of employee theft as an ordinary phenomenon that occurs among normal people responding to everyday social dynamics. Indeed, it intentionally does not shed light on the behavior of the "professional thief." Deliberately removing the matter of theft from the realm of the extraordinary marks the path for employee theft to be treated as a supervisory problem: one that can be understood and controlled using the tools of management as opposed to the tools of criminology.

Despite the promise of this approach, it is predicated on assumptions that beg for careful analysis in further research. Indeed, there has been precious little research on the social psychology of employee theft, and what little there has been is not as systematic as it would need to be to provide insight into all the underlying complexities. Yet drawing on the work that has been done has led me to propose a taxonomy that appears to do a reasonable, albeit preliminary, job of identifying some of the key issues involved in understanding and managing employee theft.

With this said, the caveat needs to be issued that the STEAL motive does not intend to tell the complete story of the social dynamics of employee theft. Rather, it intends to serve as a useful heuristic in guiding future efforts in this regard. Similarly, by focusing on the social psychological dynamics of employee theft, the STEAL motive is not meant to supplant existing approaches to this important problem. It merely intends to supplement them. And given the keen insight and focus that this approach provides, it would appear to be a very useful supplement indeed.

References

Adams, J. S. (1965). Inequity in social exchange. In L. Berkowitz (Ed.), *Advances in experimental social psychology* (Vol. 2, pp. 267-299). New York: Academic Press.

Adams, V. (1981, November). Hot to keep 'em honest: Honesty as an organizational policy can help prevent employee theft. *Psychology Today*, pp. 50, 53.

Addis, K. K. (1992, July). Company crooks on the line. *Security Management*, pp. 36, 38, 40, 42.

Altheide, D. L., Adler, P. A., Adler, P., & Altheide, D. A. (1978). The social meanings of employee theft. In J. M. Johnson & J. D. Douglas (Eds.), *Crime at the top: Deviance in business and the professions* (pp. 90-124). Philadelphia: J. B. Lippincott.

Bintliff, R. L. (1994). *Crime-proofing your business*. New York: McGraw-Hill.

Boldero, J. (1995). The prediction of household recycling of newspapers: The role of attitudes, intentions, and situational factors. *Journal of Applied Social Psychology, 25*, 440-462.

Bradford, J. A. (1976). *A general perspective on job satisfaction: The relationship between job satisfaction and sociological, psychological, and cultural variables.* Unpublished doctoral dissertation, University of California, San Diego.

Brockner, J., & Wiesenfeld, B. M. (in press). The interactive impact of procedural fairness and outcome favorability: The effect of what you do depends on how you do it. *Psychological Bulletin.*

Bullard, P. D., & Resnik, A. J. (1983). SMR forum: Too many hands in the corporate cookie jar. *Sloan Management Review, 24*(3), 51-56.

Carter, N., Holström, A., Simpanen, M., & Melin, K. (1988). Theft reduction in a grocery store through product identification and graphing of losses for employees. *Journal of Applied Behavior Analysis, 21*, 385-389.

Cartwright, D., & Zander, A. (1968). *Group dynamics: Research and theory* (3rd ed.). New York: Harper & Row.

Cherrington, D. J., & Cherrington, J. O. (1985). The climate of honesty in retail stores. In W. Terris (Ed.), *Employee theft: Research, theory, and applications* (pp. 27-39). Park Ridge, IL: London House.

Dalton, D. R., Metzger, M. B., & Wimbush, J. C. (1994). Integrity testing for personnel selection: A review and research agenda. In G. R. Ferris (Ed.), *Research in personnel and human resources management* (Vol. 12, pp. 125-160). Greenwich, CT: JAI Press.

Dalton, M. (1959). *Men who manage.* New York: John Wiley.

Delaney, J. (1993). Handcuffing employee theft. *Small Business Report, 18*(7), 29-38.

Ditton, J. (1977a). *Part-time crime: An ethnography of fiddling and pilferage.* London: Macmillan.

Ditton, J. (1977b). Perks, pilferage, and the fiddle: The historical structure of invisible wages. *Theory and Society, 4,* 39-71.

Emshwiller, J. R. (1993, December 3). Corruption in bankruptcy system injures firms in need. *Wall Street Journal,* p. B1.

Feldman, D. C. (1984). The development and enforcement of group norms. *Academy of Management Review, 9,* 47-53.

Folger, R., & Greenberg, J. (1985). Procedural justice: An interpretive analysis of personnel systems. In K. Roland & G. Ferris (Eds.), *Research in personnel and human resources management* (Vol. 3, pp. 141-183). Greenwich, CT: JAI Press.

Foushee, H. C., Lauber, J. L., Baetge, M. M., & Acomb, D. B. (1986). *Crew factors in operations III: The operational significance of exposure to short-haul air transport operations* (Tech. Mem. No. 88342). Moffett Field, CA: NASA-Ames Research Center.

Ginnett, R. C. (1993). Crews as groups: Their formation and their leadership. In E. L. Weiner, B. G. Kanki, & R. L. Helmreich (Eds.), *Cockpit resource management* (pp. 71-98). San Diego, CA: Academic Press.

Gouldner, A. W. (1954). *Wildcat strike: A study in worker-management relationships.* New York: Harper & Row.

Govoni, S. J. (1992, February). To catch a thief. *CFO,* pp. 24-32.

Greenberg, J. (1990a). Employee theft as a reaction to underpayment inequity: The hidden cost of pay cuts. *Journal of Applied Psychology, 75,* 561-568.

Greenberg, J. (1990b). Looking fair vs. being fair: Managing impressions of organizational justice. In B. M. Staw & L. L. Cummings (Eds.), *Research in organizational behavior* (Vol. 12, pp. 111-157). Greenwich, CT: JAI Press.

Greenberg, J. (1993a). The social side of fairness: Interpersonal and informational classes of organizational justice. In R. Cropanzano (Ed.), *Justice in the workplace* (pp. 79-103). Hillsdale, NJ: Lawrence Erlbaum.

Greenberg, J. (1993b). Stealing in the name of justice: Informational and interpersonal moderators of theft reactions to underpayment inequity. *Organizational Behavior and Human Decision Processes, 54,* 81-103.

Greenberg, J. (1994). *Restitution and retaliation as motives for inequity-induced pilferage.* Unpublished manuscript, Ohio State University.

Greenberg, J. (1995). Employee theft. In N. Nicholson (Ed.), *The Blackwell encyclopedic dictionary of organizational behavior* (pp. 154-155). Oxford, UK: Blackwell.

Greenberg, J., & Folger, R. (1983). Procedural justice, participation, and the fair process effect in groups and organizations. In P. Paulus (Ed.), *Basic group processes* (pp. 235-266). New York: Springer-Verlag.

Greenberg, J., & Scott, K. S. (1996). Why do workers bite the hands that feed them? Employee theft as a social exchange process. In B. M. Staw & L. L. Cummings (Eds.), *Research in organizational behavior* (Vol. 18, pp. 111-156). Greenwich, CT: JAI Press..

Hackman, J. R. (1993). Teams, leaders, and organizations: New directions for crew-oriented flight training. In E. L. Weiner, B. G. Kanki, & R. L. Helmreich (Eds.), *Cockpit resource management* (pp. 47-69). San Diego, CA: Academic Press.

Hawkins, R. (1984). Employee theft in the restaurant trade: Forms of ripping off waiters at work. *Deviant Behavior, 5,* 47-69.

Henry, S. (1981). *Can I have it in cash? A study of informal institutions and unorthodox ways of doing things.* London: Astragal.

Hollinger, R. C. (1989). *Dishonesty in the workplace: A manager's guide to preventing employee theft.* Park Ridge, IL: London House.

Hollinger, R. C., & Clark, J. P. (1982). Formal and informal social controls of employee deviance. *Sociological Quarterly, 23,* 333-343.

Hollinger, R. C., & Clark, J. P. (1983). *Theft by employees.* Lexington, MA: Lexington.

Homans, G. C. (1961). *Social behavior: Its elementary forms.* New York: Harcourt Brace & World.

Hopkins, K. (1978). *Conquerors and slaves: Sociological studies in Roman history* (Vol. 1). Cambridge, UK: Cambridge University Press.

Horning, D. N. M. (1970). Blue-collar theft: Conceptions of property, attitudes toward pilfering, and work group norms in a modern industrial plant. In E. O. Smigel & H. L. Ross (Eds.), *Crimes against bureaucracy* (pp. 46-64). New York: Van Nostrand Reinhold.

Jaspan, N. (1974). *Mind your own business.* Englewood Cliffs, NJ: Prentice Hall.

Jones, T. M., & Gautschi, F. H., III. (1988). Will the ethics of business change: A survey of future executives. *Journal of Business Ethics, 7,* 231-248.

Kanki, B. G., & Palmer, M. T. (1993). Communication and crew resource management. In E. L. Weiner, B. G. Kanki, & R. L. Helmreich (Eds.), *Cockpit resource management* (pp. 99-136). San Diego, CA: Academic Press.

Katzenbach, J. R., & Smith, D. K. (1993). *The wisdom of teams.* Boston: Harvard Business School Press.

Kemper, T. D. (1966). Representative roles and the legitimation of deviance. *Social Problems, 13,* 288-298.

Liebow, E. (1967). *Tally's corner.* Boston: Little, Brown.

Lipman, M., & McGraw, W. R. (1988). Employee theft: A $40 billion industry. *Annals of the American Academy of Political and Social Science, 498,* 51-59.

London House & Food Marketing Institute. (1993). *Fourth annual report on employee theft in the supermarket industry.* Rosemont, IL: London House.

Mars, G. (1973). Hotel pilferage: A case study in occupational theft. In M. Warner (Ed.), *The sociology of the workplace* (pp. 200-210). New York: Halsted.

Mars, G. (1974). Dock pilferage: A case study in occupational theft. In P. Rock & M. McIntosh (Eds.), *Deviance and social control* (pp. 209-228). London: Tavistock.

Mars, G. (1982). *Cheats at work: An anthropology of workplace crime.* London: Allen & Unwin.

McGurn, T. (1988, March 7). Spotting the thieves who work among us. *Wall Street Journal,* p. 16A.

Merriam, D. H. (1977). Employee theft. *Criminal Justice Abstracts, 9,* 375-406.

Murphy, K. R. (1993). *Honesty in the workplace.* Pacific Grove, CA: Brooks/Cole.

Ones, D. S., Viswesvaran, C., & Schmidt, F. L. (1993). Comprehensive meta-analysis of integrity test validities: Findings and implications for personnel selection and theories of job performance. *Journal of Applied Psychology, 78,* 679-703.

Payne, S. L. (1989). Self-presentational tactics and employee theft. In R. A. Giacalone & P. Rosenfeld (Eds.), *Impression management in the organization* (pp. 397-410). Hillsdale, NJ: Lawrence Erlbaum.

Robin, G. D. (1969). Employees as offenders. *Journal of Research on Crime and Delinquency, 6*, 17-33.

Sackett, P. R. (1994). Integrity testing for personnel selection. *Current Directions in Psychological Science, 3*, 73-76.

Sieh, E. W. (1987). Garment workers: Perceptions of inequity and employee theft. *British Journal of Criminology, 27*, 174-190.

Smigel, E. O., & Ross, H. L. (1970). Introduction. In E. O. Smigel & H. L. Ross (Eds.), *Crimes against bureaucracy* (pp. 1-14). New York: Van Nostrand Reinhold.

Snyder, N. H., & Blair, K. E. (1989, May-June). Dealing with employee theft. *Business Horizons*, pp. 27-34.

Snyder, N. H., Blair, K. E., & Arndt, T. (1990). Breaking the bad habits behind time theft. *Business, 40*(4), 31-33.

Snyder, N. H., Broome, O. W., Jr., Kehoe, W. J., McIntyre, J. T., Jr., & Blair, K. E. (1991). *Reducing employee theft: A guide to financial and organizational controls.* New York: Quorum.

Taft, W. F. (1985). Bulletin boards, exhibits, hotlines. In C. Reuss & D. Silvis (Eds.), *Inside organizational communication* (2nd ed., pp. 183-189). New York: Longman.

Taylor, R. R. (1986). Your role in the prevention of employee theft. *Management Solutions, 31*, 20-25.

Tucker, J. (1989). Employee theft as social control. *Deviant Behavior, 10*, 319-334.

Tyler, T. (1987). Conditions leading to value-expressive effects in judgments of procedural justice: A test of four models. *Journal of Personality and Social Psychology, 52*, 333-344.

Zeitlin, L. R. (1971, June). A little larceny can do a lot for employee morale. *Psychology Today*, pp. 22, 24, 26, 64.

6

Employee Sabotage

Toward a Practitioner-Scholar Understanding

Robert A. Giacalone
Catherine A. Riordan
Paul Rosenfeld

Employee sabotage occurs when people currently employed in an organization engage in *intentional* behaviors that effectively damage that organization's property, reputation, product, or service (Giacalone & Rosenfeld, 1987). From this perspective, individuals sometimes called "violent avengers" (Lee, 1989), whose aim is political and designed to bring about a change in an organizational function (e.g., alternatives to animal testing) or the very purpose of the organization itself (e.g., close an abortion clinic), would not be classified as employee saboteurs, either because they are not employees or because their aims originate from advocacy positions that often predate their employment.

Authors' Note: The opinions are our own; they are not official and do not necessarily represent the views of the Navy Department. We thank Jerry Greenberg for his many comments.

There is reason to believe that employee sabotage will increase in the future, making the need to understand sabotage increasingly critical to an organization's success (Caudron, 1995). Especially in today's computer-dependent workplace, employee sabotage has the potential to become an increasingly significant problem in both public- and private-sector organizations. Although organizations have always had to deal with sabotage, the current high-technology workplace has made the potential threat of employee sabotage greater, allowing even a single computer virus to decimate an entire organization's financial and personnel records (Crino & Leap, 1989). Likewise, the possibility of greater anonymity resulting from electronic or computer communication has reduced a saboteur's fears of being identified and getting caught. The consequence of anonymity is that those interpersonal deterrents that in the past fostered an employee's concern for "looking right" in front of coworkers may now be rapidly disintegrating due to the greater number of impersonal interactions that organizational members conduct electronically (Caudron, 1995; Giacalone & Rosenfeld, 1987).

The current literature on employee sabotage reflects a young field with two divergent approaches. Those taking one approach adopt the vantage point of the manager and security professional, offer cautionary warning and forecasts, and deal directly with the present need of organizations to deter sabotage and apprehend saboteurs. This approach constitutes most of the work being done today (Caudron, 1995). The other approach is found in the research literature, in which the development of motivational theories for sabotage has been the dominant focus (Dubois, 1979; Jermier, 1988), leaving to security professionals the more immediate, practical concerns of managers faced with the potentially devastating consequences of employee sabotage. Yet there is great potential to extend the findings from research on topics related to sabotage (e.g., aggression, vandalism, terrorism) to an understanding of sabotage. Theory and research in these other areas are multidisciplinary and quite rich in their description and prediction of the related phenomena. This work has yet to be shared with practitioners or used to guide their search for effective means to deter or apprehend saboteurs. Managers, security officers, and others working in organizations are left without the benefit of systematic theories that can integrate their observations and experiences in the discovery, analysis, and prevention of sabotage. Conversely, the research literature is limited because it has seldom looked at real instances of sabotage except as anecdotes that set the stage for the research being conducted.

In this chapter, we provide an approach to employee sabotage that embraces both the practitioner's need to apprehend and/or deter perpetrators and the researcher's potential to describe sabotage systematically through the use of multidisciplinary theory and research. In addition, we recommend ways that the researcher's need for data on real sabotage could be met while recognizing organizations' desires for confidentiality. Using the emerging research on sabotage and the rich research literature in the related area of aggression, we propose a new practitioner focus on employee sabotage that includes specific questions to be asked by managers. Questions are targeted at obtaining a full understanding of sabotage occurring while avoiding some of the natural human tendencies to blame an individual saboteur, seeing him or her as crazed, while ignoring other possible incidents, saboteurs, and organizational processes that foster sabotage. Finally, we also offer techniques and strategies that provide data to answer the questions posed and show how researchers can use managers' data to advance their scientific approaches to understanding, predicting, and controlling sabotage.

Using Scholarship to Focus Managers and Help Prevent Sabotage

The organizational literature has lagged behind organizations' interests in the topic of sabotage. Jermier (1988) noted that "well developed concepts of workplace sabotage are not incorporated into organizational social science, leaving its meaning, causes and consequences subject to folk wisdom, popular opinion, and casual conjecture" (p. 103). Despite the paucity of evidence dealing directly with sabotage, there is a wealth of related interdisciplinary work that can be used to develop prescriptions for the manager. This interdisciplinary work can increase the effectiveness of managers who must deal with employee sabotage today by guiding them to ask the right questions (Browne & Keeley, 1995)—questions that stimulate a thorough analysis of the incident and can lead to effective means of deterrence and apprehension.

Interdisciplinary Approaches

The most compelling literature that can guide a manager's questions stems from scholarship in interdisciplinary areas focusing on violent acts. Literatures outside the organizational sciences provide theory and data that also may be generalizable to the destructive intent of the employee saboteur. Table 6.1 identifies some of the interdisciplinary and management content areas that bear on sabotage. As Table 6.1 indicates, interdisciplinary literature appears to provide specific linkages to how employee sabotage can be understood and/or controlled through an organization-specific conceptualization. More important, as has been alluded to in previous work on sabotage (e.g., Dubois, 1979; Giacalone & Rosenfeld, 1987), the literature dealing with violent acts could also serve as a metaphor for understanding why employee destructiveness occurs.

As an illustration of the promise that interdisciplinary research and theory offer managers for framing the right questions about sabotage, we use the psychological theory on aggression and research. *Aggression* has been defined as "any form of behavior directed toward the goal of harming or injuring another living being who is motivated to avoid such treatment" (Baron, 1977, p. 7). Aggression and employee sabotage can be seen as conceptually similar behaviors because the intent of both involves harm (Giacalone & Rosenfeld, 1987). What the aggression literature shows clearly is that aggression is multiply determined, easily confused with other similar behaviors that do not involve an intent to harm, and understandable given a thoughtful analysis of the situation from the aggressor's point of view (see Tedeschi, Lindskold, & Rosenfeld, 1976, for a review). Below, we outline some of the various psychological theories of and research on aggression and how they might be relevant to the understanding of sabotage. The theories and research also serve as the foundation for the next section of this chapter, in which they constitute the basis for questions managers can use to guide a careful and thorough analysis of suspected instances of sabotage.

Biological explanations of aggression contend that aggression is an essential part of human nature, the so-called "dark side of human nature," and conclude that management needs to protect itself against the inevitable occurrence of employee sabotage (Crino & Leap, 1988, p. 53). *Behavioral reinforcement approaches* contend that when aggressive

Table 6.1 Interdisciplinary and Management Research and Theory Relevant to Sabotage

Type of Research/Theory	Representative Questions for Applications to Employee Sabotage
Motivation	How might traditional employee motivators serve to motivate employee sabotage?
Employee selection	In what ways might we modify the selection process so as to identify prospective saboteurs?
Job satisfaction	What is the relationship between job satisfaction and employee sabotage?
Conflict management	What conflict management strategies are effective in mitigating the use of employee sabotage?
Organizational change	When might resistance to change transform into an act of employee sabotage?
Organizational culture	What aspects of organizational culture serve to intensify or mitigate acts of employee sabotage?
Group dynamics	What aspects of groups make them likely to protect or report a member who has committed sabotage?
Aggression	How do the various theories of human aggression help to understand employee sabotage?
Psychopathology	What behavioral profile of a destructive personality can be identified that will aid in the prediction and control of sabotage?
Ethics and moral development	How might the assessment of moral development or ethical decision making help to predict employee sabotage?
Vandalism	In what ways might the hedonic motivation of a vandal's behavior translate to similar hedonic motivation in an employee saboteur?
Sociological (deviance)	How might the existence of a known employee saboteur affect the tendency to sabotage by other employees?
Political science (terrorism, guerilla warfare)	In what ways are acts of terrorism and guerilla warfare similar to employee sabotage, either in motivation or in strategy?
Criminology	How might our knowledge of the factors influencing people to report crimes help us to facilitate the report of employee sabotage?

behaviors occur and are rewarded or reinforced, they are more likely to be repeated in the future (Bandura, 1965). From this perspective, employee sabotage occurs because it has been followed by some type of reinforcement (Dubois, 1979) or results from social learning, in which employees model the aggressive actions performed by others (Wiesenthal, 1990). Similar acts that occur following highly publicized sabotage instances (e.g., Tylenol poisoning) might be due to this social learning process.

In addition to the learning approaches to aggression, there are also perspectives focusing on *internal mechanisms*, such as frustrating emotions, that instigate aggressive acts and have already been linked to employee sabotage (see Spector, Chapter 1 of this volume). Individuals, for example, whose productivity and ability to make more money are hampered by dependence on an incompetent, lazy, or overly rigid coworker are likely to feel frustration that becomes a catalyst for aggressive behaviors. In today's workplace, corporate downsizing, restructuring, and reengineering could be precipitating increasing rates of employee sabotage by frustrated, disgruntled employees (Hetzer, 1990).

Still other perspectives focus on *environmental cues* that have been found to make aggression more likely when a person is angered (Berkowitz & Page, 1967). Cued-aggression theory would argue that cues can exacerbate employee sabotage when there are highly publicized acts of sabotage, threats, or graffiti by disgruntled employees. Finally, there are perspectives focusing on interpersonal *reciprocity* that argue that being attacked is a reliable predictor of violence. When people feel attacked, they often respond with an attack that is similar or of comparable severity (Geen, 1968; Taylor & Epstein, 1967). The link between retaliation and employee sabotage has been made (Rozen, 1984), with many experts claiming that employee revenge is one of the greatest fears of corporate security and information systems specialists (Bies, Tripp, & Kramer, Chapter 2 of this volume).

As can be seen, a close conceptual relationship exists between the various perspectives on aggression and employee sabotage. Although this research-based literature can serve as a foundation for managers' questions aimed at apprehending and deterring sabotage, two significant problems arise. First, on which of the perspectives should managers focus? Which of the varied approaches would provide the appropriate theory and research? Inasmuch as sabotage research has not yet determined how to distinguish clearly the qualities peculiar to sabotage (Dubois, 1979; Jermier, 1988), the enormous theoretical and research literature on aggression can be too amorphous for managers to glean much that would help them address their particular sabotage problems.

Second, because many of the aggression findings are based on arcane and artificial laboratory studies (see Tedeschi, Smith, & Brown,

1974), some generalization problems may exist. With evidence of valid generalizations, research could offer managers promise for solving future problems.

A Different Approach: Asking Pointed Questions

Unless it is subjected to more rigorous tests, the extension of aggression work to understanding sabotage is speculative. To find out if it is mere speculation or if it has validity, we advocate that a different process take place: Managers should ask *pointed questions* based on their deterrence and apprehension needs, leading to data collection, comprehensive analysis, and, ultimately, greater rates of apprehension. The answers that the apprehension and/or conviction of the perpetrator might provide can contain data that, if ultimately made available to scholars, would allow scholars to test the generalizability of their theories in violence-related areas. The lack of such "real-world" data has been a central problem in identifying, preventing, and punishing employee sabotage (Giacalone & Rosenfeld, 1987).

On the basis of the few scientific works of sabotage and the many anecdotal reports on employee sabotage (e.g., Dubois, 1979; Giacalone & Rosenfeld, 1987; Sprouse, 1994), we have identified several questions that are often ignored in attempts to understand events that may have been sabotage. Although these questions address the practical concerns of deterrence and apprehension, they may represent the inception of a potentially fruitful alliance between the practitioner/manager and the scholar/researcher. We believe that a manager's improved ability to gain answers regarding *particular* sabotage events should lead to the apprehension of more saboteurs and increase the available database on the motivations and techniques of saboteurs. The answers to managers' questions should offer a more reality-based picture of sabotage incidents. This enhanced view would extend scholars' ability to formulate a scientific understanding by furnishing real data to clarify the competing interdisciplinary perspectives currently used as explanatory metaphors in the sabotage literature (e.g., Dubois, 1979; Taylor & Walton, 1971).

Unlike previous work, the questions we offer make no assumptions about sabotage causation and thereby allow the data to determine the means to address the problem. Some authors (e.g., DiBattista, 1989) have made a premature and unproven assumption that a poor work environment causes sabotage and have proceeded to offer generic approaches focusing on managerial strategies that foster a better overall work environment (e.g., encourage feedback from employees; establish quality circles). Others (Crino & Leap, 1988) have suggested an increase in security in addition to improved work environment as a solution. Although these generic improvements in human relations may reduce sabotage caused by human relations problems, effective deterrence of employee sabotage requires the identification of other factors as well.

We currently consider a set of critical questions on which managers need to focus to deal pragmatically with the sabotage problem. It is important to note that these questions are based on our synthesis of the sparse scientific literature on sabotage, the voluminous literature for aggression and related areas, and the more substantial anecdotal/case study literature. Essentially, this work has led us to conclude that deterrence and/or apprehension of the saboteur requires specifying a proper definition (Dubois, 1979; Flynn, 1915; Linstead, 1985; Sprouse, 1994), identifying the number of perpetrators and the internal support for sabotage (Dubois, 1979; Giacalone & Rosenfeld, 1987; Sprouse, 1994), determining the history of sabotage in the organization (Dubois, 1979; Taylor & Walton, 1971), identifying the provocation of the sabotage (Dubois, 1979; Giacalone & Rosenfeld, 1987), and targeting the saboteur (Crino & Leap, 1989; Sprouse, 1994) and the type (psychological versus physical) of damage done (Linstead, 1985; Taylor & Walton, 1971). Questions focusing on these issues will provide a basis for helping managers with their immediate deterrence/apprehension needs and serve as an essential database for scholars.

Managerial Questions About Sabotage

Question 1: Is the Event Sabotage?

A basic managerial problem is an inability to consider whether a particular event actually is sabotage (Giacalone & Rosenfeld, 1987; Sprouse, 1994). Underlying this problem are two separate issues: definitional problems and alternative explanations.

Definitional Problems

Although many definitions of *employee sabotage* have been offered (e.g., Dubois, 1979; Giacalone & Rosenfeld, 1987), a consensus has not been established. A variety of reasons may exist for the lack of definitional consensus. First, inconsistent assumptions either have been unnecessarily limited in focus (e.g., to perpetrators who are a small group of radicals (Flynn, 1915; Pouget, 1913) or have failed to limit their focus, resulting in a conceptualization of sabotage that is so broad as to encompass most work behaviors (Brown, 1977; Dubois, 1979). Second, the difficulty in defining *sabotage* is that it involves many different types of behaviors (Crino & Leap, 1989), including such divergent acts as destroying equipment and property, unleashing a computer virus, poisoning food and medicines, working slowly, and stealing. As Slora, Joy, Jones, and Terris (1991) noted, "Even fairly mundane acts, such as arguing with a customer, can result in losses in that both repeat business and the reputation of the company are threatened" (p. 171).

Categorization of forms of sabotage have been offered by Strool (1978) and Giacalone and Rosenfeld (1987). Strool's (1978) categorization results in seven types of sabotage (informational, chemical, electronic, mechanical, fire, explosive, and psychological), whereas Giacalone and Rosenfeld's (1987) analysis lends itself to four categories (slowdowns, destructiveness, dishonesty, and causing chaos). Nothing inherent in these descriptions of the forms of sabotage clearly distinguishes between an act that is sabotage and one that is not. Determining intent is essential to differentiate sabotage from other unintentional acts with similar consequences, for what looks like sabotage may not be motivated by a desire to sabotage (e.g., electronic interruptions can be caused inadvertently or by nonhuman agents). Even typologies of antisocial organizational behaviors (Robinson & Bennett, 1995) do not make the distinction much clearer. This lack of clarity has led to interpretive problems, making it difficult to determine whether an event is employee sabotage. As Linstead (1985) has noted, there is often a considerable stretch from what is observed to what is offered regarding the reason(s) for sabotage. We are left with a less-than-clear understanding of what we are trying to prevent and how we might prevent it.[1]

Alternative Explanations

A troublesome event such as a broken machine is a problem to the manager regardless of whether it was caused by employee sabotage or some other factor. From the manager's perspective, the fundamental issue is *not* whether an event is or is not sabotage, but what caused it. The answer to this question is a practical concern that will determine what action can or should be taken. If the problem is due to mechanical breakdown based on wear, the manager may enlist the help of technicians or engineers. If the problem is the result of sabotage, however, a different set of issues may arise. Managers may not wish to identify an act as sabotage. The act of labeling an occurrence as sabotage can create new public relations concerns, inspire copycat sabotage, and lower employee morale. The manager may be caught between the unhappy choices of properly investigating the act as if it may have been sabotage (and risking the aforementioned problems) or ignoring the possibility that it might be sabotage and attributing it instead to another cause.

However, as can be seen in Table 6.2, accurately diagnosing whether an event is actually employee sabotage has consequences that should result in appropriate, cost-effective measures. The failure to diagnose sabotage can lead to managerial reactions that make the impact of the act worse: exacerbating the factors that caused the original event, creating the image of managerial incompetence or paranoia, wasting resources, or spending time attempting to fix the wrong problem.

In addition to the problem of determining whether an act was sabotage is deciding what should be done if it is concluded that employee sabotage has indeed occurred. We contend that managers should consider whether the event is worth pursuing before undertaking the pains of investigating it. Some organizations decide to "write off" the milder forms of employee sabotage (e.g., graffiti), essentially concluding that although not particularly desirable, such behaviors can be tolerated (Cohen, 1973).

Question 2: Is the Perpetrator an Individual or a Group?

Assuming that sabotage has been deemed the likely cause of an event, identifying the perpetrator is crucial in preventing employee sabotage from occurring in the future (Dubois, 1979). The perpetrator

Table 6.2 Assessment of Sabotage

	Was an Intended Act of Sabotage	Was Not an Intended Act of Sabotage
Management attributes event to sabotage	The accurate assessment leads to appropriate actions undertaken, including investigation, prevention, and apprehension of the saboteur.	The inaccurate assessment leads to actions that are seen as unfair by employees, leading perhaps to lowering of morale and possibly resulting in actual sabotage as retaliation; actual problem is never addressed.
Management attributes event to another cause	The inaccurate assessment leads to the sabotage being ignored, leading to no investigation, prevention, or apprehension; resources may be expended on looking for and/or solving another problem that does not exist.	The accurate assessment leads to appropriate actions undertaken, including investigation and prevention of the problem.

can be either an individual or group. If the sabotage was executed by an individual, the manager's problem may be confined to that individual alone. However, it is possible that the destructive event was the function of a group of saboteurs. We can break group sabotage down into independent, conspiratorial, and blind-eye types. *Independent* group sabotage involves a group of people who are responsible for sabotage in the organization but who are working independently and may not know of each other's existence. One person may be sabotaging the machinery, another the product coming off the machinery, and yet another the packaging of the product. *Conspiratorial* group sabotage occurs when a group of people decide that an act of employee sabotage will be committed and engage in it together or jointly protect the perpetrator(s). *Blind-eye* group sabotage occurs when an act of employee sabotage is witnessed by others and, because of dislike of the organization or the victims of the sabotage, witnesses choose to say nothing about the event. Such sabotage can be easily identified if is known that many people witnessed the sabotage but not when all disclaim any knowledge of who the perpetrator was. Similarly, instances in which sabotage should have been easily spotted (e.g., via routine checks) but was not suggest the possibility that there is either active or passive complicity.

To apprehend the saboteur and deter future sabotage requires that managers search closely not only for the saboteur but also for those who were present at the time of the sabotage, who could have seen it, who might have seen it, and who should have seen it but did not. Such identification may often be reduced to the basic determination of who was present when an act of sabotage was committed and why it was not seen and/or reported.

Question 3: Is It an Isolated Event, or Is There a History of Organizational Sabotage?

The frequency of a particular type of sabotage, along with the past history of sabotage in the organization, is important for establishing how the current act being investigated is related to other instances of employee sabotage. Sometimes the sheer number of suspect events can provide important information of an ongoing problem for the company. For example, in one organization, a particular piece of equipment repeatedly and consistently miscut sheet metal forms by roughly an eighth of an inch, making the sheet metal form unusable. When questioned, technicians provided assurances that the equipment was operating properly. At the same time, other machines were having problems for which technicians could not find any cause. What made the technicians' assurances particularly important was that the consistency of the equipment failure was similar to previous acts of suspected sabotage during hostile union-management relations. The attention to the multiple incidents, in the historical context of similar problems during times of troubled labor relations, led management to conclude that the machines were being deliberately tampered with by employees. Such awareness of the sabotage chronology in organizations can provide valuable insights into the underlying causes of this behavior.

Question 4: Was There Provocation Prior to the Incident?

Although at first glance an act of employee sabotage may seem the irrational work of a deranged individual, the literature indicates that saboteurs are rarely unprovoked psychopaths (Giacalone, 1990; Jermier, 1988). Instead, saboteurs may be responding to perceived wrongs that accumulate and motivate them to get back at the provoking source and even the score. Thus the manager needs to know the answers to the questions: Who was provoked? Was this person capable of carrying out the act? Did the suspect have the opportunity to engage in the type of sabotage that occurred?

Question 5: Does the Target Appear to Be an Individual, a Unit, or the Whole Organization?

Because the impact of employee sabotage can be seen most clearly at the organizational level (Dubois, 1979; Giacalone & Rosenfeld, 1987), managers may inaccurately conclude that the organization, its financial well-being, or its products and services are the primary target of sabotage. Anecdotal evidence from interviews done by one of the authors indicates that the organization is typically a secondary or unintended victim. For example, in a large manufacturing plant, a particularly hostile manager had his equipment stolen and destroyed because employees wanted to torment him. This act of retaliation against the manager resulted in collateral damage to the organization. The failure to consider that the organization may not be the primary target ignores the reality that employee sabotage can be directed against a multitude of targets and reduces the likelihood of apprehending and preventing future harmful actions. In the case of the hostile manager, company officials incorrectly thought that their labor strife was the motivator and the company the intended victim.

An awareness of the distinction among individual, group, and organizational targets is important for managers addressing acts of employee sabotage. Quickly and specifically identifying the problem allows steps to be taken (e.g., increased security at specific locations) to reduce the likelihood of additional acts by the same perpetrator(s) or of copycat acts by others. Narrowing down the possible targets also may provide a better understanding of the motivation underlying the acts of employee sabotage that already have occurred.

Question 6: Was There Psychological Damage in Addition to Property Damage?

Employee sabotage may affect a company's bottom line in ways other than by causing physical damage. In addition to the destruction of property, there may also be considerable indirect, hidden impact resulting from psychological damage to individuals or the organization. Painter (1991) has noted that the impact of an aggressive act goes beyond the injury that is sustained and encompasses a host of other emotional and psychological consequences. Often, although visible damage appears negligible, the psychological damage may result in lost work time, increased stress, lowered morale, and increased turnover. Identifying the victims of both the physical and psychological damage provides yet another indicator of the potential motive for the sabotage.

For example, in one organization, after all of his employees had gone, a manager was known to go into the cleaning area and wash up in the large wash basins. Some employees who knew this pattern would periodically defecate in the wash basin simply to aggravate him. His rantings on the day following such events became legendary and were the source of much sadistic pleasure for the employees. These same employees would also take important tools or papers from the manager's workstation and move them out of sight not far from the original area, then gleefully report that the manager thought he was losing his mind. The manager (who did not find humor in any of this) lost time as a result of stress-related absence.

Techniques to Gather Data

Answering these questions is not best done by merely "guessing" the correct solutions or gathering opinions but by systematic assessment techniques that supplement opinions with data to help pinpoint the existence of the particular sabotage problem, provide an understanding of what caused the problem, and offer insights into how future incidents might be prevented. How might managers and organizations gather the data needed to answer these questions? We offer four techniques: sabotage log, archival review, ongoing surveying, and nominal group techniques. Table 6.3 provides a summary of these techniques and examples of how they might be used.

These techniques are consistent with previous work on antisocial behavior showing that sound data collection is essential to deterrence and apprehension (Giacalone, 1993; Lindsey, 1994), as well as substantive theoretical formulation (Giacalone, 1993; Giacalone & Knouse,

Table 6.3 Data Collection Techniques, Their Description, and Examples of Specific Uses

Technique	Description	Examples of Specific Uses
Sabotage log	Central information file on suspected employee sabotage, including location, methods used, number of times, preceding provocative events, personnel who had access; can provide a "trend" analysis of sabotage behavior	*Isolated or multiple event:* Logged events provide evidence of sabotage patterns, in the form of either similar or different sabotage acts. *Target—individual, unit, or organization:* Logged events allow for categorization to determine whether sabotage acts were restricted to certain units or particular managers or were widespread across the organization. *Prior provocation:* Because logged events were tagged with the description of prior provocations, trends can be seen across suspected sabotage events.
Archival review	Review of available archival data, including grievances, personnel evaluations, and exit interviews, that can help in consideration of both the current context and historical precedents	*Explanations for the event:* Review of maintenance logs, grievance cases, and personnel records, when gauged against the dates in the sabotage log, can show patterns, thereby offering potential insight into the sabotage. *Previous management reactions:* Review of management actions taken following suspected sabotage, when used in combination with the sabotage log, provides a means for determining whether particular sabotage patterns followed lenient (e.g., ignoring) versus severe (e.g., dismissal) management reactions.

(continued)

Table 6.3 Continued

Technique	Description	Examples of Specific Uses
Ongoing survey	Survey used to identify issues potentially causing sabotage (e.g., frustration with the organization)	*Explanations for the event:* When used in combination with a sabotage log, ongoing surveying of employees on particular topics (e.g., job satisfaction, frustration) allows for a database on which the relationship of the surveyed factor can be gauged against the intensity, form, and frequency of sabotage. *Isolated or multiple event:* The existence of isolated or multiple sabotage events, as recorded in the sabotage log, can be gauged against levels of the particular factor surveyed (e.g., job satisfaction).
Nominal group technique	Idea-generation process to identify problem areas/ expand potential responses to sabotage	*Perpetrator—individual or group:* When used in combination with a sabotage log, provides for multiple interpretations of access to sabotage area, motivated individuals, etc. *Damage—psychological and/or property:* When used in combination with a sabotage log, provides multiple perspectives on the damage done as a result of the sabotage.

1993). The techniques provide data that offer managers and scholars a longitudinal view of sabotage, both to track the saboteur and to assist in the formulation of a scientific understanding based on valid, well-substantiated observations. In addition, on the basis of their more extensive use in security work, these methods appear logically consistent with the interests of both managers and scholars (Giacalone, 1993; Giacalone & Knouse, 1993; Lindsey, 1994; Littlejohn, 1987; Stapleton, 1994). For example, the nominal group technique (Van de Ven & Delbecq, 1974) has been used successfully by the military to identify security weaknesses and expand possible administrative responses with which to interpret and deal with these problems (Giacalone, 1993).

Back to Theory: The Scholar's Gains

From the above, we can see how this benefits practitioners—but what about scholars? What was the primary reason for a *particular* act of employee sabotage? The answer to the question is no doubt the main cause of concern for most managers faced with an incident of employee sabotage. But the scholar recognizes that understanding a singular event usually cannot help other managers deter employee sabotage because one saboteur may act out of vengeance, another out of boredom, political agendas, or a host of other motivations (Crino & Leap, 1989; Farmer & Sundberg, 1986; Rozen, 1984). Whether employee sabotage, as a whole, can be successfully predicted and controlled will depend on whether a scientific way can be found to determine which factors motivate sabotage, the conditions that cause this motivation, and the ability to discern, reduce, and/or eliminate these factors. We contend that well-documented and focused efforts of managers attempting to answer the questions we have posed can provide researchers with much-needed real-world data that have been absent from prior sabotage research (Jermier, 1988; Linstead, 1985).

What remains problematic in bridging the gap between the scholar and practitioner is the best means for effectively communicating the data gathered by managers to scholars conducting research in the area. Both managers and their organizations may be reluctant to communicate openly the realities of what they find because they or their companies wish to avoid being blamed for or associated with negative organizational outcomes (see Rosenfeld, Giacalone, & Riordan, 1995). In fact, these impression management concerns may result in a "pact of silence" that leads to underestimating how widespread a problem employee sabotage is because management is reluctant to admit or discuss it. To gain fully the benefits of the approach we advocate, scholars will have to recognize management's hesitancy to admit or discuss openly many acts of employee sabotage because they do not want this to create a negative impression of their organization in their customers, competition, or the media (Crino & Leap, 1989; Giacalone & Rosenfeld, 1987). One possibility is some sort of employee sabotage consortium in which managers in a related industry (e.g., telecommunications) could meet with each other and with scholars to share findings, review advances in theory and practice, and discuss ways to address novel or challenging problems. Such an approach has proven successful in the organizational survey arena (see Morris & LoVerde, 1993), in advancing the survey process by sharing items and survey findings while also protecting the interests and security of each of the consortium members.

As noted, the possibility that interdisciplinary work offers can be fully realized only when it is determined which of the interdisciplinary perspectives is relevant, when the perspective is relevant, and how, if at all, the perspective must be modified to explain sabotage better. Organizational data leading to the apprehension of the saboteur provide a basis on which to make linkages between interdisciplinary theory/research and employee sabotage clear and interpretable. We believe that such linkages will yield valuable insights into employee sabotage that, *based on a pattern of actual data,* can be grounded within one or more interdisciplinary domains.

How might this process aid the scholar in his or her pursuit to explain employee sabotage scientifically? First, with actual sabotage data in hand, scholars may be better able to assess the external validity of various interdisciplinary perspectives. Working with real data on actual instances of sabotage within the multiple theories, perspectives, and research from interdisciplinary fields, scholars can gauge the generalizability of the theories and laboratory research and begin the process of focused research that isolates predictor variables and identifies preventative tactics most likely to reduce employee sabotage.

Second, actual sabotage data can assist in developing taxonomies of sabotage types, motivations, and contexts. For example, taxonomies can be considered within the context of how various forms of deterrence and managerial responses might be made more effective. The interrelationship between forms of sabotage (explosions, breaking equipment, etc.) and appropriate deterrence (e.g., closer monitoring, testing) has been absent from sabotage writings, and is reflective of the lack of theory and data on which discussions of employee sabotage have been based. Ultimately, organizational data on sabotage-related factors can provide the information with which scholars can create an appropriate framework that avoids impractical and unrealistic generic approaches (e.g., DiBattista, 1989) that do not take the complexity of the problem into account.

Conclusion

A more formalized and comprehensive process of managerial questioning can be the pilings of a bridge between the divergent approaches we have traced in the sabotage literature. Use of the pointed questions, grounded in interdisciplinary knowledge such as it is, leading to data collection and improved opportunities for apprehension, will not replace but rather should enhance scholarly research. Precedents would lead us to conclude that theoretical constructs can be applied from disciplines such as sociology (e.g. Hollinger & Clark, 1982) and social psychology (Giacalone & Knouse, 1990; Giacalone & Rosenfeld, 1987) toward effectively understanding areas of antisocial behavior such as sabotage. The requirement to respect the time constraints of managers while simultaneously structuring and utilizing their access to data on real sabotage will help direct scholarly work. Whether in the testing and application of interdisciplinary perspectives or in the development of entirely new theoretical formulations to explain employee sabotage, the use of reality-based managerial data rather than abstract conjecture will bridge the gap between scholar and manager and offer both access to a solution better tailored to satisfying each of their needs.

Note

1. Perry (1974) categorized strike-related sabotage into prestrike sabotage (actions prior to a strike deadline designed to make "scab" operations more difficult) and poststrike sabotage (actions taken by workers while on strike to make it more difficult to operate with replacement personnel). Investigators have also proposed classifications based on hypothetical reasons that sabotage occurred. Crino and Leap (1988), conversely, offered four reasons for sabotage: (a) to make a statement or send a message, (b) to gain revenge against management or coworkers, (c) to have an impact in a large and faceless bureaucracy, and (d) to satisfy a need to destroy, seek thrills, or avoid work. Dubois (1979), using a broader categorization, distinguished between *instrumental sabotage*, which is directed toward the achievement of some goal, and *demonstrative sabotage*, which is used to castigate management or protest injustice.

References

Bandura, A. (1965). Influence of models' reinforcement contingencies on the acquisition of imitative responses. *Journal of Personality and Social Psychology, 1*, 589-595.

Baron, R. A. (1977). *Human aggression*. New York: Plenum.

Berkowitz, L., & Page, A. (1967). Weapons as aggression-eliciting stimuli. *Journal of Personalty and Social Psychology, 7,* 202-207.

Brown, G. (1977). *Sabotage: A study in industrial conflict.* Nottingham, UK: Spokesman.

Browne, M. N., & Keeley, S. M. (1995). *Asking the right questions.* Englewood Cliffs, NJ: Prentice Hall.

Caudron, S. (1995, September). Fighting the enemy within. *Industry Week,* pp. 36-39.

Cohen, S. (1973). Property destruction: Motives and meanings. In C. Ward (Ed.), *Vandalism* (pp. 23-53). New York: Van Nostrand Reinhold.

Crino, M. D., & Leap, T. L. (1988). Sabotage: Protecting your company means dealing with the dark side of human nature. *Success, 35,* 52-55.

Crino, M. D., & Leap, T. L. (1989). What HR managers must know about employee sabotage. *Personnel, 14,* 31-38.

DiBattista, R. A. (1989, October). Designing a program to manage the risk of sabotage. *Supervision,* pp. 6-8.

Dubois, P. (1979). *Sabotage in industry.* Harmondsworth, UK: Pelican.

Farmer, R., & Sundberg, N. D. (1986). Boredom proneness: The development and correlates of a new scale. *Journal of Personality Assessment, 50,* 4-17.

Flynn, E. G. (1915). *Sabotage.* Cleveland, OH: Guardian.

Geen, R. G. (1968). Effects of frustration, attack and prior training in aggressiveness on aggressive behavior. *Journal of Personality and Social Psychology, 9,* 316-321.

Giacalone, R. A. (1990, July). Employee sabotage: The enemy within. *Supervisory Management,* pp. 6-7.

Giacalone, R. A. (1993). *Developing an exit survey instrument for identifying and decreasing theft susceptibility risks in the Department of Defense: The results at SIMA, Norfolk* (ONR-TN-N00014-91-J-4172). Monterey, CA: Defense Personnel Security Research Center.

Giacalone, R. A., & Knouse, S. B. (1990). Justifying wrongful employee behavior: The role of personality in organizational sabotage. *Journal of Business Ethics, 9,* 55-61.

Giacalone, R. A., & Knouse, S. B. (1993). Identifying security risks in organizations: Development and use of a security exit survey instrument. In P. Rosenfeld, J. E. Edwards, & M. D. Thomas (Eds.), *Improving organizational surveys* (pp. 240-256). Newbury Park, CA: Sage.

Giacalone, R. A., & Rosenfeld, P. (1987). Reasons for employee sabotage in the workplace. *Journal of Business Psychology, 1,* 367-378.

Hetzer, J. (1990, October). Preventing sneak attacks from the enemy within. *Business Month, 136,* 21.

Hollinger, R. C., & Clark, J. P. (1982). Formal and informal social controls of employee deviance. *Sociological Quarterly, 23,* 333-343.

Jermier, J. M. (1988). Sabotage at work: The rational view. In S. B. Bachrach (Ed.), *Research in the sociology of organizations* (Vol. 6, pp. 101-134). Greenwich, CT: JAI Press.

Lee, E. L. (1989, September). Violent avengers. *Security Management,* pp. 39-42.

Lindsey, D. (1994, September). Of sound mind? Evaluating the workforce. *Security Management,* pp. 69-71.

Linstead, S. (1985). Breaking the purity rule: Industrial sabotage and the symbolic process. *Personnel Review, 15,* 12-19.

Littlejohn, R. F. (1987, April). Managing the unthinkable. *Security Management,* pp. 73-78.

Morris, G. W., & LoVerde, M. A. (1993). Consortium surveys. In P. Rosenfeld, J. E. Edwards, & M. D. Thomas (Eds.), *Improving organizational surveys: New directions, methods, and applications* (pp. 122-142). Newbury Park, CA: Sage.

Painter, K. (1991). Violence and vulnerability in the workplace: Psychosocial and legal implications. In M. J. Davidson & J. Earnshaw (Eds.), *Vulnerable workers: Psychosocial and legal issues* (pp. 159-178). New York: John Wiley.

Perry, C. R. (1974). *Operating during strikes.* Philadelphia: University of Pennsylvania Press.

Pouget, E. (1913). *Sabotage.* Chicago: Charles H. Kerr.

Robinson, S. L., & Bennett, R. J. (1995). A typology of deviant workplace behaviors: A multidimensional scaling study. *Academy of Management Journal, 38,* 555-572.

Rosenfeld, P., Giacalone, R. A., & Riordan, C. A. (1995). *Impression management in organizations: Theory, measurement, practice.* New York: Routledge.

Rozen, M. E. (1984, Summer). Sabotage, anomie and the economy. *Dissent, 31,* 362-365.

Slora, K. B., Joy, D. S., Jones, J. W., & Terris, W. (1991). The prediction of on-the-job violence. In J. W. Jones (Ed.), *Preemployment honesty testing* (pp. 171-181). New York: Quorum.

Sprouse, M. (1994). *Sabotage in the American workplace: Anecdotes of dissatisfaction, mischief, and revenge.* San Francisco: Pressure Drop.

Stapleton, B. (1994, September). Maximizing the margin for sabotage safety. *Security Management,* pp. 62-67.

Strool, W. M. (1978). *Crime prevention through physical security.* New York: Marcel Dekker.

Taylor, L., & Walton, P. (1971). *Images of deviance. Industrial sabotage: Motives and meanings.* New York: Penguin.

Taylor, S. P., & Epstein, S. (1967). Aggression as a function of the interaction of the sex of aggressor and the sex of the victim. *Journal of Personality, 35,* 474-486.

Tedeschi, J. T., Lindskold, S., & Rosenfeld, P. (1976). *Introduction to social psychology.* St. Paul, MN: West.

Tedeschi, J. T., Smith, R. B., & Brown, R. C. (1974). A reinterpretation of research on aggression. *Psychological Bulletin, 81,* 540-563.

Van de Ven, A. H., & Delbecq, A. L. (1974). The effectiveness of nominal, Delphi, and interacting group decision making processes. *Academy of Management Journal, 17,* 605-621.

Wiesenthal, D. L. (1990). Psychological aspects of vandalism. In P. J. D. Drenth, J. A. Sergeant, & R. J. Takens (Eds.), *European perspectives in psychology* (Vol. 3, pp. 279-297). Chichester, England: John Wiley.

7

Whistle-Blowing
as Antisocial Behavior

Marcia P. Miceli
Janet P. Near

There are many indications that whistle-blowing is viewed as desirable from a societal perspective in the United States. We define whistle-blowers to be people who "disclose illegal, immoral, or illegitimate practices under the control of their employers, to persons or organizations that may be able to effect action" (Near & Miceli, 1985, p. 5). On television talk shows and in news reports, whistle-blowers often are presented as heroes, thus suggesting that whistle-blowers are viewed favorably. Further, many states have enacted laws to protect whistle-blowers, and efforts to strengthen these and federal laws are underway (Dworkin & Near, 1987).

_____

Authors' Note: We thank Brian Burton for his comments on an earlier draft of this manuscript.

But whistle-blowing can have negative consequences as well, and the intentions of those who say they are engaging in it may be far from altruistic. For example, organizational and societal resources may be wasted in responding to frivolous complaints. Creation of reporting mechanisms and codification of rules and procedures can damage organizational climate, reduce trust, reduce flexibility, or increase organization and societal members' sense that they are overly controlled (Clark, 1992). The reputations of innocent "wrongdoers" targeted by the whistle-blower because of a wish for revenge may be damaged, or an organization may be driven out of business (Clark, 1992).

Previously published work on whistle-blowing has tended to emphasize its potential positive societal, and sometimes organizational, consequences: For example, production of hazardous goods may be halted, or managerial fraud may be revealed (Brief & Motowidlo, 1986; Dozier & Miceli, 1985). However, in previous empirical work, predictor variables explain relatively little variance in whistle-blowing, and the observed consequences of whistle-blowing rarely play out precisely as hypothesized (Miceli & Near, 1992). One possible explanation is that some whistle-blowing is essentially antisocial and thus likely to have different antecedents and consequences from other types of whistle-blowing. If so, then we need to understand these differences better.

Accordingly, there are two purposes of this chapter. First, we construct a simple typology that may provide guidance in classifying some whistle-blowing incidents as antisocial. Second, we offer research propositions identifying potential predictors and consequences of antisocial whistle-blowing. It is hoped that researchers will test these propositions and increase our understanding of whistle-blowing.

Definitions

Whistle-Blowing

As noted above, the most commonly used definition of whistle-blowing (Near & Miceli, 1985) includes several elements: (a) the disclosure, by organization employees (past or present), of practices under the control of their employers that they believe to be illegal, immoral, or illegitimate to (b) persons or organizations that these employees believe may be able to effect action. These elements of the definition necessarily rely on the perceptions of the whistle-blower. Yet these perceptions may differ from those of other observers, and both sets of perceptions are often very difficult to measure accurately—problems faced by investigators of many phenomena in the field!

To illustrate, consider the case of Karen Silkwood, as portrayed in the motion picture *Silkwood*. Silkwood was a factory worker who believed that she and her fellow workers were being asked to handle radioactive materials in an unsafe manner. When she reported this concern, first to coworkers, then to the union, then to members of Congress, several of her coworkers felt that her perception of unsafe working practices was inaccurate. Furthermore, they were concerned that their employer would be irreparably harmed by this allegation and that their jobs and livelihood might be jeopardized. Thus Silkwood's belief that illegitimate behavior had occurred was questioned. She reported her allegation to several persons and organizations who might be expected to take action, and clearly she thought that they would do so. Some of these, however, felt that it was outside their defined roles to take action and failed to react.

We define whistle-blowing from the perspective of the whistle-blower, but clearly others' views of the act or its elements may differ from those of the whistle-blower. There is some disadvantage to this limitation, but we think it is necessary for one simple reason: Probably all whistle-blowing is viewed as antisocial by some observer. Yet classifying all whistle-blowing as inherently antisocial defeats our purpose of trying to distinguish whistle-blowing that is relatively antisocial from that which is relatively prosocial. We need to draw these distinctions conceptually before we can test empirically whether they actually exist. Relying primarily on the whistle-blower's perception facilitates this effort.

Prosocial Versus Antisocial Organizational Behavior

We and others (Brief & Motowidlo, 1986; Dozier & Miceli, 1985; Kolarska & Aldrich, 1980; Miceli & Near, 1988) have shown that many, if not most, incidents of whistle-blowing can be classified as prosocial organizational behavior. Prosocial organizational behavior is behavior that is "(a) performed by a member of an organization; (b) directed toward an individual, group, or organization with whom he or she interacts while carrying out his or her organizational role; and (c) performed with the intention of promoting the welfare of the individual, group, or organization toward which it is directed" (Brief & Motowidlo, 1986, p. 711).

One defining characteristic of whistle-blowing is the observer's intention to stop perceived wrongdoing (Near & Miceli, 1985); thus all whistle-blowers must have this motive. However, stopping wrongdoing from occurring may not be the only, or even the primary, motive for whistle-blowing. Previous research has shown that there can be multiple or mixed motives (e.g., Dozier & Miceli, 1985). For example, a whistle-blower might pursue a discrimination suit with the intentions of rectifying wrongful discrimination; making management less likely to discriminate against others in the future; obtaining not only a "make whole" remedy but punitive damages; and embarrassing, punishing, or controlling those perceived to be responsible. To the extent that the primary motive for action is to improve only one's own position, through alleviated wrongdoing or concomitant consequences, at the expense of others or without regard to the harm caused to others, then whistle-blowing is less prosocial and more antisocial. Thus some whistle-blowing may not fit the definition of prosocial organizational behavior in that the whistle-blower's intentions may not include promotion of the welfare of the target. Rather, these intentions may be quite the opposite and may involve harming others.

Unlike prosocial organizational behavior, little research attention has been paid to the topic of antisocial organizational behavior. Although sociologists have studied deviance, we consider this a somewhat broader category of behavior. In fact, we could find no existing definition in the organizational literature. Webster's dictionary (1990) provides the following definition of *antisocial:* "1. averse to the society of others: unsociable. 2. hostile or harmful to society, esp.: being or marked by behavior deviating sharply from the social norm." This definition is useful in that it clarifies the central role of harm, but obviously it does not deal with organizational behaviors and their implications. Accordingly, we have modified the Brief and Motowidlo (1986) definition quoted above: Antisocial organizational behavior is behavior that is (a) performed by a member of an organization; (b) directed toward an individual, group, or organization with whom he or she interacts while carrying out his or her organizational role; and (c) performed with the intention of harming the welfare of the individual, group, or organization toward which it is directed.

Building a Preliminary Typology

We assume that whistle-blowing is a dynamic process, following a sequence of steps (Dozier & Miceli, 1985). Three factors useful in building a preliminary typology emerge from further consideration of the definitions of *prosocial* and *antisocial behavior* in whistle-blowing contexts. We propose that these factors are (a) the intentions of the whistle-blower; (b) the process used by the whistle-blower to report the wrongdoing, whether procedurally just or unjust; and (c) the actual consequences of whistle-blowing for other organizational members. The reader will note that only the first of these three is expressly included in the definitions of prosocial and antisocial behavior. Research is needed to examine whether either of the other two factors should be added to the definition, whether all conditions must be present for the whistle-blowing to be seen by most people as antisocial, and whether there is a hierarchy of importance attached to these factors.

Intentions of the Whistle-Blower

Greenberg (Chapter 5 of this volume) has examined the importance of intentions in classifying motives for employee theft. Similarly, intentions are viewed as important in classifying whistle-blowing as antisocial. The intention to help versus harm others is viewed as a key factor in determining the extent to which whistle-blowing is prosocial or antisocial.

Before addressing this point, we wish to clarify that intending to help oneself probably does not distinguish antisocial from prosocial whistle-blowing. Although a few observers maintain or imply that prosocial behavior must be purely altruistic (e.g., Graham, 1984, 1986), most observers agree that some benefit can accrue to the prosocial actor (for a review, see Miceli & Near, 1992). Studies have shown that whistle-blowers seek some benefit for themselves in fully half the cases, whether an archival method is used after the fact to assess motivation (Dworkin & Near, 1987) or whether whistle-blowers are asked who was harmed by the wrongdoing or who benefited from their actions (Miceli & Near, 1984). Similarly, studies of organizational citizenship behavior (OCB; e.g., Organ, 1988), a concept related to prosocial organizational behavior, do not usually attempt to distinguish those workers who engage in OCBs and benefit in some way from those who engage in OCBs with absolutely no benefit, not even an expression of gratitude from those helped. Thus it seems reasonable to claim that whistle-blowers can be prosocial actors even if they intend to benefit or actually benefit from their acts of whistle-blowing.

Antisocial whistle-blowers act to stop perceived wrongdoing, and they may do so with the intention of benefiting themselves. To be considered antisocial, however, the whistle-blowing must be pursued with the intention of harming *others*.

The Procedural Justice of the Process Used by the Whistle-Blower

Merton (1957) pioneered the study of deviance in society. In his famous typology, he distinguished those deviants who held goals deviant from those of society versus those who used deviant means to achieve their goals. Similarly, the literature on justice in organizations (e.g., Greenberg, 1987) distinguishes distributive justice from procedural justice, in that the former is concerned primarily with perceptions and evaluations of outcomes, whereas the latter is concerned with perceptions and evaluations of processes. This distinction can be applied to whistle-blowers engaged in antisocial behavior as well. One can easily picture whistle-blowing cases in which the means used are viewed as clearly violating norms of procedural justice. For example, one such norm (Leventhal, Karuza, & Fry, 1980) concerns the correctibility of procedures; organizations that provide an opportunity for wrongs to be corrected, perhaps through appeals procedures, are more procedurally just than those that provide no opportunity for correctibility. If a whistle-blower appears to refuse to utilize properly these legitimate procedures, others may perceive that his or her actions are procedurally unfair.

As one potential illustration, a General Electric employee blew the whistle when senior managers provided weapons systems to Israel that violated national security rules (Naj, 1992). Although observers of this case rarely disputed that the wrongdoing took place, they did disagree on the whistle-blower's method. Most firms would prefer that whistle-blowers use internal rather than external channels to prevent negative publicity. Because the whistle-blower did not use the straightforward internal reporting procedures available at GE but instead used external channels for reporting—which ultimately resulted in his receiving a multimillion dollar award from the federal government—many observers felt that his behavior was antisocial in that it seemed to violate norms of procedural justice. In this instance, the whistle-blower claimed that he did not use the internal channels for reporting the wrongdoing because he felt that the story would have been quashed. Further, he continued to wait long beyond the point at which he first learned of the wrongdoing, purportedly to collect more detailed evidence that the wrongdoing had occurred. The judge in his case, however, felt that the waiting period might be more properly ascribed to the fact that the employee knew his award would increase over time. Therefore he benefited more handsomely by waiting to report the wrongdoing. Accordingly, the judge reduced the award to the whistle-blower to the percentage of federal savings that would have been awarded to him at the point at which he first began to document the wrongdoing.

In this case, the whistle-blower's actions probably were not intended to harm the firm or most coworkers, and the outcome was indeed beneficial in the long run. However, the procedure used might be viewed as unjust because he may have violated procedural norms. In fact, it appears that two norms may have been violated here. First, whistle-blowers are expected to utilize available internal channels to provide the wrongdoers with the opportunity to take corrective action. Second, reporting must be timely, particularly when monetary consequences are at stake. It is also possible that to the extent that internal procedures are viewed with distrust by many others, no violation will be perceived. To the extent that adherence to norms of procedural justice appears to be important in differentiating whistle-blowing incidents—or individuals' reactions to them—the norms that may be relevant should be articulated.

Consequences of Whistle-Blowing
for Other Organizational Members

The term *prosocial organizational behavior* is defined with respect to intentions rather than outcomes. Yet outcomes seem important. For example, the so-called "good Samaritan" who stops to help an injured motorist on the highway but—through ignorance—harms the injured person further is not protected by law because his or her intentions were pure; the fact is that this do-gooder has caused harm. Unfortunately, the literature on prosocial behavior has not distinguished intended consequences from actual consequences. Studies of prosocial behavior (e.g., Latané & Darley, 1968) have frequently involved carefully staged events in which the altruistic behavior appears to have actually benefited the recipient. Likewise, the literature on OCBs largely assumes that the OCB is undertaken for purposes of helping and that it is successful in this regard (Organ, 1988).

We argue that the perceived potential or actual consequences are also important and should be distinguished from intent. In the case of whistle-blowing, two key issues remain to be addressed: (a) Who is the target of concern—society, the organization, or an individual or group? and (b) Given that multiple persons may be involved, how is harm to be determined?

Who Is the Target?

As noted earlier, antisocial organizational behavior may be related to deviant behavior, a topic that has been widely studied by sociologists beginning with Merton (1957). Extending this work to the organizational setting, Robinson and Bennett (1995) defined *workplace* or *employee deviance* as "voluntary behavior that violates significant organizational norms and in so doing threatens the well-being of an organization, its members or both" (p. 556). They distinguished deviant behavior from (un)ethical behavior because in the latter the employee relies on societal rather than organizational standards to define wrongdoing. Insofar as societal and organization norms may conflict, unethical behavior is not always deviant.

For example, Robinson and Bennett (1995) noted that

> dumping toxic waste in a river is not deviant if it conforms with the policies of one's organization. However, most people would probably agree that this act is unethical. Conversely, reporting this dumping to authorities may be an ethical act, but it would also be a deviant act in this particular example if it violated organizational norms. (pp. 556-557)

But which constitutes antisocial organizational behavior? Following Robinson and Bennett, we focus on harm to organizations and their members only, rather than stakeholders external to the organization, including society at large. This decision is admittedly simplistic, but we feel that the question of who is harmed needs to be limited in some way. Without this limitation, almost any case of whistle-blowing could be found to be beneficial to one stakeholder and harmful to another—thus preventing us from comparing those cases that are relatively harmful to those that are not.

In many instances, however, whistle-blowing helps some organiza-tion members and harms others. For example, as portrayed in the film *Silkwood*, several of Karen Silkwood's coworkers felt that her reporting of the alleged wrongdoing harmed them directly; others felt that she acted on their behalf. From a societal point of view, we might argue that she benefited society and some coworkers because her actions to im-prove workplace safety might ultimately reduce the number of workers who suffered from cancer and other diseases and who might seek medical attention and public assistance to pay for this care. On the other hand, a viable employer was harmed, thereby resulting in unemployed workers and an important product not produced. In cases in which ultimate determination of whether wrongdoing has occurred can be made, of course, assessing harm is less difficult. This brings us to the second question.

What Constitutes Net Harm?

We assume that causing harm is in some sense a "net" concept, meaning that a greater number of people are harmed by the action than the number helped, or that the quality of the harm is more severe. This is obviously a variation of the philosophical basis of utilitarian theory (Mill, 1861, in Mill & Sher, 1979): Actions that benefit the greatest number of people the most are considered to be helpful. Given our focus on the organization and its members, in determining net harm, we would need to apply stakeholder theory (Freeman, 1984), basically to determine the number of internal stakeholders affected by the action and how strongly they were affected.

Summary

Three factors may distinguish the most antisocial of whistle-blowing cases. Using these factors, we can attempt a preliminary classification of whistle-blowers as "purely" prosocial, "purely" antisocial, or somewhere in between on the continuum: that is, mixed with respect to having both antisocial and prosocial elements. We view as most purely prosocial those incidents in which whistle-blowers (a) intended to benefit their fellow organization members or the organization itself, (b) used procedures seen as just in pursuing the complaint, and (c) helped the greatest number of organization members and harmed the fewest. (An exception to this might be the case in which a small number of organizational members benefits greatly while little harm is caused to the majority of members.) Most purely antisocial whistle-blowers are those who (a) act to harm their fellow organization members or the organization itself (regardless of whether they also benefit), (b) use procedures seen as unjust in pursuing the complaint, and (c) have the effect of harming the greatest number of organization members and helping the fewest. (As in the case of prosocial behavior, an exception to this might be the case in which a small number of people are greatly harmed while the majority are benefited only slightly.) We would label these as "purely prosocial" and "purely antisocial" whistle-blowing, respectively. Mixed cases would be neither purely prosocial nor purely antisocial.

One might argue that the typology could be simplified further by reclassifying the procedural justice factor under one of the other two factors. However, it is not clear to us that this factor fits well under either. Notably, one could violate others' standards of procedural justice without intending to do harm, and/or one could violate procedural norms even when the complaint is actually one that, when corrected, leads to positive outcomes for many other organization members. For example, an individual who goes over the perceived wrongdoer's head rather than providing an opportunity for him or her to respond to the charge, or who distorts information in making the report, could anger some coworkers or managers and waste their time. But, despite the bad process, the whistle-blower may have a good case, and the wrongdoing ultimately may be corrected, leading to net positive outcomes for most coworkers and managers. Thus, whereas in one sense the actual consequences could include the consequences of the bad process as well as the consequences of the content of the complaint itself, in another sense these factors should be separated.

Propositions: Predictors and Effects
of Prosocial Versus Antisocial Whistle-Blowing

Assuming that antisocial whistle-blowing can be distinguished from prosocial whistle-blowing on the basis of the three criteria we have described, we are left with the question: So what? In other words, the real issue here is not coming up with a definition or typology but making predictions about the effects of the two different kinds of whistle-blowing. If there truly is a continuum of whistle-blowing types that runs from antisocial to prosocial, as suggested above, then we should expect to see differential effects associated with different points on the continuum. For example, whistle-blowing that is more purely antisocial may be less likely to lead to the correction of wrongdoing than whistle-blowing that is more purely prosocial. As we did above, here we focus on the pure types at the ends of the continuum: purely antisocial whistle-blowing and purely prosocial whistle-blowing.

We have argued that whistle-blowing is purely antisocial if the whistle-blower's intention is to harm fellow employees and/or the organization, if the procedure used to blow the whistle is unfair, and if the consequence of the whistle-blowing is actually harmful to employees or the organization at large. Below, we consider the effects of each of these criteria on the whistle-blowing process. Our propositions are listed in Table 7.1.

Earlier research on whistle-blowing has focused on three general research questions (see Miceli & Near, 1992, for a review): (a) What causes people to blow the whistle? (e.g., Miceli & Near, 1984, 1988; Miceli, Near, & Schwenk, 1991); (b) What are the effects on whistle-blowers, especially in terms of retaliation? (Miceli & Near, 1994; Ryan, Near, & Miceli, 1995); and (c) Under what conditions is whistle-blowing most effective? (Near & Miceli, 1995). If the antisocial versus prosocial construct is useful, it should allow us to speculate about each of these three research questions.

Table 7.1 Propositions

Proposition 1: Whistle-blowers who intend to harm coworkers by blowing the whistle are more to be likely motivated by a wish for revenge on coworkers than are other whistle-blowers.

Proposition 2: Whistle-blowers who intend to harm the organization by blowing the whistle are more likely to be motivated by a wish for revenge on the organization than are other whistle-blowers.

Proposition 3: Whistle-blowers who intend to harm the organization by blowing the whistle are more likely to be motivated by fear of the consequences of having been involved in the wrongdoing than are other whistle-blowers.

Proposition 4: Potential whistle-blowers may be persuaded by rewards to report wrongdoing, even though the result will be to cause harm rather than benefit to the organization or its employees.

Proposition 5: Whistle-blowers who intend to harm the organization by blowing the whistle are more likely to suffer retaliation from managers than other whistle-blowers.

Proposition 6: Whistle-blowers whose actions cause harm to the organization or its employees are more likely to suffer retaliation than those whose actions benefit the organization or its employees.

Proposition 7: Whistle-blowers whose actions violate norms of procedural justice are more likely to suffer retaliation from coworkers and managers than those whose actions do not violate norms of procedural justice.

Proposition 8: Whistle-blowers who intend to harm the organization or its employees by their actions are less likely to be effective than whistle-blowers who intend to benefit the organization or its employees.

Proposition 9: Anonymous whistle-blowers are less likely to be effective than identified whistle-blowers.

Proposition 10: Whistle-blowers who cause benefit to the organization or its employees are more likely to be effective than those who cause harm to the organization or its employees.

Predictors of Whistle-Blowing

We would expect that antisocial whistle-blowers who intend to harm others are different kinds of people, or perhaps people who have experienced very different organizational situations, than prosocial whistle-blowers who intend to help others. The literature on prosocial behavior generally would suggest expected differences here, but there are specific conditions that we consider most likely to increase intent to do harm.

A variety of motives for reporting wrongdoing could be seen, in isolation, as harmful to others. Whistle-blowers may be angry, perhaps "chronically" or because they have experienced perceived injustice at the hands of others, and they may seek revenge on individual wrong-doers who hold powerful positions. One example was the "now infamous" ZZZZ Best case, in which revenge was at least part of the motive for a report to the external audit team (Ponemon, 1994, p. 120). Such whistle-blowers may hope to embarrass the target or to ruin his or her career. These may be justifiable and understandable reactions, or they may not be. According to an attorney who has represented whistle-blowers and an author of the amended False Claims Act, prior to the act, many whistle-blowers "had a 'need to confess' or to 'point the finger at someone' " (Singer, 1992, p. 21).

Proposition 1: Whistle-blowers who intend to harm coworkers by blowing the whistle are more likely to be motivated by a wish for revenge on coworkers than are other whistle-blowers.

Other whistle-blowers may be angry with their organizations. They may feel underrewarded or punished, for example, in being denied a promotion or credit for a recent success and thus may want to exert countercontrol. These instances are probably fairly common and likely to increase in the future. As organizations transform and "reengineer," laying off long-term employees and causing substantial workplace change, there are many stresses on the job survivors, such as increased responsibility, overtime hours, insecurity, and fears of job loss (Leana & Feldman, 1992). The sense of personal control may be diminished; a documented reaction to diminished personal control is for the organizational member to want to regain control over his or her job (Greenberger & Strasser, 1986). The organizational member may then engage in sabotage or other antisocial acts (Giacalone, Riordan, & Rosenfeld Chapter 6 of this volume; Greenberger & Strasser, 1986). And one of these may be antisocial whistle-blowing, aimed at lashing out in retribution or preventing the organization from moving forward with reengineering or other change.

Proposition 2: Whistle-blowers who intend to harm the organization by blowing the whistle are more likely to be motivated by a wish for revenge on the organization than are other whistle-blowers.

Wrongdoers (or would-be wrongdoers) sometimes may fear being caught in the act, or they may actually find themselves observed. They may then reveal to authorities other wrongdoers—partly to get the wrongdoing stopped, partly to salve their consciences, and partly to avoid some punishment (e.g., Ivan Boesky and the SEC). Although this action may not always constitute antisocial behavior in terms of harm to the wrongdoer's or whistle-blower's organization, it seems less prosocial than the report of wrongdoing in which the whistle-blower has refused to take part. Finally, whistle-blowing may be a "subterfuge to disguise an employee's incompetence or illegal activity, and it may be a spurious counterclaim to disciplinary action taken against the employee" (Vinten, 1992, p. 48).

> *Proposition 3:* Whistle-blowers who intend to harm the organization by blowing the whistle are more likely to be motivated by fear of the consequences of having been involved in the wrongdoing than are other whistle-blowers.

There are many available rewards for certain whistle-blowers, including cash, fame, movie contracts, even Pulitzer Prizes, for their action (Gilbert, 1994b; Ponemon, 1994; Smardz, 1994). Whistle-blowers can act primarily because they hope to obtain these rewards. And cash rewards can be sizable. For example, under the False Claims Act, whistle-blowers can receive 15% to 25% of any money recovered by the government. In the United Technologies case, a whistle-blower took home $22.5 million (Gilbert, 1994b), and in another case a whistle-blower stood to receive up to $62 million (Singer, 1992).

However, although some may disapprove of such awards, it is not clear that there is anything inherently antisocial about accepting (or offering, for that matter) cash awards for heroic acts, even when pursuit of such rewards is seen as a primary motive. As we argued earlier, a desire to help oneself is not the same as desiring to harm others and can even be part of a prosocial motive (e.g., to correct unsafe conditions at work for everyone in the work group, including the whistle-blower). Further, cash or other awards may be appropriate to offset the risks many whistle-blowers may be forced to take, and there is some evidence that the awards have the desired effect, which is to convince organizations to correct problems voluntarily (Singer, 1992). Moreover, although relieving an organization of a large sum of cash when it is found guilty of wrongdoing may be harmful to that organization, such an outcome may seem justifiable to many observers. Finally, organizations can reduce fines levied by the U.S. government under federal sentencing guidelines by showing that they provide an "allegedly effective compliance program" encompassing codes of ethics, employee training, a system for detecting and punishing errors that removes fear of retribution, and other factors (Gilbert, 1994a, p. 22).

On the other hand, there is some reason to propose that employees will be motivated by rewards to engage in antisocial whistle-blowing. Some observers have argued that a healthy climate in the organization is undermined when people are encouraged through incentives to "fink" on one another: For example, Charles Barber, former chairman and CEO of a Fortune 500 company, has been quoted as saying, "Encouraging tittle-tattles is destructive; the integrity of the organization has to be built another way. You can't run a defense company if everyone is being watched" (Singer, 1992, p. 18). Trust is undermined, and members may be distracted from working together to achieve common goals. And any whistle-blowing incident can spawn a proliferation of organizational control mechanisms or rules for preventing or reacting to wrongdoing that may be overly restrictive, preventing the organization from responding effectively and quickly to unique situations. At a societal level, concerns that offering rewards simply increases an already overly litigious culture are often expressed (e.g., Singer, 1992). Thus:

> *Proposition 4:* Potential whistle-blowers may be persuaded by rewards to report wrongdoing, even though the result will be to cause harm rather than benefit to the organization or its employees.

Predictors of Retaliation

Previous research suggests that whistle-blowers are more likely to suffer retaliation if they lack power, defined in broad terms (for a review, see Miceli & Near, 1992). The strongest single predictors of retaliation, across multiple studies, are lack of support from upper management and the immediate supervisor to the whistle-blower (Near & Miceli, 1995). Coworkers may also engage in retaliation independently of management (Miceli & Near, 1992). Because it is often difficult to separate perceptions of the whistle-blower from perceptions of the case itself (Miceli & Near, 1992), one source of power for whistle-blowers is credibility. Here perceived intention is critical: If managers perceive that the whistle-blower is motivated to harm rather than to benefit the organization or its employees, they will assume that the case itself is not credible or valid. In such an instance, they may retaliate either as a way of venting anger toward the suspect whistle-blower or to discourage other employees from engaging in future whistle-blowing.

Proposition 5: Whistle-blowers who intend to harm the organization by blowing the whistle are more likely to suffer retaliation from managers than other whistle-blowers.

Coworkers, as well as managers, are likely to be concerned about the expected effect of the whistle-blowing on themselves and the health of the organization. The film *Silkwood* presents a clear example of such a situation. Coworkers resented interference from government agencies called in to investigate workplace safety because they felt their jobs were in possible jeopardy if the firm had to cut back or even close its doors. In such a case, they may retaliate against whistle-blowers to silence them or to discourage other potential whistle-blowers from acting. Again, the whistle-blower has little power, in this case because of the expected or actual detrimental effect of the whistle-blowing on coworkers or the organization at large. Missing this key source of power, the whistle-blower is more likely to suffer retaliation than is a whistle-blower whose actions are perceived to benefit the organization or its employees.

Proposition 6: Whistle-blowers whose actions cause harm to the organization or its employees are more likely to suffer retaliation than those whose actions benefit the organization or its employees.

Finally, whistle-blowers perceived as antisocial because they use unjust procedures for reporting wrongdoing may be expected to suffer greater retaliation than those who use just procedures. As noted by Near, Dworkin, and Miceli (1993), "Procedural justice [is perceived] when the whistle-blower follows 'fair' reporting procedures, probably reporting the wrongdoing through internal channels rather than making it public knowledge by reporting it to some outside agency or the media" (pp. 395-396). Near et al. (1993) proposed that maintaining procedural justice would increase coworker satisfaction. We extend this by proposing that following fair procedures may reduce the likelihood of retaliation from coworkers or managers. As an example of procedural justice, many state laws provide protection for external whistle-blowing only under limited circumstances, for instance, for certain types of illegal activity or after all internal remedies have been exhausted (e.g., Dworkin & Near, 1987). Some professional standards, such as those for internal auditors, support internal but not external reporting (Miceli et al., 1991). Both these cases suggest that one norm of "fair reporting" is to use the internal channels for reporting rather than external. Whistle-blowers who fail to do so may be viewed as unfair and therefore appropriate targets of retaliation. Thus:

> *Proposition 7:* Whistle-blowers whose actions violate norms of procedural justice are more likely to suffer retaliation from coworkers and managers than those whose actions do not violate norms of procedural justice.

Predictors of Effectiveness

Recently Near and Miceli (1995) argued that researchers should focus more specifically on variables that predict effective whistle-blowing rather than whistle-blowing in general because only effective whistle-blowing benefits society, organizations, and their employees. Two key variables were expected to increase whistle-blowers' effectiveness: their credibility and their power. To the extent that antisocial whistle-blowers lack credibility and power, we can expect that they will not be effective (i.e., the organization will not terminate the wrongdoing).

Specifically, we expect that whistle-blowers who intend to harm the organization or its employees will be perceived to lack credibility; they will be seen as acting from self-interest, and their evidence will be viewed as suspect because it is tainted by antisocial motivations. As a result, their evidence will be discounted, and the organization will be less likely to terminate the wrongdoing.

> *Proposition 8:* Whistle-blowers who intend to harm the organization or its employees by their actions are less likely to be effective than whistle-blowers who intend to benefit the organization or its employees.

Another variable that increases credibility is the decision by whistle-blowers to identify themselves rather than report the wrongdoing anonymously (Near & Miceli, 1995). One likely reason for this is that anonymous whistle-blowers are viewed as violating a norm of procedural justice commonly held in our society: that accused wrongdoers have the right to confront their accusers (Elliston, 1982). As a result, anonymous whistle-blowers, who violate this norm of procedural justice, are less likely to be effective than identified whistle-blowers.

Proposition 9: Anonymous whistle-blowers are less likely to be effective than identified whistle-blowers.

Finally, whistle-blowers who lack power are likely to be relatively ineffective compared to their peers with greater power (Near & Miceli, 1995). If, as argued above, blowing the whistle in such a way as to benefit the organization or its employees conveys power, then whistle-blowers who wreak negative consequences on the organization or its employees are less likely to be effective. In short, whistle-blowers who benefit the organization are more likely to gain support from employees and therefore to be more persuasive in pushing the dominant coalition to terminate the wrongdoing. Thus:

Proposition 10: Whistle-blowers who cause benefit to the organization or its employees are more likely to be effective than those who cause harm to the organization or its employees.

Conclusion

Research is needed to identify differences between antisocial and prosocial whistle-blowers. Our propositions are intended to provide a starting point for such investigation. If empirical evidence of real differences can be found, then it will be important to distinguish between prosocial and antisocial whistle-blowers in future research.

References

Brief, A. P., & Motowidlo, S. (1986). Prosocial organizational behaviors. *Academy of Management Review, 11*, 710-725.

Clark, F. P. (1992, March 2). Unfounded "whistle blower" suit can kill a small defense company. *Aviation Week and Space Technology*, pp. 65-66.

Dozier, J. B., & Miceli, M. P. (1985). Potential predictors of whistle-blowing: A prosocial behavior perspective. *Academy of Management Review, 10*, 823-836.

Dworkin, T., & Near, J. P. (1987). Whistle-blowing statutes: Are they working? *American Business Law Journal, 25*, 241-264.

Elliston, F. (1982). Anonymity and whistle-blowing. *Journal of Business Ethics, 1*, 167-177.

Freeman, R. E. (1984). *Strategic management: A stakeholder approach*. Boston: Pittman.

Gilbert, N. (1994a, Fall). 1-800-222-Ethic. *Financial World*, pp. 20-25.

Gilbert, N. (1994b, Fall). Toot toot for the jackpot. *Financial World*, pp. 30-31.

Graham, J. W. (1984, August). *Organizational response to principled organizational dissent.* Paper presented at the 44th annual meeting of the Academy of Management, Boston.

Graham, J. W. (1986). Principled organizational dissent: A theoretical essay. In L. L. Cummings & B. M. Staw (Eds.), *Research in organizational behavior* (Vol. 8, pp. 1-52). Greenwich, CT: JAI Press.

Greenberg, J. (1987). A taxonomy of organizational justice theories. *Academy of Management Review, 12*, 9-22.

Greenberger, D. B., & Strasser, S. (1986). The development and application of a model of personal control in organizations. *Academy of Management Review, 11*, 164-177.

Kolarska, L., & Aldrich, H. (1980). Exit, voice, and silence: Consumers' and managers' responses to organizational decline. *Organizational Studies, 1*, 41-58.

Latané, B., & Darley, J. M. (1968). Group inhibition of bystander intervention. *Journal of Personality and Social Psychology, 10*, 215-221.

Leana, C. R., & Feldman, D. C. (1992). *Coping with job loss.* New York: Lexington.

Leventhal, G. S., Karuza, J., & Fry, W. R. (1980). Beyond fairness: A theory of allocation preferences. In J. Mikula (Ed.), *Justice and social interaction* (pp. 127-218). New York: Springer-Verlag.

Merton, R. K. (1957). *Social theory and social structure* (2nd ed.). Glencoe, IL: Free Press.

Miceli, M. P., & Near, J. P. (1984). The relationships among beliefs, organizational position, and whistle-blowing status: A discriminant analysis. *Academy of Management Journal, 27*, 687-705.

Miceli, M. P., & Near, J. P. (1988). Individual and situational correlates of whistle-blowing. *Personnel Psychology, 41*, 267-282.

Miceli, M. P., & Near, J. P. (1992). *Blowing the whistle: The organizational and legal implications for companies and employees.* Lexington, MA: Lexington.

Miceli, M. P., & Near, J. P. (1994). Relationships among value congruence, perceived victimization, and retaliation against whistle-blowers. *Journal of Management, 20*, 773-794.

Miceli, M. P., Near, J. P., & Schwenk, C. (1991). Who blows the whistle and why? *Industrial and Labor Relations Review, 45*, 113-130.

Mill, J. S., & Sher, G. (Eds.). (1979). *Utilitarianism.* Indianapolis: Hackett.

Naj, A. K. (1992, December 7). Federal judge awards ex-GE staffers record amount in whistle-blower case. *Wall Street Journal*, p. A5.

Near, J. P., Dworkin, T., & Miceli, M. P. (1993). Explaining the whistle-blowing process: Suggestions from power theory and justice theory. *Organization Science, 4,* 393-411.

Near, J. P., & Miceli, M. P. (1985). Organizational dissidence: The case of whistle-blowing. *Journal of Business Ethics, 4,* 1-16.

Near, J. P., & Miceli, M. P. (1995). Effective whistle-blowing. *Academy of Management Review, 20,* 679-708.

Organ, D. W. (1988). *Organizational citizenship behavior: The good soldier syndrome.* Lexington, MA: Lexington.

Ponemon, L. A. (1994). Whistle-blowing as an internal control mechanism: Individual and organizational considerations. *Auditing: A Journal of Practice and Theory, 13*(2), 118-130.

Robinson, S. L., & Bennett, R. J. (1995). A typology of deviant workplace behaviors: A multidimensional scaling study. *Academy of Management Journal, 38,* 555-572.

Ryan, K., Near, J. P., & Miceli, M. P. (1995). Results of a human resource management "experiment": Whistle-blowing in the federal bureaucracy, 1980-1992. In D. P. Moore (Ed.), *Proceedings of the 55th annual meeting of the Academy of Management* (pp. 369-370). Madison, WI: Omnipress.

Singer, A. W. (1992, November). The whistle-blower: Patriot or bounty hunter? *Across the Board,* pp. 16-22.

Smardz, Z. (1994, June). The payoff for a whistle-blower. *Working Woman,* p. 16.

Vinten, G. (1992). Whistle-blowing: Corporate help or hindrance? *Management Decision, 30,* 44-48.

Webster's New Collegiate Dictionary (10th ed.). (1990). Springfield, MA: Merriam-Webster.

8

Litigation and Claiming in Organizations

Antisocial Behavior or Quest for Justice?

E. Allan Lind

Litigation, and to an even greater extent the fear of litigation, is arguably a driving force in many organizational decisions. Recruitment practices, procedures, and tests are often developed with an eye to defending against claims of bias. Employee evaluation and compensation procedures today often take into account the possibility that unfavorable evaluations can lead to lawsuits, that inequalities in remuneration can be seen as bias, and that past favorable evaluations can be used as evidence in wrongful termination claims. Layoffs and firings are seen as minefields of potential Equal Employment Opportunity Commission complaints and civil lawsuits. The design and enforcement of organizational procedures and practices, and supervisory practices from the factory floor to the boardroom, must now be sensitive to the possibility of sexual harassment and lawsuits deriving from inappropriate actions.

Concerns about litigation are understandable. There is, of course, the cost associated with losing a lawsuit. Not long ago, General Motors settled a discrimination lawsuit for more than $3 million in direct payments, more than $13 million in raises for employees who said they had been discriminated against, and changes in pay raise practices that were estimated to cost between $20 million and $40 million over several years ("Closing a Color Gap," 1989). An interesting aspect of the GM suit, in light of some points to be explored here, is that it started with a grievance by a single employee and grew to a class action with more than 3,800 plaintiffs. More recently, Polaroid Corporation was ordered to pay $400,000 to a black employee who claimed that injurious job assignments were prompted by racism ("Ex-Polaroid Employee," 1995). It is not uncommon for commentary on the organizational side of the "litigation explosion" to focus on such awards in giving the impression that litigation poses a threat to the operation of most corporations.

A lawsuit not only exposes an organization to possible losses from an unfavorable verdict but also brings with it steep costs for paying defense attorneys. Additional costs of being sued include the time and resources expended within the firm to gather evidence and the "down-time" of employees and supervisors, often ranging well up the organizational hierarchy, as representatives of the firm advise attorneys, give depositions, and prepare to testify. Modern discovery law requires not only that the firm expend resources on its own case but also that it gather information and documents requested by the opposing side in the lawsuit.

Even for firms that are not engaged in current litigation, there are costs of the climate of litigation. As I noted at the outset, many aspects of organizational life have been affected by efforts to avoid litigation and to ensure that litigation will not be successful if it does arise. These indirect costs of litigation are perhaps the most expensive and most pernicious. Specific policy and supervisory actions may be decided on not so much because the policy or action is the best one available but because that policy or action minimizes the perceived likelihood of lawsuits. Thus inept or even dishonest employees are kept on, raises are given that have little to do with either need or merit, and promotions are made on easily quantified or documented but sometimes invalid criteria—all in the interest of avoiding potential lawsuits (Dertouzos, Holland, & Ebener, 1988). An especially ironic aspect of efforts to control litigation is that they may, in fact, be encouraging more litigation, for reasons noted below.

For all the importance that business people accord to lawsuits and potential lawsuits, however, organizational behavior scholars have not paid much attention to what predisposes a potential, current, or former employee to sue. For all that is written in personnel and business law journals about the dangers of various sorts of lawsuits, there are no hard empirical investigations of claiming, suing, and their consequences for organizations and management. Fortunately, there is a literature in the social and behavioral sciences generally about why and when people sue. Most of the research on this topic concerns what is termed "tort" claiming—claims for compensation for injuries, which is not much of a problem in intraorganizational settings in the United States[1]—but the general findings and theory that emerge can provide some good leads to understanding claiming and litigation in organizations. Later in this chapter, I review three theories about litigation behavior, introducing the empirical literature as I discuss the support that each theory has received. Although additional research on organizational claiming per se is clearly needed (and, fortunately, such research is underway), the current state of knowledge is such that we can make some tentative statements about how litigation arises in organizations and about how procedures and practices might be structured to reduce the likelihood of unnecessary litigation.

Some Background Issues

This last phrase—"unnecessary litigation"—raises a point that deserves discussion at the outset of this chapter. Executives and managers might prefer that there be no litigation at all and no possibility of litigation in their workforce, but we must not forget that discriminatory, dangerous, biased, and just plain wrongheaded practices certainly exist and that some of these practices deserve to be complained and litigated against. We also should not forget that much of the progress that women and minorities have made in the past 40 years has come about not voluntarily, but under threat of litigation. No small part of the "humanization" of the workplace can be traced to lawsuits about practices that now seem to us antiquated but that posed a very real threat to the safety, security, and well-being of employees. We need to keep firmly in mind that not all litigation behavior is "antisocial" in nature.

But just as there are legitimate claims, there are also certainly claims that an objective observer would say are unjustified. A point that is really the theme of this chapter is that claiming, litigating, and the perceptions and choices that surround these actions are psychologically and socially conditioned. That is, the perception of injury or injustice gets people thinking about suing, the perception of avenues for claiming directs their actions, and the perception of restitution leads people to settle or abandon claims and lawsuits. These perceptions can be accurate or inaccurate, but whether accurate or not, they determine what people do. Some claims will be legitimate, in some objective sense, and some will not be. If the legal system does its job well, most of the legitimate claims will be successful and most of the illegitimate ones will not be successful, but this certainly does not mean that removing any legitimate basis for claims will remove claiming. Unless one can ensure that no employee feels unjustly treated, regardless of whether he or she is in fact unjustly treated, there will still be claiming. And one must remember that even unjustified claims consume organizational resources until they are abandoned or until the legal machinery works.

Given the perceptual underpinnings of claiming and litigation in organizations, a far better way to think about unnecessary litigation is to view it in much the same way we view organizational conflict. That is, unnecessary litigation is "unnecessary" when better management could have avoided it. To place all of the responsibility for unnecessary litigation on the employee by labeling claiming and litigation behavior as "antisocial" is not only at variance with what we know about the history and psychology of litigation against organizations; it is simply counterproductive for modern organizations. Only by understanding what leads an employee to consider claiming and by taking some responsibility for counteracting the beliefs that are the basis for claims can employers lessen their exposure to claims.

In fact, as will be seen below, our knowledge of the psychology of claiming suggests that the first and greatest rule of how to avoid litigation should be to treat people fairly, to be considerate, and to seek to humanize and dignify the organizational experience for one's employees and subordinates. If decisions are made honestly, with human as well as economic values in mind, and if these aspects of the decision-making process are obvious to the potential litigant, litigation rates will drop substantially. Another way of saying this is that lawsuits are generally the result of someone's feeling that he or she has suffered an injustice and that the best way to avoid lawsuits is to make workplace justice a major criterion for organizational decisions. I will argue below that this approach to justice may well yield better financial payoffs than does the conventional approach of making decisions on purely economic criteria and then trying on a post hoc basis to cope with claiming and litigation problems that arise from economically oriented decisions. Before the validity of these suggestions can be demonstrated, however, we need to review what is known about litigation and the psychology of claiming.

Social and behavioral scientists engaged in the study of "law and society" have long been interested in what makes people seek out legal forums to resolve their grievances. Over the years, three rather distinct models of claiming have arisen: (a) an economic model of claiming behavior based on the costs, benefits, and risks associated with initiating and pursuing a lawsuit; (b) a psychosocial model of what leads people to perceive an injury and to attribute it to others; and (c) a model that describes how people define fair and unfair treatment and the role of perceived unfairness in motivating claiming and litigation. Each of these three approaches is discussed in the sections that follow.

Economic and Quasi-Economic Models of Claiming

The idea that people will sue if they think it will benefit them underlies both lay and economic explanations of what is termed "the litigation explosion."[2] The basic argument is that people see the opportunity to get money if they sue their employer, that lawyers are happy to help them (for a fee), and that there is really very little disincentive to suing. At the level of lay analysis, this explanation seems to have a lot going for it. It is bolstered by news accounts of the substantial sums that some plaintiffs win from their former employers (including the reports cited at the beginning of this chapter), and it fits well with what has been termed "the myth of self-interest," the great belief in our culture that most people do what they do for personal gain (Miller & Ratner, in press).[3]

At a more sophisticated level, social exchange theorists (MacCoun, Lind, & Tyler, 1992), sociologists, and economists (Posner, 1986; Priest & Klein, 1984) have analyzed the probabilities, costs, and benefits associated with initiating a lawsuit and with continuing with the suit or terminating it at various points in the litigation process. Unlike the lay accounts, these analyses include examinations of the significant costs associated with litigation from the plaintiff's perspective, as well as analyses of the impact of differences between plaintiffs and defendants in assessments of the likelihood of various outcomes and analyses of the impact of various levels of defendant wealth on the likelihood that a particular verdict can be collected. For example, many commentators have speculated about a "deep pockets" effect on claiming: Potential defendants, such as large corporations, who can pay large awards are more likely to be sued than are defendants with lesser resources. One psychological account of personal injury claiming uses a similar argument (Harris et al., 1984) to explain that those who are most likely to pay are also most likely to be seen as responsible for the injury. Thus automobile accidents are blamed on other drivers, whose insurance can be made to pay for injuries, rather than on the governmental entity that built the road, which is generally a far less promising target for a lawsuit.

Economic models of litigation behavior often analyze the benefits and costs associated with various options: initiating a suit, negotiating a settlement, and continuing to trial (see, e.g., Bebchuck, 1984; Cooter, Marks, & Mnookin, 1982; Danzon & Lillard, 1982; King & Smith, 1988; Landes, 1982; P'ng, 1983; Posner, 1986; Priest & Klein, 1984; Whittman, 1985). The general prediction is that lawsuits will be started when defendants refuse prelitigation demands of the plaintiffs and that defendants will refuse demands that exceed the expected value of the trial, which is a function of estimates of the likelihood of various possible trial events (e.g., favorable or unfavorable trial verdicts) multiplied by the estimated costs associated with each event. Factors that alter either the likelihood of a given outcome or the costs associated with it are predicted to change litigation behavior. Thus, for example, it is expected that if government policy provides less costly access to lawyers by assigning Justice Department lawyers to represent work discrimination plaintiffs, then people will sue more often.

Clearly, these economic models of litigation can be applied to litigation against employers as easily as they can be applied to tort litigation, and indeed, some economic analysts have turned their attention to issues such as wrongful termination (Dertouzos et al., 1988). If "deep pockets" incentives do exist for litigation in general, the phenomenon will certainly play out in litigation against employers. As noted below, however, the existing research does not suggest that richer defendants are really any more at risk than poorer defendants.

Economic analyses of claiming generally stick to the financial costs and benefits associated with claiming and suing actions, but other social science disciplines predict that the social costs associated with claiming will enter into the equation (e.g., Black, 1987). Thus it is not unusual for empirical studies of claiming to find that people are less likely to engage in litigation against family and friends than against people with whom they have more distant relations (see, e.g., Harris et al., 1984).

The empirical evidence that exists on the impact of economic and quasi-economic factors suggests that economic analyses have some validity with respect to gross trends in litigation but that these analyses miss the mark with respect to many aspects of claiming. It is likely that economic considerations figure relatively powerfully in plaintiffs' lawyers' decisions about whether to accept a case as well as their assessments of the wisdom of settling or continuing a lawsuit. For example, in the area of personal injury claiming, it is difficult to get a lawyer to represent one in a lawsuit over an injury that will not result in a substantial payoff.[4] In the areas we are most concerned with here, economic considerations may play a role in determining when litigation will be pursued or abandoned by making legal representation more or less easy to obtain or by influencing the settlement offers proffered by the defendant corporation.

There is, however, a growing body of research that shows that the decisions of both individual and corporate litigants with respect to initiating and pursuing legal claims are not explained very well by the payoffs and probabilities associated with these courses of action (Lind, Kulik, Ambrose, & Park, 1993). When researchers attempt to predict claiming actions from either the actual or the perceived outcomes attached to various actions, only a small proportion of the variance in behavior is explained. Only when one adds noneconomic factors, such as judgments of wrongdoing, responsibility, and injustice, to the equation does one begin to explain much claiming behavior. These issues are addressed in the remaining two models of claiming.

The "PIE" Model of Claiming

There have been several important conceptual analyses of the claiming process by sociologists and political scientists (e.g., Felstiner, 1974, 1975; Felstiner, Abel, & Sarat, 1981; Kritzer, Bogart, & Vidmar, 1991; Kritzer, Vidmar, & Bogart, 1991). Most of these "sociolegal" analyses have followed the seminal work of Felstiner et al. (1981) in distinguishing at least three stages of claiming: *naming* the event as an injury or harm, *blaming* someone or some organization or institution for causing the harm, and *claiming* compensation or restitution through a legal or administrative forum. The key target of these analyses is the "perceived injurious event" or "PIE," which must be identified, attributed, and acted on before it becomes a cause of action in a lawsuit.

Naming

Felstiner et al. (1981) argued that before any thought of claiming can occur, a person must decide that he or she actually has been hurt: That is, he or she must "name" the event an injury. Just because someone has in fact been injured—or discriminated against, or otherwise harmed—does not mean that he or she necessarily *knows* that he or she has been harmed. A prime example of how the absence of naming can forestall claiming outside organizational contexts is a recent study of potential medical malpractice claims (Harvard Medical Malpractice Study, 1990). The researchers found that most potential claims are never realized because the patient does not know that he or she has been injured. Apparently, many patients who might have had real, legitimate claims simply thought that the longer recoveries or additional surgery they experienced were part of the normal consequences of their original problem. This type of error, which might be compared to Type I error in statistical inference, involves not seeing a harm when one is in fact there.

Clearly, such errors can occur with respect to organizational claims just as they do with respect to medical claims. Consider, for example, the example of the discrimination claims by black GM employees, which I mentioned at the beginning of the chapter. The claim began with a single employee deciding that he or she had been discriminated against in pay, but it spread to include more than 3,800 other employees as they too named their pay discriminatory.

Not part of the Harvard Medical Malpractice Study but equally interesting are instances in which "naming" of injuries does occur but in which the perception of harm is inaccurate. These would correspond to Type II errors in statistical inference. For example, in the realm of medical malpractice a person might think that some pain, inconvenience, or other negative event was not part of his or her original illness when in fact it was.

Similar naming problems can arise in organizational contexts. An African American employee might not notice that he or she was not receiving deserved raises or promotions because of corporate policies of keeping pay information secret, or the employee might know that he or she was earning less that a European American employee but nonetheless have a difficult time deciding that discrimination was going on because of a desire to avoid being seen as a victim of bias. Similar errors in naming have been documented empirically. Crosby (1984) reported that working women often resist seeing themselves as victims of gender discrimination, even though they admit that most other working women are discriminated against.

Blaming

Once a "perceived injurious event," or PIE, has occurred, one must decide whether someone is to blame for the injury. The "blaming" part of the sequence involves the injured person's deciding not only that the injury is caused by someone's actions but that the person is somehow at fault. If I lose a prize position in the firm to a harder-working coworker, the other's actions are the cause of my loss, but there is no blame because that person is simply doing what a good employee is supposed to do. On the other hand, if the person's actions were somehow outside the realm of normal, and normative, conduct, the loss could more readily give rise to blaming. Blaming involves the judgment that actions or consequences are somehow outside the normal scope of things. And blaming seems to be one of the key elements in the development of a claim. Recent research (Hensler et al., 1991) shows that the attribution of blame is one of the most important single factors in personal injury claiming. It seems very likely that blaming is just as central to claiming in organizational contexts, although I am aware of no research at this time that demonstrates such an effect.

Claiming

The final step in the psychological and institutional process described by Felstiner et al. (1981) is claiming recompense for the PIE. Felstiner et al. referred to variations in "claims consciousness," meaning that a person with a legitimate claim has to be aware of the avenues and possibilities for claiming before a claim can occur. Research on claiming for personal injuries suggests that often it is not the claimant him- or herself who comes up with the idea of claiming, but instead someone else who suggests the possibility to the injured person (Harris et al., 1984; Hensler et al., 1991). For example, Hensler et al. (1991) found that more than half of the people who file claims for personal injuries say that the idea of claiming came from someone else, usually a relative or a doctor. Presumably because the social and normative factors surrounding a PIE are generally less than perfectly clear, people may well want and engage in some social reality checking before they take action. The same process seems likely to occur in organizational settings: Employees may talk to others about the fairness or reasonableness of their experiences and only after discussion decide that they have been treated badly and that they should sue. Advertising by lawyers about the possibility of discrimination claims or knowledge that others in the organization have successfully pursued such claims could also provoke a transition from "blaming" to "claiming." Again, however, the organizational research literature has not yet shown that such "contagion" or "suggestion" effects do in fact occur.

An additional factor that bears on the transformation of a potential claim into a real claim or lawsuit is the willingness of an attorney to take the case. As noted above, it is at this stage in the claiming process that economic incentives and disincentives for claiming seem likely to be most important. An individual with a legitimate claim may not be able to pursue it if he or she cannot find an attorney who views the case as profitable enough to justify the cost of litigating it. Of course, part of the attorney's consideration is whether there is likely to be adequate legal basis for the lawsuit.

Claiming Versus Complaining

In recent work building on the PIE model of claiming, scholars have begun to distinguish between "complaining" to a wrongdoer about his or her actions and "claiming" compensation from a third party (e.g., Kritzer, Vidmar, & Bogart, 1991). Kritzer, Bogart, and Vidmar (1991) have built on earlier conceptualizations of the claiming process (Felstiner, 1974, 1975; Felstiner et al., 1981) to examine the transitions and barriers involved in moving from one state to the next in the development of a claim. Kritzer, Bogart, and Vidmar (1991) used the label *recognition* to describe the transition from the raw experience of some injury to the perception of the experience as injurious (i.e., to what Felstiner et al., 1981, called *naming* the experience), *attribution* to describe the transition from knowing that one has been injured to deciding that one has been injured by someone (i.e., to *blaming*), *confrontation* to describe the transition from blaming someone to deciding that one has a claim (i.e., the move from blaming to *claiming*), and *litigation* to describe the transition from having an informal or nonlegal claim to initiating a lawsuit. In this construction, as in the original Felstiner et al. (1981) model, the principal point is that as people move from one stage to another, disputes can be pursued, abandoned, or resolved. This leads researchers (e.g., Hensler et al., 1991) to talk about the "claiming pyramid": There are many more injurious incidents than there are PIEs with blame attached, many more instances of blame than confrontations, and many more confrontations than lawsuits.

The distinction between "claiming" and "complaining" may have special significance for intraorganizational disputes. There is some evidence in medical malpractice research that people who complain rarely sue (S. Lloyd-Bostock, personal communication, March 1989). In organizational contexts, this argues for the provision of a readily available avenue for internal complaints concerning discrimination, sexual harassment, and other problems that might give rise to litigation. It may be possible to divert to internal resolution channels disputes and charges of wrongdoing, even after naming and blaming have occurred. As we will see in the next section, there are other reasons to suspect that an internal process that is seen as fair can do a great deal to remove the impetus to claim.

The Justice Model

Over the past several years, Tom Tyler and I have developed a theory of justice judgments in organizations (Lind, 1994, 1995; Lind &

Tyler, 1988; Tyler & Lind, 1992) that offers a new perspective on the question of when people can be expected to litigate over grievances. The theory dovetails nicely with the recent thinking and research of other scholars who work on organizational justice issues (e.g., Greenberg, 1993) in that it focuses on links between the way people are treated, the perception of justice or injustice, and behavioral responses such as those involved in initiating, pursuing, or abandoning a claim.

The Relational Model of Organizational Justice

The Tyler and Lind (1992) relational model of justice begins with a new perspective on what motivates people in organizations and on what leads employees to view their treatment as fair or unfair. We begin by arguing that people use their membership in organizations not only as a way of obtaining financial remuneration but also as a way of validating their social self-identity. For most of us, our membership in various social entities is a large part of who we are. People who are employed tend to see themselves in terms of their jobs and the organizations to which they belong.

We argue that because people depend on their organization for both their livelihoods and their self-identities, they are extremely attentive to their relationships with their organizations and with its authorities.[5] The theory predicts that if an employee feels that his or her relationship with the organization is fundamentally positive, that he or she is viewed positively by the organization and protected from arbitrary power or rejection, the employee will tend to adopt a very cooperative orientation toward the organization. If, on the other hand, the employee feels subject to exploitation or not valued by the organization, he or she will adopt a much less cooperative, more self-interested orientation toward the organization. We argue that employees' perceptions that their treatment is fair or unfair serves as a global evaluation of their positive or negative relationship with the organization. Thus justice is considered "relational" because what people mean by "just" or "fair" treatment is treatment that tells them whether their relation with the organization is positive or negative.

With this relational view of organizational justice in mind, we have done a good bit of research and theorizing concerning how people arrive at these relational justice judgments (e.g., Lind, MacCoun, et al.,

1990; Tyler, 1990, 1994; Tyler & Lind, 1992). What we have found is that people tend to use the nuances of interpersonal process to arrive at the justice judgments. They look to such things as whether they are treated politely and with dignity, whether they feel that their views are listened to and considered, and whether they feel that decisions they care about are being made on a factual, rather than a biased, basis. Three aspects of process have emerged as being particularly important. We term these elements *status recognition, trust in benevolence,* and *neutrality.*

Status recognition is the belief that others in the organization, especially those in positions of authority, view the person as a full-fledged member of the organization. The most humble employee can feel substantial status recognition if he or she receives positive messages from his or her treatment by others in the organization, and high-level executives can feel little status recognition if their superiors treat them in a disrespectful or demeaning fashion. A number of studies (e.g., Lind, Kanfer, & Earley, 1990; Lind et al., 1993; Lind, MacCoun, et al., 1990; Tyler, 1990) have shown that people who are treated with dignity emerge from experiences, even experiences that entail substantial negative outcomes, with a feeling of fairness.

Trust in benevolence refers to the belief, again usually engendered by the quality of interpersonal treatment, that authorities and those with power in the organization are well intentioned and honest in their decision-making process. Trust involves attributions about the motives of authorities and inferences about their motives. One of the strongest sources of these inferences is the feeling that one is being listened to and that one's views are being considered. If authorities give the impression that they are trying to do the right thing and are considering all points of view, this sort of trust is engendered.

The final relational aspect of organizational justice judgments is neutrality. As with the other two elements, the perception of neutrality turns on inferences drawn from interpersonal process and treatment. Some elements of process can lead directly to inferences of bias, as when one hears a superior use racial or gender epithets, but sometimes the issue is more complex, involving an interplay of social cognition and ideological elements. On the one hand, if there is a playing out, in process or in process-related rules and symbols, of the idea that the organization wants a level playing field and that organizational decision makers will base their judgments on facts rather than personalities, then people will feel fairly treated. On the other hand, if cronyism or favoritism seems to be a major factor in decision making, as evidenced by the way organizational authorities act or by the unavailability of information on the way in which decisions are made, then people will feel that their treatment has been less than fair.

A strong theme in recent research on organizational justice judgments, and a key element of the relational model of justice, is the idea that most of the perceptions that determine whether a person will feel fairly or unfairly treated are drawn not from factors traditionally thought to be essential elements of fairness—such things as equitable allocations or formally unbiased procedures. Instead, when people feel they are being treated fairly or unfairly, they base their judgment on the patterning of everyday social interaction.

Turning from the antecedents of a feeling of justice or injustice to the consequences of that feeling, there is a growing body of evidence that fairness judgments are what might be called "pivotal cognitions" with respect to many social and organizational behaviors. Unlike many other dimensions of attitude and belief that seem to have little effect on behavior, justice judgments have been found to exert a profound influence on such behaviors as acceptance of and obedience to the mandates of authorities (Lind, Kanfer, & Earley, 1990; Lind et al., 1993; Tyler, 1990), protest behavior (Greenberg, 1987), and theft (Greenberg, 1993, Chapter 5 of this volume; Greenberg & Scott, 1996). Building on the ideas included in the relational model, I have suggested that people use fairness judgments as a decision heuristic in a variety of social contexts (Lind, 1994, 1995): That is, they refer to their perceptions of fairness to decide whether to behave cooperatively or competitively, whether to obey or ignore authorities, and whether to extend themselves in the interest of the organization or to look after their own narrow self-interest.

Justice Judgments and Claiming

We can apply the relational model to the issue of litigation and claiming in organization by considering the implications of a sense of injustice for decisions about whether to claim and whether to pursue claims and lawsuits. If we assume that feelings of unfair treatment can result in complaining, claiming, and lawsuits, then we should look to the antecedents of justice judgments for clues as to what might predispose people to claim or not to claim. In any given claim-prone situation, the relational model of justice suggests, the likelihood of claiming will be enhanced if the person feels that he or she has been denied dignified treatment (i.e., if the employee feels denied his or her due as a member of the organization), if his or her views and needs seem to have been ignored (which would lead the employee to feel little trust in the benevolence of organizational superiors), or if the employee feels that decisions and decision makers have not been neutral. Because feelings of unfair treatment shift people from cooperative, accepting modes of interacting with the organization to competitive, self-interested modes of interacting, the model predicts that a person who feels unfairly treated will want to complain and to pursue his or her complaint until a feeling of fairness has been restored. In other words, once an employee feels that he or she has suffered a substantial injustice, he or she will engage in a search for some forum or action that will restore justice.

The relational model suggests that this "quest for justice" can take on major proportions in the person's life because the unjust treatment that instigates it carries with it the message that the person's social self-identity is being denied. Because self-identity can often be far more important to a person than even substantial monetary gains or losses, the search for a restoration of a sense of justice may well be continued even when it appears to be against the person's own best interests.

Implications of the Models
for Avoiding Unnecessary Litigation

The models just described, especially the PIE and justice models of claiming, have some rather straightforward implications for how to avoid litigation. (The implications of the economic models are less certain because, as I noted above, the claiming research that does exist is not very supportive of economic models as predictors of when people will claim.) The strong prediction of all three models described above is that the best time to resolve an injury, from the perspective of all involved, is at the time it occurs or, better still, before it occurs. The data on costs and compensation in tort litigation, if applicable to the economics of organizational litigation, make it clear that everyone stands to lose, relative to a host of other possibilities, if the issue goes to court.

The PIE model makes it clear that the social construction of injury, blame, and complaint offers opportunities for those involved to negotiate an understanding of what happened and how injuries can be accounted for and compensated in ways that are mutually productive. And the justice-judgment model gives us some rather specific clues about how perceived justice can be restored short of litigation.

The PIE model argues that what matters is what people think has happened to them and how they interpret this perceived state of affairs. For this reason, organizational claiming will be affected profoundly by such things as suggestion or contagion concerning what is a harm and what are appropriate ways to pursue one's grievances. When one claim occurs, it is not unreasonable to expect that other, similar claims will occur. When the outside world labels some action a harm, it is unreasonable for those within an organization to expect that their own employees will know better than to interpret a long-standing practice as wrong.

When claims do arise, the newer versions of the PIE model suggest that a good, well-accepted, and obviously fair internal process may well be able to handle most or all of the claims. There is not room here to discuss the issue at length, but we know a great deal about what is needed to convince people that a claims-handling procedure is fair (e.g., MacCoun et al., 1992). Formal processes are not needed. Instead, what is crucial is a hearing process, formal or informal, in which the complainant is allowed (and assisted in realizing) a full opportunity to tell his or her story to a truly impartial third party without fear of reprisal or bias.

The relational model also tells us a good bit about what might predispose people *not* to claim, complain, or sue. If people experience some treatment that reassures them about their relation vis-à-vis the organization, a feeling of fairness may be restored, and the inclination to claim may disappear. Other organizational justice researchers have shown the capacity of explanations and accounts to dissipate the effects of unjust treatment (e.g., Bies & Shapiro, 1988; Greenberg, 1990), and it seems likely that such actions can ameliorate feelings of injustice in claim-prone situations. If management explains the reasons for treatment that seems unfair (and if the explanation is seen as honest and reflecting unbiased decision making), or if the organization offers an apology or acts quickly and convincingly to remedy the situation, the injured person may feel reassured about his or her standing with respect to the organization, and the claim may die at that point. Absent some restoration of dignity or trust or some reassurance of neutrality via either explanations, apologies, or a grievance process of the sort described above, people may feel that they can find reassurance of their personal worth only by prevailing over the organization in court.

Taken together, all that we know about the social and psychological dynamics of organizational litigation suggests that a personal, proactive approach to remedying injuries and resolving complaints will work better than do current approaches that seek to hide decision-making processes or quantify and document every organizational decision. As I noted earlier, the lesson from the whole body of claiming research is that if one wants to avoid litigation, one must both be fair and be seen to be fair. If instead of worrying about whether any given decision might be objectively actionable, managers worried about whether each decision was fair and was viewed as fair, litigation would be a far smaller problem. If mistakes are made, apologies and explanations should be forthcoming, quickly and publicly. In other words, if more attention were paid to the issues commonly raised by organizational behavior researchers in general and organizational justice researchers in particular, and if less attention were paid to the issues commonly raised by lawyers, the company in question might be better off in financial, as well as human, terms.

Ironically, the actions that the relational model suggest include options that most lawyers or insurers would consider dangerous. Accounts and explanations can be fuel for lawsuits, so many employers tend to let injurious events take place with little or no communication from higher management. In termination actions, for example, giving the person a reason for laying him or her off might be seen as dangerous because an enterprising lawyer can often twist the reason to give the impression of bias, making the reason evidence against the organization. But the option of giving no explanation may be worse because this compounds the injury of being laid off with the insult of being given no reason for the injury.[6] It is arguable that it would be in the organization's interests to give explanations and forestall many lawsuits, even if the policy worked against the organization in the few lawsuits that were not forestalled.

Only one study has looked in any detail at the role of justice judgments on organizational litigation. Bies and Tyler (1993) interviewed employed people in the Chicago area about their experiences with their organizations and supervisors. Focusing on people who reported negative experiences and who said that they believed there was some agency or court to whom they might complain, Bies and Tyler compared the relationship between their respondents' reports that they considered suing their employers and seven possible antecedents of claiming: (a) process justice judgments, (b) outcome justice judgments, (c) the favorability of the outcome of the experience relative to the respondent's initial expectations, (d) the favorability of the outcome of the experience in absolute terms, (e) the probability of winning in court, (f) organizational commitment, and (g) job satisfaction.

The Bies and Tyler (1993) study used structural equation modeling to test which of the possible antecedent factors showed a strong enough link to consideration of claiming to be judged as causes of consideration of claiming. They found that only two factors, process justice judgments and job satisfaction, showed significant links to the consideration-of-claiming measure. To a small extent, people who were satisfied with their jobs showed less inclination to think about claiming in response to these negative experiences.[7] To a much greater extent, people who felt that they had been fairly treated and that rules and procedures were fair were less likely to consider claiming.

Bies and Tyler (1993) then turned to the question of what factors led their respondents to experience feelings of process fairness or unfairness. They examined the relationships linking process fairness ratings to four potential antecedents of that variable: (a) status recognition, (b) trust in benevolence, (c) neutrality, and (d) perceived control over the information considered in making decisions and influence over the decisions. They found significant links between all four factors and process fairness, with trust and neutrality showing very strong links and status recognition and control showing less strong links. Together, the four antecedent factors accounted for more than 80% of the variation in process fairness ratings.

The findings of the Bies and Tyler (1993) study offer substantial support for interpersonal justice models of claiming, such as the relational model described above. By showing that process fairness was more important than outcome-oriented factors such as the absolute or relative favorability of the experience and more important than traditional organizational life factors such as organizational commitment or job satisfaction, the study provides good reason for additional investigations of fairness-based models of organizational claiming. By showing that much of the variation in process fairness is attributable to impressions of relationships and nuances of treatment, the study suggests that much of the story of what makes people sue their organizations lies in the quality of treatment that people receive when they experience negative events.

Conclusion

We have only just begun to study what causes litigation behavior within organizations. The theories, models, and research I describe above have started us on the road to a fuller understanding of litigation behavior, but much of the material can be applied to organizations only by inference. What is clearly needed is more research drawing on ideas such as those described above but sited in employment and organizational settings. The Bies and Tyler (1993) study is a start in this regard, and more studies of this sort are getting underway (e.g., Greenberg, Lind, Scott, & Welchans, 1995), so there is reason to hope that 4 or 5 years from now we will able to draw far stronger conclusions about the social, economic, and organizational dynamics that increase or decrease the likelihood of litigation.

Notes

1. Workers' compensation laws mandate what amounts to a no-fault insurance scheme, in which workers are compensated for on-the-job injuries, and these same laws generally make it difficult or impossible for the worker to seek damages from his or her employer outside the workers' compensation system.

2. In fact, it is far from clear that there has been much of a litigation explosion. With the exception of new causes of action, such as sexual harassment or employment discrimination claims, where there was no possibility of lawsuits until the statutes or common law permitted, lawsuits are growing at a rate not very much faster than the population; see, for example, Galanter (1983) and Selvin and Ebener (1984). There is also evidence that reports in personnel and business law journals concerning the threat posed by wrongful termination litigation are much overblown (Edelman, Abraham, & Erlanger, 1992).

3. As Miller and Ratner (in press) pointed out, in many areas of life, people are driven by considerations that have little to do with self-interest, although these true determinants of behavior are often not acknowledged either by lay observers or by the

people themselves. As we shall see below, there is a considerable and growing body of research that suggests that factors other than self-interest play a substantial, often predominant role in determining whether people sue.

4. Plaintiffs' lawyers in personal injury cases generally work on contingent fees, usually about one third of the final payoff to the plaintiff. If the lawyer's business is to survive, he or she must make the determination that the likely payoff is sufficient to justify the effort and expense of litigating the case.

5. All of this assumes that the person identifies positively with the organization. Although this is generally the case, there are certainly instances in which an employee has little or no real identification with the organization. In such instances, the justice judgment process is different. See, for example, Huo, Smith, Tyler, and Lind (1996).

6. Layoffs pose an interesting problem from the perspective of the relational model of justice. Because a person is, by definition, being removed from his or her relationship with the organization, one might question whether relational concerns still apply. I would argue that *at the time of the layoff* the potential claimant still has a relationship with the organization and that therefore relational concerns will still rule the justice judgment process. If at this point a sense of some fairness is imbued, the person will be very unlikely indeed to claim. Actions such as expressions of concern, efforts at outplacement, or severance packages will do a great deal to engender this feeling of concern. This prediction is born out by some very recent, unpublished data by Greenberg, Lind, Scott and Welchans, who interviewed recently laid-off employees about their desire and actions in claiming against their former employers. Of the more than 700 former employees interviewed, not a single respondent who felt that he or she had been treated with a great deal of dignity and respect at the time of his or her dismissal sued his or her former employer.

7. Other significant causal links in the Bies and Tyler (1993) study include a negative link between perceptions of process justice and assessments of the probability of winning in court, a positive link between outcome justice and organizational commitment, and a negative link between absolute outcome favorability and job satisfaction.

References

Bebchuck, L. A. (1984). Litigation and settlement under uncertain information. *RAND Journal of Economics, 15,* 404-415.

Bies, R. J., & Shapiro, D. L. (1988). Voice and justification: Their influence on procedural fairness judgments. *Academy of Management Journal, 31,* 676-685.

Bies, R. J., & Tyler, T. R. (1993). The "litigation mentality" in organizations: A test of alternative psychological explanations. *Organizational Science, 4,* 352-366.

Black, D. (1987). Compensation and the social structure of misfortune. *Law and Society Review, 21,* 563-584.

Closing a color gap. (1989, February 13). *Time,* p. 63.

Cooter, R., Marks, S., & Mnookin, R. (1982). Bargaining in the shadow of the law: A testable model of strategic behavior. *Journal of Legal Studies, 11,* 225-251.

Crosby, F. (1984). The denial of personal discrimination. *American Behavioral Scientist, 27,* 371-386.

Danzon, P. M., & Lillard, L. A. (1982). *The resolution of medical malpractice claims: Modeling the bargaining process.* Santa Monica, CA: RAND.

Dertouzos, J. N., Holland, E., & Ebener, P. (1988). *The legal and economic consequences of wrongful termination.* Santa Monica, CA: RAND.

Edelman, L. B., Abraham, S. E., & Erlanger, H. S. (1992). Professional construction of law: The inflated threat of wrongful discharge. *Law and Society Review, 26,* 47-83.

Ex-Polaroid employee awarded $400,000 in suit. (1995, November 3). *Wall Street Journal,* p. A6.

Felstiner, W. L. F. (1974). Influences of social organization on dispute processing. *Law and Society Review, 9,* 63-94.

Felstiner, W. L. F. (1975). Avoidance as dispute processing: An elaboration. *Law and Society Review, 9,* 695-755.

Felstiner, W. L. F., Abel, R. L., & Sarat, A. (1981). The emergence and transformation of disputes: Naming, blaming, and claiming. *Law and Society Review, 15,* 631-644.

Galanter, M. (1983). Reading the landscape of disputes: What we know and don't know (and think we know) about our allegedly contentious and litigious society. *UCLA Law Review, 31,* 4-95.

Greenberg, J. (1987). Reactions to procedural injustice in payment distributions: Do the means justify the ends? *Journal of Applied Psychology, 72,* 55-61.

Greenberg, J. (1990). Employee theft as a reaction to underpayment inequity: The hidden cost of pay cuts. *Journal of Applied Psychology, 75,* 561-568.

Greenberg, J. (1993). The social side of fairness: Interpersonal and informational classes of organizational justice. In R. Cropanzano (Ed.), *Justice in the workplace: Approaching fairness in human resource management* (pp. 79-103). Hillsdale, NJ: Lawrence Erlbaum.

Greenberg, J., Lind, E. A., Scott, K., & Welchans, T. (1995). *Final report on "Collaborative Research on Layoffs and Wrongful Termination Litigation."* Columbus: Ohio State University, Fisher College of Management.

Greenberg, J., & Scott, K. S. (1996). Why do workers bite the hands that feed them? Employee theft as a social exchange process. In B. M. Staw & L. L. Cummings (Eds.), *Research in organizational behavior* (Vol. 18, pp. 111-156). Greenwich, CT: JAI Press.

Harris, D., McLean, M., Genn, H., Lloyd-Bostock, S., Genn, P., Corfield, P., & Brittan, Y. (1984). *Compensation and support of illness and injury.* Oxford, UK: Clarendon.

Harvard Medical Malpractice Study. (1990). *Patients, doctors and lawyers: Medical injury, malpractice litigation and patient compensation in New York.* Cambridge, MA: Harvard University, School of Public Policy.

Hensler, D. R., Marquis, M. S., Abrahamse, A. F., Berry, S. H., Ebener, P. A., Lewis, E. G., Lind, E. A., MacCoun, R. J., Manning, W. G., Rogowski, J. A., & Vaiana, M. E. (1991). *Compensation for accidental injuries in the United States.* Santa Monica, CA: RAND.

Huo, Y. J., Smith, H., Tyler, T. R., & Lind, E. A. (1996). Superordinate identification, subgroup identification, and justice concerns: Is separatism the problem; is assimilation the answer? *Psychological Science, 7,* 40-45.

King, E. M., & Smith, J. P. (1988). *Dispute resolution following airplane crashes.* Santa Monica, CA: RAND.

Kritzer, H. M., Bogart, W. A., & Vidmar, N. (1991). To confront or not to confront: Measuring claiming rates in discrimination grievances. *Law and Society Review, 25,* 101-115.

Kritzer, H. M., Vidmar, N., & Bogart, W. A. (1991). The aftermath of injury: Cultural factors in compensation seeking in Canada and the United States. *Law and Society Review, 25,* 499-545.

Landes, E. M. (1982). Compensation for automobile accident injuries: Is the tort system fair? *Journal of Legal Studies, 11,* 253-260.

Lind, E. A. (1994). Procedural justice and culture: Evidence for ubiquitous process concerns. *Zeitschift für Rechtssoziologie, 15,* 24-36.

Lind, E. A. (1995). Justice and authority in organizations. In R. Cropanzano & K. M. Kacmar (Eds.), *Politics, justice, and support: Managing the social climate of work organizations* (pp. 83-96). Westport, CT: Quorum.

Lind, E. A., Kanfer, R., & Earley, P. C. (1990). Voice, control, and procedural justice: Instrumental and noninstrumental concerns in fairness judgments. *Journal of Personality and Social Psychology, 59,* 952-959.

Lind, E. A., Kulik, C., Ambrose, M., & Park, M. (1993). Individual and corporate dispute resolution: Using procedural fairness as a decision heuristic. *Administrative Science Quarterly, 38,* 224-251.

Lind, E. A., MacCoun, R. J., Ebener, P. E., Felstiner, W. L. F., Hensler, D. R., Resnik, J., & Tyler, T. R. (1990). In the eye of the beholder: Tort litigants' evaluations of their experiences in the civil justice system. *Law and Society Review, 24,* 953-996.

Lind, E. A., & Tyler, T. R. (1988). *The social psychology of procedural justice.* New York: Plenum.

MacCoun, R. J., Lind, E. A., & Tyler, T. R. (1992). Alternative dispute resolution in the courts. In D. Kagehiro & W. Laufer (Eds.), *The handbook of law and psychology* (pp. 95-118). New York: Springer-Verlag.

Miller, D., & Ratner, R. K. (in press). The power of the myth of self-interest. In L. Montada & M. J. Lerner (Eds.), *Current societal issues in justice.* New York: Plenum.

P'ng, I. P. L. (1983). Strategic behavior in suit, settlement, and trial. *Bell Journal of Economics, 14,* 539-550.

Posner, R. A. (1986). *Economic analysis of the law.* Boston: Little, Brown.

Priest, G. L., & Klein, B. (1984). The selection of disputes for litigation. *Journal of Legal Studies, 13,* 1-56.

Selvin, M., & Ebener, P. A. (1984). *Managing the unmanageable: A history of civil delay in the Los Angeles Superior Court.* Santa Monica, CA: RAND.

Tyler, T. R. (1990). *Why people obey the law.* New Haven, CT: Yale University Press.

Tyler, T. R. (1994). Psychological models of the justice motive: Antecedents of distributive and procedural justice. *Journal of Personality and Social Psychology, 67,* 850-863.

Tyler, T. R., & Lind, E. A. (1992). A relational model of authority in groups. In M. Zanna (Ed.), *Advances in experimental social psychology* (Vol. 25, pp. 115-192). New York: Academic Press.

Whittman, D. (1985). Is the selection of cases for trial biased? *Journal of Legal Studies, 14,* 185-214.

9

Organizational Culture and Employee Counterproductivity

Michael W. Boye
John W. Jones

Recent research indicates that counterproductive employee behavior such as theft and sick-day abuse is prevalent in a variety of industries. For instance, a recent survey of supermarket employees revealed that 42% had taken cash, merchandise, and/or property from their employer in the last 6 months (London House & Food Marketing Institute, 1995). Twenty-nine percent of the respondents said they had abused sick days, and 20% admitted that they had come to work hung over from alcohol. A study conducted with restaurant employees found that 60% admitted to some type of theft in the last 6 months (Hollinger, Slora, & Terris, 1992). Moreover, 80% of the overall sample admitted that they had engaged in some type of counterproductive behavior other than theft. Such behaviors included using illicit drugs or alcohol at work, intentionally working in a slow or sloppy manner, and engaging in unsafe workplace behavior, to name a few.

Using multidimensional scaling techniques, Robinson and Bennett (1995) developed a typology of deviant workplace behavior. These researchers defined *counterproductive behavior* as voluntary behavior that violates significant organizational norms and in so doing threatens the well-being of the organization, its members, or both. This definition is adopted throughout this chapter and includes counterproductive behavior that could be considered nonserious (e.g., tardiness) as well as more serious types of counterproductivity (e.g., theft of cash, sabotage).

Counterproductive behavior by employees can be broadly viewed as resulting from (a) economic factors, (b) individual factors, and (c) organizational factors (see Jones, 1995).

Economic factors include variables such as prices and interest rates that lead many dishonest employees to conclude that it is a good time to benefit from acting in a counterproductive manner. For example, on the basis of economic factors, an employee may steal to improve a reduced standard of living or may abuse substances to reduce financially related stress. However, despite the long-term success that an organization may achieve in its attempts to influence economic factors, the influence of such factors would obviously not be considered effective as a primary strategy for reducing counterproductive behavior by employees.

Individual factors include a number of characteristics that are common among employees who engage in counterproductive behavior at work, such as the belief that a large proportion of employees act in a similar manner and the tendency to rationalize this type of behavior. These attitudinal factors can be addressed through personnel selection. The topic of reducing counterproductive behavior by means of employee selection has been addressed extensively elsewhere (e.g., Jones, 1991; Jones & Terris, 1991).

A number of studies suggest that modifying the *organizational climate* is effective in reducing deviant employee behavior (e.g., Cherrington & Cherrington, 1985; Jones & Boye, 1995; Parilla, Hollinger, & Clark, 1988). However, this research indicates that better results will be obtained by altering the organizational climate to address employee motivations and perceptions rather than merely to decrease employee opportunities to engage in such behavior. This chapter considers the modification of organizational factors and employee reactions to these factors to reduce theft and other types of counterproductive behavior at work.

Definitions

The definition of *organizational climate* has changed to some extent over the past 30 years (Rentsch, 1990). Early researchers defined *climate* as enduring organizational or situational characteristics that organizational members perceived, whereas *climate* was later defined in terms of individuals' perceptions. *Organizational climate* has recently been defined as a shared or summary perception that people attach to particular features of the work setting (Ostroff, 1993). On the basis of this definition, climate can be modified directly by addressing employee perceptions of organizational characteristics but also indirectly by changing objective characteristics of the working environment. The present discussion will consider each of these methods of modifying climate.

Organizational Factors

A number of organizational factors have the potential to influence the extent to which employees engage in counterproductive behavior. These factors are the values of the organization, the company's formal antitheft policy, the norms of the work group, organizational security, and the company's record of handling offenders.

Organizational Values

A number of recent studies indicate that the values communicated by an organization have a significant effect on the extent to which employees engage in counterproductive activity. For example, London House & Food Marketing Institute (1995) concluded that 10 organizational values were related to lower levels of counterproductive workplace behavior. These values were (a) fairness with employees, (b) caring and empathy, (c) employee empowerment, (d) career-enriching opportunities, (e) equitable pay and benefits, (f) interpersonal cooperation, (g) accurate job-person matching, (h) honesty and ethics, (i) safe working conditions, and (j) job security. Thus the findings indicated that employers were likely to minimize counterproductive employee behavior when they treated employees with dignity and respect, paid and treated them fairly, modeled integrity, and attempted to improve their job. Parenthetically, these findings were replicated in a recent restaurant industry survey (London House and National Food Services Security Council, 1996).

As part of the same study, Jones and Boye (1995) found that employees from organizations communicating at least 8 of these 10 values stole significantly less from their company (an annual average of $27.58 per employee) than employees from organizations that did not communicate at least 8 of these values (average annual theft of $75.82 per employee; $t = 1.91$, $p < .05$). Hollinger and Clark's (1983b) results also indicated that low employee theft is one result of management efforts to be responsive to the perceptions, attitudes, and needs of its workforce.

Formal Antitheft Policy

A formal antitheft policy is one method of communicating the organizational value of intolerance to theft by employees. Parilla et al. (1988) pointed out that a formal antitheft policy serves two deterrence-related functions. First, an antitheft policy is a formal announcement that stealing company merchandise or property is considered to be a serious matter and will be punished. Employees do respond to this threat. Second, an antitheft policy increases the likelihood that supervisors will react when employee theft is discovered. Parilla et al. (1988) found that the presence of a formal antitheft policy was significantly associated with lower theft rates in retail organizations ($r = -.62$, $p < .001$).

Work Group Norms

Many studies have shown that the norms of the work group can also influence the level of counterproductive behavior engaged in by employees. For example, Hawkins (1984) found that workers in restaurants collaborated with one another to steal from employers, customers and other coworkers. Horning (1970) found that the norms of the work group in a television assembly plant determined the amount and types of company property that workers could take without sanction from the group. The work group also defined the conditions under which theft would be tolerated by its members. Mars (1974) found that those who loaded and unloaded ships regularly stole enough of the contents for everyone involved in the loading and unloading process. The findings of Hollinger and Clark (1982) indicated that the perceived threat of informal sanctions by coworkers had even more impact on theft and other counterproductive behavior than the perceived severity of formal sanctions by management.

Organizational Security

Organizational theft rates are to a large extent contingent on the opportunities for employees to steal. Security measures are used to reduce these opportunities substantially and are perhaps the most obvious organizational climate factors affecting employee theft. Some of these methods (e.g., security guards, video cameras) may also be beneficial for reducing other types of counterproductive behavior.

Research evaluating the impact of security measures, however, has not conclusively determined that these measures are effective in reducing counterproductivity. Parilla et al. (1988) studied the relationship of the size and sophistication of security departments with organizational theft rates. The relationship of the priority of theft reduction (as compared with other responsibilities of the department) with theft rates was also examined. None of these security department attributes were found to be significantly correlated with company theft rates. This finding was consistent across all three industries represented by the study (i.e., retail, hospital, and manufacturing).

Hollinger and Clark (1983b) discovered that worker morale decreases significantly when employees feel unduly harassed by security systems. Many of these employees may then behave in a counterproductive manner to confirm what they perceive to be management's lack of trust. It appears that the extent to which security measures are effective depends in part on their unobtrusiveness and on whether employees believe that their counterproductive behavior will be detected by these measures.

Company Record of Handling Offenders

Employees draw conclusions about the consequences of their own theft and counterproductive activity based on what happens to other employees who engage in such behavior. Inconsistent or lenient handling of employee theft and rule violations is likely to reinforce the belief commonly held among those who engage in high levels of employee deviance: that they will not be punished very severely if they are caught. The deterrent effect of a formal policy concerning counterproductive behavior can be negated when employees see that the policy is not consistently enforced. In addition, the problem of counterproductive behavior may be exacerbated when employees see that the violations of some employees (e.g., lower-level workers) are punished more regularly or severely than the violations of others (e.g., supervisors and management personnel).

Parilla et al. (1988) examined the effect of various types of sanctions (i.e., number of thieves apprehended, percentage terminated, percentage prosecuted, and percentage who made restitution to the organization) on organizational theft rates. Although their sample of organizations was small, they found that apprehensions for theft were significantly correlated with lower theft rates in retail companies ($r = -.54, p < .01$). Terminations for theft were also significantly correlated with lower theft rates in hospitals ($r = -.61, p < .001$). The obtained correlations also provided some evidence that prosecutions were effective in hospitals and restitution was effective in retail organizations, although these correlations were not statistically significant ($r = -.18$ and $-.10$ respectively).

Employee Reactions to Organizational Factors

A large body of research (e.g., Hollinger & Clark, 1982, 1983a, 1983b; Kamp & Brooks, 1991; London House & Food Marketing Institute, 1991, 1992, 1993, 1995) has identified a number of employee characteristics that are associated with counterproductive employee behavior (e.g., job satisfaction, perceptions of the integrity of the organization). This research suggests that the effectiveness of any organizational climate modification in reducing counterproductive behavior depends largely on the extent to which the modification alters several employee characteristics. These characteristics are reviewed below.

Job Satisfaction

A commonly expressed theory of counterproductive behavior is that certain employees engage in such behavior because they are dissatisfied with their jobs. Research evidence does provide some support for this hypothesis. Correlations of job satisfaction with theft and other types of counterproductivity have typically ranged from about $-.10$ to $-.25$ (e.g., Berte, Moretti, Jusko, & Leonard, 1981; Hollinger & Clark, 1983b; Kamp & Brooks, 1991; London House & Food Marketing Institute, 1991, 1992, 1993, 1995). Hollinger and Clark (1983b) obtained significant correlations with theft using very large samples from the retail and hospital industries ($r = -.11$ and $-.09$ respectively, $p < .05$) but not with employees of manufacturing companies ($r = .06$, ns). These investigators did, however, find that job satisfaction was significantly correlated with counterproductive behavior other than theft in all three industries (r ranged from $-.19$ to $-.23$, $p < .05$). In four large studies conducted in the supermarket industry (London House & Food Marketing Institute, 1991, 1992, 1993, 1995), correlations with theft ranged from $-.10$ to $-.15$ ($p < .01$), and correlations with counterproductive behavior other than theft ranged from $-.21$ to $-.28$ ($p < .001$). Thus employees who were dissatisfied with their jobs engaged more often than others in theft and other counterproductive activity.

Perceived Integrity of the Organization

The problem of counterproductive behavior is often exacerbated when employees believe that their managers are dishonest or unethical. Supervisors who engage in counterproductive behaviors or unethical practices can influence many of their subordinates to behave in ways that are detrimental to the organization. In a study of three retail organizations, Cherrington and Cherrington (1985) found that employee perceptions of management integrity were associated with company shrinkage rates. London House & Food Marketing Institute (1992, 1993, 1995) found that employees who believed their employer was dishonest engaged more often in many counterproductive workplace behaviors. These included stealing merchandise or equipment, eating food without paying, changing company records to receive unearned pay, and doing slow or sloppy work intentionally.

Perceived Certainty of Detection

A major factor influencing employees' decisions to steal or engage in other counterproductive activities at work is whether they believe they will get caught. Hollinger and Clark (1983a) found that employees who perceive that they are unlikely to be caught if they steal from their employer were over three and one-half times more likely than others to engage in theft at work. These investigators also obtained correlations of perceived certainty of detection with theft ranging from $-.24$ to $-.29$ ($p < .001$) in three industry sectors (Hollinger & Clark, 1983b). In four separate studies conducted in supermarkets (London House & Food Marketing Institute, 1991, 1992, 1993, 1995), correlations between perceived certainty of detection and theft ranged from $-.22$ to $-.32$ ($p < .001$). Thus those who did not believe they would be caught if they stole from their employer consistently stole from the company more frequently than others.

Perceived Severity of Sanctions

Empirical evidence also indicates that the severity of sanctions is a factor influencing the decision to behave in a counterproductive manner (Grasmick & Milligan, 1976; Hollinger & Clark, 1982, 1983a). Hollinger and Clark (1983a) found that employees who perceive little severity in management's response to theft behavior were almost twice as likely to report above-average levels of theft from their employers. In another study, perceived severity of sanctions from management and from coworkers were both significantly correlated with theft and other counterproductive behavior (Hollinger & Clark, 1982). However, the perceived severity of informal sanctions from coworkers was more strongly related to counterproductive behavior than the perceived severity of formal sanctions from management. This indicates that the influence of work group attitudes on employee involvement in counterproductive behavior is equal to or greater than the influence of management sanctions. It appears that programs designed to get all employees involved in minimizing counterproductivity among their coworkers may be highly effective in reducing such behavior. It also appears that management sanctions against those caught engaging in unacceptable counterproductive activities should be consistent, severe, and known to all employees.

Perceived Job Stress

A large body of research has documented the relationship between perceived job stress and counterproductive behavior (see Jones, Steffy, & Bray, 1991, for a review). In a study conducted with 507 retail employees, Lavelli (1986) found that perceived job stress was significantly correlated with theft admissions ($r = .38$, $p < .05$), illegitimate absenteeism ($r = .33$, $p < .01$), and emotional outbursts during the workday ($r = .35$, $p < .01$). Jones (1981b) found that perceived job stress was significantly correlated with theft admissions ($r = .39$, $p < .05$) among hospital workers. Jones (1981a, 1996) found that employees experiencing high levels of job stress and also possessing a predisposition to steal (based on their attitudes, values, and perceptions) admitted stealing far more from their employer (in terms of dollar value) than others. These findings indicate that stress-related feelings of anger, frustration, and disappointment may build up over time and result in counterproductive activity against the company. This may be especially likely when employees perceiving high levels of job stress project blame for their resultant feelings onto management. Terris and Jones (1981) found that revenge is a major motivation to steal. Feelings resulting from job stress can conceivably weaken and eventually override the cognitive controls that prevent counterproductive behavior, especially if an employee already has tolerant attitudes toward such behavior (see Jones, 1981b).

Climate Modification for Counterproductivity Reduction

The aforementioned findings have several implications for organizations interested in reducing counterproductive behavior by their employees. Research indicates that managers should strive to create a work environment that communicates to employees that they are appreciated, that their contribution is significant, and that honesty in the workplace is expected. In addition, coworkers should be helped to recognize the personal benefits that they receive by stopping their own counterproductive behavior and helping to reduce the counterproductivity of others. These practices should reduce employee deviance not only by instilling loyalty and rewarding employees but also by shaping the norms of the work group so that employees will discourage counterproductivity among themselves. A number of organizational climate modifications based on these findings are reviewed below.

- *Set the example.* An organizational climate of honesty begins at the top. Supervisory personnel must set a good example for their employees. How can employers expect honesty and ethics from their employees when they themselves engage in dishonest or unethical practices? When supervisors engage in counterproductive or unethical behavior, they give workers a perfect rationalization to do likewise ("If my boss does it, why shouldn't I?"). When hiring supervisory personnel from outside the organization, care should be taken to hire those who will model a standard of integrity. Personnel selection tests that assess the ethics of managerial job candidates can be used for this purpose (see Nerad & Orban, 1989). (An organizational climate of integrity is further enhanced by assessing the integrity of all applicants for positions with the company.)
- *Treat employees with trust, respect and dignity.* Employees are less likely to act in a counterproductive manner when they are valued by the company and satisfied with the quality of their work experience. Therefore managers should be encouraged to build congenial relationships with employees and to be respectful and sensitive to their needs.
- *Attempt to enrich employees' jobs.* Job improvements such as increasing decision-making responsibility or job autonomy also demonstrate to employees that they are appreciated. Hence these programs are likely to reduce counterproductive behavior in the work setting.
- *Provide fair and adequate compensation.* Employers should also communicate to employees in a tangible way that they are valued. A fair and adequate compensation system generally contributes to satisfaction with the employer and minimizes feelings that the employer is unfair, thus reducing the likelihood of counterproductive behavior on the part of many employees. One feature of the compensation system that should be especially effective in reducing counterproductive employee activity is profit sharing. This method of compensation should help make clear to employees the reward they can obtain by reducing counterproductive behavior and thus helping the company to increase its profitability.

- *Adopt and communicate a policy concerning counterproductive behavior.* A policy concerning counterproductive behavior should thoroughly inform employees as to what counterproductive activities upper management regards as unacceptable. The policy should also specify what will happen to employees caught engaging in such activities. This information should be conveyed to employees soon after hire (i.e., in the employee orientation program). In addition, management's concern with counterproductive behavior should periodically be emphasized to employees.
- *Consistently punish unacceptable counterproductive acts.* A policy regarding counterproductive behavior is of little value if the policy is not consistently enforced. Employees will be less likely to act in a counterproductive manner if they believe that such behavior will be punished when caught.
- *Reduce job stress.* Employee assistance programs provide workers with a constructive way of dealing with job stress that provides an alternative to counterproductive behavior. Teaching stress reduction skills such as the "instant calming sequence" (Cooper, 1991) and other relaxation techniques can also help employees to reduce job stress and consequently the propensity to steal.

Conclusion

Counterproductive employee behavior is a difficult and pervasive problem for many organizations. However, research suggests a number of effective methods for reducing employee counterproductivity (Jones, 1996). Several of these methods (e.g., treating employees with respect and dignity, adopting and communicating a policy concerning deviant behavior, and consistently punishing unacceptable counterproductive acts) are likely to be less costly and perhaps more effective than conventional methods of theft reduction, such as closed-circuit video cameras and security guards. Use of personnel selection tests can help managers create an honest culture by hiring the most dependable and productive employees. Finally, managers can routinely use organizational surveys to determine if their employee groups do possess counterproductive values and high levels of job stress. Hopefully, by better understanding the psychology of employee deviance, managers will be able to implement contemporary loss control programs that will improve corporate culture *and* reduce employee counterproductivity.

References

Berte, D. L., Moretti, D. M., Jusko, R., & Leonard, J. (1981, August). *An investigation of a combined withdrawal and counterproductive behavior decision process model.* Paper presented at the annual meeting of the American Academy of Management, San Diego.

Cherrington, D. J., & Cherrington, J. O. (1985). The climate of honesty in retail stores. In W. Terris (Ed.), *Employee theft: Research, theory, and applications* (pp. 27-39). Rosemont, IL: London House.

Cooper, R. K. (1991). *The performance edge.* Boston: Houghton Mifflin.

Grasmick, H. G., & Milligan, H., Jr. (1976). Deterrence theory approach to socioeconomic/demographic correlates of crime. *Social Science Quarterly, 57,* 608-617.

Hawkins, R. (1984). Employee theft in the restaurant trade: Forms of ripping off by waiters at work. *Deviant Behavior, 5,* 47-69.

Hollinger, R. C., & Clark, J. P. (1982). Formal and informal social controls of employee deviance. *Sociological Quarterly, 23,* 333-343.

Hollinger, R. C., & Clark, J. P. (1983a). Deterrence in the workplace: Perceived certainty, perceived severity, and employee theft. *Social Forces, 62,* 398-418.

Hollinger, R. C., & Clark, J. P. (1983b). *Theft by employees.* Lexington, MA: Lexington.

Hollinger, R. C., Slora, K. B., & Terris, W. (1992). Deviance in the fast-food restaurant: Correlates of employee theft, altruism, and counterproductivity. *Deviant Behavior: An Interdisciplinary Journal, 13,* 155-184.

Horning, D. N. M. (1970). Blue collar theft: Conceptions of property, attitudes toward pilfering, and work group norms in a modern industrial plant. In E. O. Smigel & H. L. Ross (Eds.), *Crimes against bureaucracy* (pp. 46-64). New York: Van Nostrand Reinhold.

Jones, J. W. (1981a). Attitudinal correlates of employee theft of drugs and hospital supplies among nursing personnel. *Journal of Nursing Research, 30,* 349-351.

Jones, J. W. (1981b, August). *Dishonesty, staff burnout, and employee theft.* Paper presented at the 89th annual meeting of the American Psychological Association, Division of Industrial Psychology, Los Angeles.

Jones, J. W. (1991). *Preemployment honesty testing: Current research and future directions.* Greenwood, CT: Greenwood.

Jones, J. W. (1995, July). Mind over motive with employee theft. *Security,* pp. 55-57.

Jones, J. W. (1996, April). Creating an honest corporate culture: A 10-step approach. *Security Management,* pp. 23-26.

Jones, J. W., & Boye, M. W. (1995, April). *Hiring honest and productive employees.* Presentation delivered at the Loss Prevention Conference of the Retail Council of Canada, Toronto.

Jones, J. W., Steffy, B. D., & Bray, D. W. (1991). *Applying psychology in business: The handbook for managers and human resource professionals.* Lexington, MA: Lexington.

Jones, J. W., & Terris, W. (1991). Personnel selection to control employee theft and counterproductivity. In J. W. Jones, B. D. Steffy, & D. W. Bray (Eds.), *Applying psychology in business: The handbook for managers and human resource professionals* (pp. 851-861). Lexington, MA: Lexington.

Kamp, J., & Brooks, P. (1991). Perceived organizational climate and employee counterproductivity. *Journal of Business and Psychology, 5,* 447-458.

Lavelli, M. (1986). *Psychological predictors of employee counterproductivity.* Master's thesis, DePaul University, Chicago.

London House & Food Marketing Institute. (1991). *Second annual report on employee theft in the supermarket industry: 1990 summary of findings*. Rosemont, IL: London House.

London House & Food Marketing Institute. (1992). *Third annual report on employee theft in the supermarket industry: 1991 findings*. Rosemont, IL: London House.

London House & Food Marketing Institute. (1993). *Fourth annual report on employee theft in the supermarket industry*. Rosemont, IL: London House.

London House & Food Marketing Institute. (1995). *Fifth annual report of supermarket employee behavior*. Rosemont, IL: London House.

London House & National Food Services Security Council. (1996). *First annual report on restaurant employee behavior*. Rosemont, IL: London House.

Mars, G. (1974). Dock pilferage: A case study in occupational theft. In P. Rock & M. McIntosh (Eds.), *Deviance and social control* (pp. 209-228). London: Tavistock.

Nerad, A. J., & Orban, J. A. (1989). *Prediction of restaurant manager performance using the Retail Management Assessment Inventory* (Tech. Rep. No. 37). Rosemont, IL: McGraw-Hill/London House.

Ostroff, C. (1993). The effects of climate and personal influences on individual behavior and attitudes in organizations. *Organizational Behavior and Human Decision Processes, 56*, 56-90.

Parilla, P. F., Hollinger, R. C., & Clark, J. P. (1988). Organizational control of deviant behavior: The case of employee theft. *Social Science Quarterly, 69*, 261-280.

Rentsch, J. R. (1990). Climate and culture: Interaction and qualitative differences in organizational meanings. *Journal of Applied Psychology, 75*, 668-681.

Robinson, S. L., & Bennett, R. J. (1995). A typology of deviant workplace behaviors: A multidimensional scaling study. *Academy of Management Journal, 38*, 555-572.

Terris, W., & Jones, J. W. (1981, October). *Psychological factors related to employee theft in the convenience store industry*. Paper presented at the seventh annual meeting of the Society of Police and Criminal Psychology, Baton Rouge, LA.

Index

About the Authors

Robert A. Baron, PhD (Iowa, 1968), is Professor of Management and Professor of Psychology at Rensselaer Polytechnic Institute. He has been a Visiting Fellow at Oxford University (1982) and has served as a Program Director at the National Science Foundation (1979-1981). He has been a Fellow of the American Psychological Association since 1978. He is the author or coauthor of several major textbooks (e.g., *Social Psychology*, 7th ed.; *Behavior in Organizations*, 5th ed.; and *Human Aggression*, 2nd ed.). He is a member of the Board of Directors of the Albany Symphony Orchestra and is President of Innovative Environmental Products, Inc., a company that designs equipment for enhancing the physical environment of work settings and living spaces. He holds two U.S. patents for a desktop device combining air filtration, noise control, and other features. His research activities focus mainly on (a) the impact of the physical environment on productivity, (b) organizational conflict, and (c) workplace aggression.

Robert J. Bies is Associate Professor of Management in the School of Business, Georgetown University, Washington, DC. He received his PhD in business administration (organizational behavior) in 1982 from Stanford University. He is a member of the Academy of Management, the American Psychological Association, and the Society for the Advancement of Socio-Economics. His research interests include leadership and the delivery of bad news, revenge in the workplace, the "litigation mentality," privacy, and organizational justice. He has published articles on these topics in *Academy of Management Journal*, *Academy of Management Review*, *Journal of Behavioral Decision Making*, *Research in Organizational Behavior*, *Research on Negotiation in Organizations*, *Organization Science*, and *Organizational Behavior and Human Decision Processes*. In addition, he has coedited a book of analytical essays entitled *The Legalistic Organization* (Sage, 1993).

Michael W. Boye is Personnel Research Coordinator for McGraw-Hill/London House in Rosemont, IL. He has conducted research in a variety of areas including job stress, employee theft management, industrial accident prevention and turnover reduction. He is also the senior author of the Annual Study of Supermarket Employee Behavior, a national study conducted by McGraw-Hill/London House and the Food Marketing Institute.

He received his BA in psychology from Grand Rapids Baptist College and his MA and PhD in industrial and organizational psychology from DePaul University. He received the Grand Rapids Baptist College Academic Scholarship for outstanding academic achievement. He is a member of the American Psychological Association and the Society of Industrial and Organizational Psychology. His clients have included Burger King, Circle K, and Spiegel.

Robert A. Giacalone is Associate Professor of Management Systems at the E. Clairborne Robins School of Business, University of Richmond. He was named to *Outstanding Young Men in America* in 1985, *Distinguished Educator* in 1991, and *Who's Who in America* in 1992. He has been a consultant to both the private and public sectors and is a frequently requested speaker on a variety of management topics. He is coeditor of two books, *Impression Management in the Organization* (1989) and *Applied Impression Management: How Image Making Affects Managerial Decisions*

(Sage, 1991), and coauthor of *Impression Management in Organizations: Theory, Measurement, Practice.* He is currently Series Editor for the Sage Series in Business Ethics. In addition, he has served as Guest Editor of a special issue on behavioral aspects of business ethics in the *Journal of Business Ethics* and a special issue on diversity and impression management in *American Behavioral Scientist.* He has also authored over 40 papers on ethics, employee sabotage, and exit interviewing, appearing in *Human Relations, Business and Society Review, Journal of Business Ethics, Group and Organization Studies, Journal of Social Psychology,* and a variety of other journals.

Jerald Greenberg is the Abramowitz Professor of Business Ethics and Professor of Management and Human Resources at The Ohio State University (OSU). He is a Fellow of both the American Psychological Association (Division 14, Society for Industrial/Organizational Psychology) and the American Psychological Society, as well as a member of the Society for Organizational Behavior. Among the professional honors he has received are a Fulbright Senior Research Fellowship (1980), the New Concept Award of the Organizational Behavior Division of the Academy of Management (1986), and the Pace Setter's Research Award from OSU's College of Business (1989). He has also been awarded several grants by the National Science Foundation. An active member of several committees of the Academy of Management— most notably, its Ethics Task Force and the Executive Committee of the Organizational Behavior Division—he also serves as a review board member of several professional journals, including the *Journal of Applied Psychology, Organizational Behavior and Human Decision Processes, Basic and Applied Social Psychology, Journal of Applied Social Psychology,* and *Social Justice Research.* He is the author of more than 100 publications specializing in the topic of organizational justice, including *Behavior in Organizations* (5th ed., with Robert Baron) and *Controversial Issues in Social Research Methods* (with Robert Folger). He has been on the faculties of Case Western Reserve University and Tulane University, and was a visiting professor at the University of California at Berkeley.

Steven L. Grover (PhD, Columbia University) is Associate Professor of Management at Georgia State University. In addition to his research on lying in organizations, he has conducted research on family-friendly human resource policies, and he publishes both streams of research in a variety of management journals. His current work on lying investigates the cross-cultural influences on lying. His other work now examines how the way people devote time to self-oriented activities, such as reading and exercise, affects their work and nonwork attitudes and behavior.

John W. Jones, PhD, is Vice President of Research and Services for McGraw-Hill/London House in Rosemont, IL. Well known for his work in risk management, especially in the areas of employee theft, substance abuse, industrial safety, and job stress, he has extensive experience in industrial/organizational psychology. He is also founder and Editor-in-Chief of the *Journal of Business and Psychology,* a scholarly periodical devoted to articles on all aspects of psychology that apply to business settings. His most recent books are *High-Speed Management* (1993) and *Personnel Testing: A Manager's Guide* (1994). He is Senior Editor of *Applying Psychology in Business: The Handbook for Managers and Human Resource Professionals* (1991). He holds a BA in psychology from the University of Cincinnati; an M.A. in applied experimental psychology from DePaul University, Chicago; and a PhD in psychology, specializing in industrial/organizational psychology, applied research, and counseling psychology, also from DePaul University. He was awarded the Diplomate in Industrial/Organizational Psychology by the American Board of Professional Psychology.

Roderick M. Kramer is Associate Professor of Organizational Behavior at the Graduate School of Business. He received his PhD in social psychology from the University of California at Los Angeles. He joined the faculty of the Stanford Business School in 1985. His research focuses primarily on decision making in conflict situations, such as social dilemmas, negotiations, and international disputes. Most recently, his research has focused on the role of cognitive illusions in conflicts and the dynamics of trust and distrust in organizations. His work has appeared in journals such as the *Annual Review of Psychology, Journal of Personality and Social Psychology, Journal of Experimental Social Psychology, Journal of Conflict Resolution,* and *Organizational Behavior and Human Decision Processes.* He teaches courses on negotiation, group decision making, and power and politics, as well as the introductory course on organizational behavior.

E. Allan Lind is Professor at Duke University. He received his PhD in social psychology from the University of North Carolina. He has served on the faculties of the University of New Hampshire and the University of Illinois at Urbana-Champaign, and he currently holds a Special Professorship at Leiden University in the Netherlands. He has also worked for the American Bar Foundation, the Federal Judicial Center, and the RAND Corporation. He is coauthor of the book *The Social Psychology of Procedural Justice,* and he is active in research and theory on social justice, claiming and litigating, and alternative dispute resolution.

Marcia P. Miceli obtained her DBA from Indiana University at Bloomington. She is Professor of Human Resources in the Fisher College of Business at The Ohio State University. Her research interests include pay systems, whistle-blowing in organizations, and human resources effectiveness.

Janet P. Near is Dow Professor of Management and Chairperson of the Management Department, School of Business, and Adjunct Professor in the Sociology Department and Philanthropic Studies Department of Indiana University. Her research interests focus on (a) whistle-blowing in organizations and (b) the relationship between job and life satisfaction. She has published several articles on these and, with Marcia P. Miceli, a book entitled *Blowing the Whistle: The Organizational and Legal Implications for Companies and Employees.*

Joel H. Neuman, PhD (State University of New York at Albany, 1990), is Assistant Professor of Management and Organizational Behavior in the School of Engineering and Business Administration at the State University of New York at New Paltz. His research interests involve the application of the principles and findings of social psychology to behaviors in work settings. This includes a focus on workplace aggression, the effects of organizational and technological change on worker productivity, and interpersonal relations and group processes. From 1970 through 1983, prior to his entry into the teaching profession, he was employed as an executive in the consumer electronics industry, and he continues to serve as a management consultant to both public- and private-sector organizations.

Catherine Riordan, PhD, is Professor of Psychology and Director of Management Systems at the University of Missouri-Rolla. She has conducted research on individuals' use of impression management to negotiate identities in situations in which their desired identity is threatened or questioned. As a consultant, she has applied this work to diversity and ethical issues in organizations. In addition to the chapter in this volume, she has co-authored with Paul Rosenfeld and Robert Giacalone the book *Impression Management in Organizations* (1995). She has also published interdisciplinary research on the use of computers supporting collaborative work, innovations in higher education, and the lives of commercial fishermen in the United States.

Paul Rosenfeld (PhD, State University of New York at Albany) is a personnel research psychologist at the Navy Personnel Research and Development Center in San Diego and Adjunct Professor of Psychology at the California School of Professional Psychology. He has authored two books: *Impression Management in Organizations* (with Robert Giacalone and Catherine Riordan; 1995) and *Introduction to Social Psychology* (with Jim Tedeschi and Svenn Lindskold; 1985). He has also edited four books: *Improving Organizational Surveys* (with J. E. Edwards and M. D. Thomas; Sage, 1993), *Applied Impression Management: How Image-Making Affects Managerial Decisions* (with Robert Giacalone; Sage, 1991), *Impression Management in the Organization* (with Robert Giacalone; 1989), and *Hispanics in the Workplace* (with Steven Knouse and Amy Culbertson; Sage, 1992).

Paul E. Spector received his PhD in industrial/organizational psychology from the University of South Florida in 1975 and is now a professor in the Department of Psychology there. His research interests encompass both content and methodology. His content interests include antisocial behavior at work, employee turnover, job satisfaction, job stress, and personality. He has published methodological articles on both complex statistics and psychometrics. He was listed in a 1992 study by the Institute for Scientific Information as one of the 50 highest-impact authors in the entire field of psychology on the basis of number of articles and citations to those articles during the years 1986 through 1990.

Thomas M. Tripp received his PhD in organization behavior from Northwestern University in 1991. Since then, he has conducted laboratory experiments and field studies investigating how people use fairness to mitigate power differentials during negotiations. Also, he has written on related issues of power abuse, distrust, defamation within organizations, and, currently, revenge in the workplace. His work has appeared in *Organizational Behavior and Human Decision Processes, Journal of Behavioral Decision Making, Social Justice Research, Employee Responsibilities and Rights Journal, Research on Negotiations in Organizations, Trust in Organizations, Journal of Applied Social Psychology,* and *Organizational Politics Justice and Support.*